TRIBAL THOUGHT AND CULTURE

About the Editor

Baidyanath Saraswati (b. 1932) is Research Professor in Indira Gandhi National Centre for the Arts, New Delhi; former Professor of Anthropology in North Eastern Hill University, Shillong. Professor Saraswati's major publications include: *Contributions to the understanding of Indian civilization; Pottery making cultures and Indian civilization; Kashi: myth and reality of a classical cultural tradition; Brahmanic ritual traditions; The spectrum of the sacred;* and *Ascetics of Kashi: an anthropological exploration (with Surajit Sinha.*

TRIBAL THOUGHT AND CULTURE

Essays in Honour of SURAJIT CHANDRA SINHA

Edited by
BAIDYANATH SARASWATI

CONCEPT PUBLISHING COMPANY PVT. LTD.
NEW DELHI-110059

ISBN-13: 978-81-7022-340-5

Edition 2017

Published and Printed by

Concept
Since 1974

Concept Publishing Company Pvt. Ltd.
A/15-16, Commercial Block, Mohan Garden
New Delhi-110059 (India)
T: 25351460, 25351794, *F*: 091-11-25357109
E: publishing@conceptpub.com, W: www.conceptpub.com
Editorial Office: H-13, Bali Nagar, New Delhi-110 015, India.

Cataloging in Publication Data--Courtesy: D.K. Agencies (P) Ltd. <docinfo@dkagencies.com>

Tribal thought and culture : essays in honour of Surajit Chandra Sinha / edited by Baidyanath Saraswati.
pages cm
Includes bibliographical references and index.
ISBN 9788170223405

1. Ethnology--India. 2. India--Scheduled tribes. 3. India--Civilization. 4. Philosophy, Indic. 5. India--Social life and customs. 6. Sinha, Surajit, 1926- I. Sinha, Surajit, 1926- honouree. II. Saraswati, Baidyanath, editor. III. NK Bose Memorial Foundation.

GN635.I4T75 2017 DDC 305.800954 23

Prof. Surajit Chandra Sinha

PREFACE

The plan for this *Festschrift* was initially made at Shillong in 1986, in consultation with two of my great friends, P.K. Misra and Arabinda Basu. Both of them had very kindly accepted the responsibility for collecting the essays which constitute this volume. I am most, most grateful to them and to all my collaborators, whose names are in the Contents, for their stimulating contributions and, particularly, for the patience with which they have borne with delays.

Surajit Chandra Sinha (*b.* 1926) is a pioneering anthropologist of Indian civilization. Born a prince of Susanga Raj, a quasi-sovereign estate in tribal Mymensingh district of Bangladesh, he has shown special interest in the study of primary civilization. Acclaimed for originality, penetrating insight and jargon-free subtle analysis, he has drawn concepts and themes from fairly long extensive fieldwork, especially among the tribes of India, as also from his preceptors, N.K. Bose, T.C. Das and Robert Redfield, the great masters of Anthropology. He was previously Director of the Anthropological Survey of India, where he initiated several young anthropologists to a series of critical and imaginative themes in the study of Indian society and civilization: complex societies and religious institutions, nomads, fisherfolk, weaker section, culture of poverty, ethical aspirations, aesthetic forms, and so on. He also served as Vice-Chancellor of Tagore's Visva-Bharati, where he continued guiding doctoral research, delivering lectures, and addressing intellectual conventions. In his search for interpretations of Indian civilization, Sinha, in close collaboration with his highly talented wife Purnima, is at present plunged into a more profound writings on tribe, civilization, nation building and Bose, in his homely cloister at Santiniketan.

The Foundation's concern in this project was not only to felicitate its distinguished founder President but to offer an insightful evaluation of the scientific work of a superb researcher, a natural teacher, a thinker and a noble leader who, by consensus among his colleagues, is one of the greatest anthropologists of our time. This volume on *Tribal Thought and Culture* was designed also to feed new ideas in his chosen field

Sinha has intellectual kinship with Bose and, as he acknowledges very often, his thoughts are firmly grounded in the Bosean tradition. For us at the Bose Foundation it is a matter of very great satisfaction that all the thirteen essays collected here belong to that tradition, and that in them emerge the richness of empirical data, the daring speculations and the diversity of viewpoints that reflect the true spirit of the man in whose honour these essays have been written.

The photograph of the Varli mural painting from Maharashtra, that adorns the jacket of this book, has been taken by Shri Parthiv Shah, a talented young artist from Gujarat and the son of my esteemed friend Professor Haku Bhai Shah, the renowned artist and author. My gratefulness and best wishes for Parthiv. The picture symbolizes 'life' and 'tradition'.

N.K. Bose Memorial Foundation
Varanasi on the Ganga

BAIDYANATH SARASWATI
General Secretary

CONTENTS

Preface 7
Notes on Contributors 11

Introduction
Baidyanath Saraswati 13

Man Greater Than Theorists of Human Science

Anthropology of Surajit Chandra Sinha
— *P.K. Misra* 27

The Implicit Philosophy and Worldview

1. Tribal cosmogony: primal vision of man and cosmos
— *Baidyanath Saraswati* 63
2. Tribal cosmology: displacing and replacing processes in Andamanese places
— *Vishvajit Pandya* 85
3. The tribal worldview: changing perspective
— *Ashim Kumar Adhikary* 105
4. Understanding tribal lore by means of intention theory of meaning
— *S.C. Daniel* 121

Tribal Aesthetics and Science

5. Tribal music: its proper context
— *Onkar Prasad* 131
6. Tribal medicine: a study in Irular science and superstition
— *P.R.G. Mathur* 151

Biological, Psychological Interpretations

7. Small tribal populations: observed patterns of fertility and mortality
— *Arabinda Basu* 169
8. Tribal value pattern: a case study of the Santals
— *Lal Bahadur Singh* and *Balanand Sinha* 183
9. Polyethnic behaviour: Hindu, Muslim and Tribal
— *Kumkum Bhattacharya* 193

The Changing, the Unchanging Tribes

10. Hinduization of tribes: critique and perspective
— *H.K. Bhat* 217
11. Private property formation among highland tribal communities of northeast India
— *S.N. Mishra* 225
12. Industrialization and the nature of tribal transformation
— *Pranab Kumar Das Gupta* 239
13. Kinjoli: a tribal village floating beyond the new wind
— *Raghunath Singh Negi* 247

Index of tribes 254

NOTES ON CONTRIBUTORS

ASHIM KUMAR ADHIKARY (*b.* 1943), Ph.D. Reader in Social Anthropology, Visva-Bharati, Santiniketan. Author of one book and twenty articles.

ARABINDA BASU (*b.* 1931), Ph.D. Executive Editor, *Journal of the Indian Anthropological Society* (Calcutta); former Senior Physical Anthropologist, Anthropological Survey of India. Author of four books and thirty articles.

H.K. BHAT (*b.* 1949), Ph.D. Reader in Anthropology, Mysore University. Specialization in Medical Anthropology.

KUMKUM BHATTACHARYA (*b.* 1955), Ph.D. Reader in Psychology, Visva-Bharati, Santiniketan. Author of three articles.

S.C. DANIEL (*b.* 1938), Ph.D. Reader in Philosophy, North-Eastern Hill University, Shillong. Specialization in Western Philosophy.

PRANAB KUMAR DAS GUPTA (*b.* 1938), Ph.D. Deputy Director, Anthropological Survey of India. Author of four books and several papers.

P.R.G. MATHUR (*b.* 1934), M.A. in Sociology, Ph.D. in Anthropology. Former Director, Kerala Institute for Research Training and Development Studies of Scheduled Castes and Scheduled Tribes. Author of four books and several papers.

S.N. MISHRA (*b.* 1935), Ph.D. Professor of Economics and Director, Institute of Economic Growth, Delhi; recipient of Jawaharlal Nehru Fellowship 1982-84. Author of five books and several papers on development planning and tribal transformation.

P.K. Misra (*b.* 1936), Ph.D. Professor of Anthropology, North-Eastern Hill University, Shillong; founder Director, Tribal Research. Tamil University, Udhagamandalam. Author of nine books and several papers.

Raghunath Singh Negi (*b.* 1932), Ph.D. Professor of Anthropology, Gadhawal University, Srinagar (U.P.); founder Director, Rashtriya Manava Sangrahalaya, Bhopal. Author of several important papers in Physical Anthropology.

Vishvajit Pandya (*b.* 1956), M.A. in Sociology, Ph.D. in Anthropology. Assistant Professor of Anthropology, Westminster College, Fulton USA. Forthcoming publications: one book and six papers concerning ethnohistory of the Andaman and Nicobar Islands.

Onkar Prasad (*b.* 1948), Ph.D. Reader in Rural Sociology, Visva-Bharati, Santiniketan. Author of two books and several papers. Specialization in Ethnomusicology.

Baidyanath Saraswati (*b.* 1932), Ph.D. Research Professor, Indira Gandhi National Centre for the Arts, New Delhi; former Professor of Anthropology, North-Eastern Hill University, Shillong. Author of seven books and several papers.

Lal Bahadur Singh (*b.* 1949), Ph.D. Reader in Psychology, Bhagalpur University. Author of two books and forty papers.

Balanand Sinha (*b.* 1953), M.A. in Psychology, Ph.D. in Anthropology. Reader in Psychology, Bhagalpur University. Author of one book and thirty papers. Specialization in Psychological Anthropology.

INTRODUCTION

Baidyanath Saraswati

Anthropology of Tribe

Tribe, a separate humanity

Anthropologically speaking, man is the product of an evolutionary process which determines his nature, talents and power. Civilization is postulated as an historic form of social life that has evolved along a measured line of savagery, barbarism and civilization. The contemporary human groups in a state of, or carrying traces of, the original conditions of life are the survivals of the lower grades of culture, namely, savagery and barbarism. They are branded as 'primitive', characterized as: a complete world; a mental universe; with its own special cast or character; autonomous; isolated, remaining always within a small territory; a single biological type; in a state of homogeneity and uncritical mind; with norms and behaviour conventionally patterned; strongly ethnocentric; etc. But, as anthropologists realized that few real society could correspond to the ideal type 'primitive', they began using an alternative term 'tribe'. Tribe refers to a 'constellation of somewhat reformed aspects of primitive life, generally constituting a homogeneous unit, speaking a common language, claiming a common ancestry, living in a particular geographical area, lacking in scientific knowledge and modern technology, and having a social structure based on kinship'. The subtlity of the definition is that tribe in relation to modern society is a separate humanity.

Tribe, an unfettered life to be left alone

Traditional Indian society is a challenge to the anthropological definition of tribe. India's major population is organized into a highly intellectualized *varna-jati* system within which there are a large number of non-literate groups clearly identifiable with the so-called 'primitive' or 'tribal'. Many of the beliefs and practices of the *varna-jati* people are indistinguishable from the relatively isolated forest-dwelling primitive groups. The British administrator-anthropologists, who were the first to introduce anthropology in India, could not comprehend the complexity of the Indian situation. It was on their recommendations that, for administrative purposes, the Indian population was divided into caste and tribe, and certain parts of the country were reserved as aboriginal areas, or what was technically known as Excluded Area and Partially Excluded Area. Indian anthropologists of that time supported the British policy, unfortunately, not so much in the zeal of science and independent thinking as in the romantic spirit of misplaced emotions. They were enamoured by the free and unfettered life of the jungle tribes, and hence pleaded that the tribes be left alone. In their opinion contact with the 'outside' world has proved fatal for the tribe: 'disintegration and degradation' (S.C. Roy) and 'rapid disappearance' (D.N. Majumdar). Verrier Elwin suggested the establishment of a national park in which the tribes might take refuge. On the other hand, the nationalist social workers like A.V. Thakkar Bapa vehemently opposed the anthropological theory of separation and isolation. The Indian National Congress also held the view that the Excluded Areas were a trick of the anthropologists to preserve the aboriginals as museum specimen for the exercise of their 'blessed science'.

Tribe, an interdependent structure of Indian civilization

Anthropology of tribes in India entered into a new theoretical debate with N.K. Bose identifying the Hindu method of tribal absorption and G.S. Ghurye considering tribe as a Hindu subsystem. Surajit Chandra Sinha followed it up systematically and profoundly and has since made significant contributions to both theory and method (see P.K. Misra). His theoretical thrust has been evolutionary; but he has always laid emphasis on a natural historical (nomothetic) approach, with descriptive integration in his ethnographic presentation of the tribal cultures. He tried to place the social formations in a historical perspective, and yet retaining a core concern about the evolutionary levels. He views the ethnic groups in India – tribe or caste – as one species, *homo sapiens*. His special interest has been in the primary civilization. He has described the vital elements of continuity between the tribal cultures and the Hindu caste-peasants, and has noted the possibility of an orthogenetic development of civilization in India from a 'tribal' culture base. He identifies among the tribal groups the unique processes of adaptations, such as devolution, secondary primitivization, withdrawal, oscillation, and regional universalization and participation in the caste-peasant base of Indian civilization through the intervention of state-formation. Subsequently, he has emphasized that the tribes in the Indian mainland should be looked as 'interdependent historic structures'. However, he still keeps up his predilections for looking at tribe as a quality of socio-cultural integration, as having a distinct lifestyle, a state of mind and worldview. Sinha has stimulated a whole generation of Indian anthropologists to develop finer insights on tribe in the broader context of Indian civilization.

Tribe, not the 'other'

The next step, now, is to raise a more fundamental methodological question. Is there anything in the classical Indian thought structure, or in the traditional organization of Indian society, that may correspond to the evolutionary anthropological notion of tribe? I would say, there is absolutely nothing. Then, is there anything in the tribal thought structure, or in the tribal culture itself, that stands in opposition to the classical Indian vision of man and culture? I personally don't think so. But, then, how will this be ascertained? Tribal cultures are essentially oral, unwritten and 'without explanation'. Can anthropologists truly interpret tribal tradition? They do interpret. But to what extent are their interpretations relevant and authentic, especially for those people whose tradition has been interpreted? The problem takes a keen edge in anthropological assumption. Is the interpretation of the observer same as that of the observed? If the answer is yes, then the anthropologists' interpretation is misleading, because the relationship between the observer and the observed is asymmetrical. Following the anthropologists' own argument, the 'civilized mind' (the observer) is logical, rational, supremely abstract and scientific, while the 'savage mind' (the observed) is prelogical, irrational, supremely concrete and superstitious. Consequently, there can be no possible, or proper, communication between the observer and the observed. If so, then all anthropological interpretations, howsoever sound and invaluable they may be in their own right, are of little relevance for the tribe, and, perhaps, also intrinsically false because they do not present the true state of the tribal tradition. Thus, interpretation by the 'other' – be he a philosopher or a psychologist or an anthropologist, be it rosy or derogatory – is a caricature. This general problem has caused methodological discussion in anthropology for the past few years, and the importance of the 'native's point of view' has now been acclaimed.

I have myself been an advocate of the anthropological use of the 'self-interpretation' of cultures. But it seems to me now that the question of the 'other' has to be addressed more realistically. What difference will the 'native's viewpoint' make in anthropological interpretation as long as the natives are considered the 'other', and their way of life looked upon from outside? What good will it serve as long as the evolutionary anthropological theory of man, history and civilization is treated as sacrosanct? Obviously, then, the notion of the 'other' needs reconsideration. At some point, the 'self' of the anthropologist, I suggest, will have to grow into a *vishvarupa,* encompassing all the 'other'. This necessitates a further search for alternatives to the modern science of man. In such a venture, of course, there will be no room for a monolithic universal theory of man that can be applied to all cultures. Perhaps, there is no need to pursue that end.

Tribal Thought

The knowledge-system

In the tribal knowledge-system, myth is entry into unthought and unthinkable and ritual is an act that leads into direct contact with the experiential reality. Tribal myths say that priests of all creatures were born at the beginning of the creation and that primordial knowledge came to human beings from birds and animals. The significance of this belief is that the universal knowability lies with the transcendence and man is not unique in the possession of knowledge. This is contrary to the professed anthropological theory.

In tribal cultures, intellectual construction has been given no pride of place, and hence, it may be characterized as "culture without explanation". This statement may, of course, be taken with some caution. For, tribal creation myths are of wide-ranging variations; but in them there is an implicit philosophy that points to the same reality.

The text of a myth multiplies in course of time through a natural process of reinterpretation and reformation, leaving the core tradition unaffected. This has been possible because the tribes do not manipulate their myths as an intellectual game. For them, all descriptions, explanations and interpretations have only secondary value; what is central in the myth is the fulfilment of the original 'intention'. Hence, as S.C. Daniel suggests, tribal lore can be understood best by the intention theory of meaning.

The vision of man and cosmos

The tribal notion of man stands in sharp contrast to the Western anthropocentric-turned-ethnocentric-turned-technocentric theory of man. An analysis of the cosmogonic myths of the North-East tribes, has shown (B. Saraswati) that in tribal perception, neither man nor god is unique. Nobody reigns supreme, one is only different from the other. Every creature performs the same paradigmatic act of creation, preservation and destruction. The cosmic order is maintained by a harmonious functioning of each one of them. The first principle of the cosmos is 'one-two-and-many', and what makes the cosmos one undifferentiated reality is its eternal law of nonduality. Tribal eschatological beliefs support the theory that the ontological experience of life and death is the same. This truth of unity of all experiences was visualized and stated exactly in the same form also by the Upanisadic *Risis*.

Anthropologists have reported on the tribes making perceptible differentiation in the existential contexts of life situations. A.K. Adhikary finds that the Birhor distinguish between *disum*, their own territory in the jungle, and *muluk*, the territory dominated by the caste peasants. They also distinguish themselves as *hor* from others as *diku*. It would, however, be unrealistic to expect the tribes not making differentiation between the ontological reality and the existential reality. V. Pandya provides a good example of the Ongee idea of hierarchically differentiated relations among the spirits, humans and animals. If in the Ongee worldview every relation and phenomenon has a place and every place has a particular relation and phenomenon to it, then the principle of hierarchy can easily be understood in terms of maintaining the cosmic order. Here hierarchy means the sacred order (*hieros*) rather than the social idea, or the ideal, of gradation. The spirits, humans and animals are differentiated at the existential level, but there is nothing in the Ongee cosmology that may convey the ontological separateness between the three. Perhaps, the best way to grasp the differentiation is to think of the functional aspect of interrelatedness of all existing things and beings in the larger context of the cosmic process.

The changing worldview

Adhikary has observed that elements of the tribal worldview change as the tribes come in contact with the wider world but the experiences of the new world, though enter into their consciousness, lack meanings in the context of their life and culture. Anthropological position about the changing worldview of the tribes must, therefore, be taken with caution. Unlike the 'modern' societies, a basic characteristic of all traditional societies is that there is no gap in their knowledge and existence. The moment a tribal society loses this unique feature, its purity and distinction are lost for ever. But this does not mean that the tribal world is static and closed. There has always been active incorporation of the new elements and reformation of the old, the evidence of which can be found in the elaboration of myths and general beliefs. However, affirmation of new ideas is possible only within the basic ontological categories. Difficulties arise when cosmologies are in conflict. The following autobiographical statements by B.M. Pugh (*The story of a tribal: an autobiography*, Calcutta, 1976), a Christian Khasi by birth, trained in agricultural science in the USA, and a public man of high repute, are relevant :

> . . . the conversion of my father to Christianity, to a very large extent, explains why I am a Christian. As I ponder over the faith of my forebears, the earlier Khasis, I feel ashamed that my faith in god and my belief in prayers are not as strong as theirs. . . . There are spirits and demons in the Khasi belief which are responsible for evils, sufferings, and disease in the world and have to be appeased, but they are lesser deities, and there are many of them, very often associated with peaks or valleys and even with trees. My faith and belief have now become diluted. If there is heaven I am sure that my non-Christian grand-father will be sitting in the higher heavens while I, a professed Christian, may not even find a place in the lower heavens.
>
> As a religious man I believe in God and being a man, my God

also is anthropomorphic, while in my heart of hearts, I do not believe that it can be so. Jesus himself has said: 'God is a spirit' or 'God is spirit'. But being also a Khasi tribal who live in a Khasi land, in spite of my science and Christian theology, I continue to pray to God who seems to me circumscribed in the environment in which I live.

When I stand there on Mawthohrew Peak (on the outskirts of Shillong) above the green pine forests I imagine that when I die my soul will fly and go down beyond Diengiei – the peak to the West – as I can never imagine that the spirit at the end of a life could ever go East (according to Khasi belief).

When I die, my desire is that I may be cremated as I do not wish that my body should lie in close company with the saints, neither do I wish that my mortal remains should unnecessarily encumber the ground which is so hard pressed because of the increasing population.

Tribal Culture

The perfect form

If culture is defined as a human form of life aesthetically harmonic and spiritually tuned with Nature, I submit, many of the so-called primitive tribes are still in their 'perfect form'. 'The perfect form' of a culture is that which has a critical mass and within which perfect identification with the Nature is established, a self-organizing system is developed, and a self-generating, self-experiencing and self-perpetuating bliss is reached. When a self-willing and self-thinking culture loses its autonomy, the 'perfect form' is destroyed, and when the 'perfect form' is destroyed the bliss is lost for ever.

A. Basu draws our attention to the problems of survivality of some of the small populations such as Jarva, Sentinelese and Ongee. Among the possible factors responsible for the decline of a population, the ABO(H) blood incompatibility causing infertility, and inadequate nutrition and poor health leading to low fertility and high mortality have been identified.

As the studies of palaeontologists have proved, biological extinction of species is a natural phenomenon. Certain forms of life have disappeared in course of their evolution, many of them on account of ecological imbalances. Cultural imbalance, I think, is yet another contributing factor in the decline of human populations. It appears that the Ongee and other small populations in the Andaman Islands have lost interest in life because their 'perfect form' has been endangered by a mighty technocentric culture whose lifestyle does not correspond with the tribal vision of life.

Thought and behaviour

A consideration of tribal thought and behaviour (action) is doubly necessary: first, to focus on the relationship between the mythic thought and wisdom, and secondly, to find out the connection between ideology and behaviour.

L.B. Singh and B. Sinha have observed that while the tribals (the Santal) have significantly lower theoretical, political and economic value, they are well-endowed with social, aesthetic, religious and moral values, and that their deficiency in scientific zeal and aptitude – the ingredients of theoretical value – are attributed to inherent traditionality, superstitions and orthodoxy. What one may draw from this field-tested psychological statement is that the mythic thought (inherent traditionality) is in no way a hindrance to 'wisdom' (high social, aesthetic, religious, moral values). Extending the argument further, it can as well be said that there is no positive correspondence between the logical thought (theory, science, rationality) and wisdom.

Another psychological study of the same tribe by K. Bhattacharya shows that in a polyethnic interaction between Hindu, Muslim and Santal, the first two groups maintain social hierarchy and distance within and between themselves: the Hindu have encapsulated the Santal but the Muslim maintain social distance with them; the Santal are, however, contained within themselves and there is no overt expression of their feelings towards the Hindu and the Muslim. Thus, what seems as an incontestable conclusion is that the more theoretically oriented and ideologically perfect a society (the Advaitin Hindu, the egalitarian Muslim), the greater the gap between its thought and behaviour. In other words, in a tribal society, behaviour, or practice, takes primacy over thought, and ideology is identified with action. In short, there is no room for inconsistency in tribal thought and action.

The musical model

A 'perfect form' organizes itself on the model of sound. Sound is the primordial substance of the world. Creation began with the Big Bang, say the ancient philosophers and modern scientists. In man's life, sound enters at the stage of foetus, stays in the mother's womb, comes out with the first cry of the baby, and later gets interiorized and structured as a creative principle for all human actions. The rhythm of life flows with the heart-beat, and as the sound of breath stops the light of life is gone. The vital functions of life-experiencing and -expressing are grounded in sound. Sound brings awareness, helps communication, and plays a pivotal role in the organization of social life. Music is its finest fruition. There is something divine about music. It is the essence of life, the fragrance of all cultures. There is no culture without music.

O. Prasad's ethnomusicological essay on the Santal is an invitation to consider a theory that musical cosmology conforms to the basic pattern of a culture in which it is grounded. Metaphorically speaking, as are the *svara* embodied in the *svara-mandala* (the tone-circle) so are the members of the Santal community organically connected with one another. Their collective and total participation in the musical performance is an empirical affirmation of the visible tribal 'harmony'. Similarly, the sexual differentiation of role, with regard to the use of musical instrument, has a function which is analogous to that of a *sruti* and a *jati* in the *svara-mandala*; and the collective ownership of musical instrument symbolizes the tribal bond of 'unity'. The Santal perception of music – 'always good' – corresponds with the theory of *rasa* that hinges on the ontological meaning of 'perfection'. The statement that the proper contexts of tribal music are both social and ritual – conforming to the *desi* and *marga* classification – affirms the existence of 'symmetrical' relationship between the sacred and the secular. The *dasae* music, which is aimed at establishing direct contact with the spirits, calls the principle of "balance" into play. Thus, it follows from the musical model of the Santal that the texture of tribal culture is woven by such fine strings as 'symmetry', 'balance', 'unity', 'harmony' and 'perfection'.

P.R.G. Mathur's study of the Irular science of medicine is a further support to the musical model of tribal culture. His concluding statements are: 'In the tribal worldview body, mind and spirit are inseparable. As and when the harmony between them is broken sickness and misfortune arise. To bring things to order one has to return to the primordial sources of existence, the Nature.' To say differently, the tribals believe that disunity, disharmony and imbalance bring disorder and threaten the well-being of all.

Let me sum-up. In musical terms, 'tasting' (experiencing) and 'tuning' (expressing) are the stimulus of all cultures; and ideally speaking, 'symmetry', 'balance', 'harmony', 'unity' and 'perfection' constitute the tone-circle of a tribal culture.

Culture change

Discussions on culture change are usually set within the context of 'modern' culture. For, the parameters of progress and change are invariably those that have been determined by the cosmological view of the modern technocentric society. The whole enterprise of action and applied anthropology is centred around a discussion on modern versus traditional, where 'tradition' is defined in terms of immobility and 'modern' represents the ideal model of change. But this is not what I propose to do here. I wish to concentrate on a description purely from the tribal point of view.

The expression 'tribes have a perfect form' is linked with the question of whether the 'perfect form' is subject to change. Or do tribes recognize the factors and forces of change? Obviously, there is hardly any society that does not change, or profit from the experiences of time. But cultures may differ in their attitudes towards change, depending on how they conceptualize time, history and man. To tribes, time and space are interrelated, man's activities are synchronous with the cosmic forces. And hence, the tribal people experience time in a continuous present, that is, past (ancestral tradition) is lived in (reactualization of myths) and the future (collective needs) encountered by such means as rituals and oracular practices. My point is that tribes do have the fundamental intuition of change, but in terms of both emphasis and perception they differ significantly from the 'modern' societies stimulated by the idea of breathless change and limitless progress. Their thought is rooted in the unchanging 'real'. They see moon wax and wane, and all other natural phenomena undergoing a similar process of deformation and reformation. Hence, in the tribal cosmology the form is 'Real' (permanent) and changes occur only within the limits of an unalterable form. The limits are defined by the natural law of harmony which a culture may seek and obtain through the avenue of life-experiences. There are two types of change: endogenous, and exogenous. Endogenous change maintains the natural rhythm of a culture; exogenous change creates an artificial rhythm. Both may occur simultaneously, in some cases contributing to the enrichment of human life and in others creating confusion and impoverishment.

Endogenous change is normally so smooth and silent, as also gracious and harmonious, that it may, at times, be difficult to comprehend the reality of change. R. S. Negi has visited a Bastar tribal village several times over a period of two decades and finds that the communication system in the Bastar region has improved significantly, the modern institutional buildings have come up conspicuously, the shops have grown phenomenally, and the business houses have made inroads right into the village; and yet the eternal tribal life flows there, unaffected by the new wind. It has also been reported that while the traditional institutions and landmarks in the village are well-maintained the new features introduced by the State agency are ill-maintained, and that there has been no change in the village settlement pattern and no change in women's hairstyle. Clearly, no tribe wants to lose its self-generating and self-organizing ability, and no woman is willing to give up her enduring aesthetic sense. Assessing the opportunity structure and tribal situation in time, Negi seems to be overwhelmed by the deeper paradox of unchangeability. But a closer look at the situation will reveal that unchangeability is more apparent than real. Negi's own reference to the villagers' ardent concern for the visiting anthropologists is a clear pointer to the broadening horizon of the tribal psyche. If tribals are ideally 'a complete world, a mental universe, where members live in intimacy with one another and with no other', then the Kinjoli tribes' sentimental yearnings for the outsiders – Tandon, Hasin, Negi – are surely a perceptible evidence of the endogenous change in their fundamental view on life.

However, the complexity of the tribal situation in India is such that, more often than not, it is difficult to comprehend as to whether a particular change is endogenous or exogenous. H.K. Bhat has reviewed the anthropological literature on what he calls Hinduization of tribes, and has also given his own ideas on the universal process of Hinduization. In this context what seems to me worth questioning is the directionality of the very process of Hinduization. If Hinduization is not a process of conversion, and if tribe is a Hindu sub-system then the question of its Hinduization does not really arise. Should caste and tribe be admitted as separate categories, it would become obligatory to determine as to whether the degree of Hinduization of tribe is greater than the degree of tribalization of caste. This, as we know, is neither easy nor worth pursuing a task. If Hinduization refers to an internal process of revitalization, then such changes in tribal cultures as resulting from the process of Hinduization will have to be considered endogenous.

Exogenous change, from the point of view of the tribal tradition, is generally degenerative in nature, the evidence of which comes from S.N. Mishra's study of the highland tribes of North-East India and P.K. Das Gupta's report on the industrialization of the tribes. The highlanders' time-honoured tradition of corporate life and common ownership of land was broken as soon as the British penetrated into their territory, and subsequently as they introduced money economy and conferred private property rights in land to the chiefs. Privatization of property received tremendous boost in the post-Independence period, when money flew into private hands in several different ways. Under the circumstances, the very foundation of the tribal culture was shaken and eventually all aspects of tribal life were adversely affected. Following the industrialization of their homeland, the tribes were uprooted from their cultural moorings. It reduced them to a state of cultural subjection, placed them marginally in the industrial organization, and forced them to a bi-cultural way of existence.

Changes originating from radically different cosmologies prevent the endogenous growth of a culture. In the case of tribal cultures, its consequences are far more disastrous: a loss of cultural autonomy, that is, the self-contained tribal system becoming a sub-system; tribesmen live a double-life; becoming depersonalized, individualized, emotionally shallow, atomized, unstable and other-directed; and, finally, suffer from identity crisis. From the 'modernist' viewpoint, the exogenous change brings the tribe a new form of life, a new social type, a new outlook, an enlarged universal consciousness, and a civilization to be identified with.

In any case, it is neither the endogenous nor the exogenous change itself which can be taken as an ultimate value, or goal of life. Change is only a process of becoming. More important is the vision of a culture that makes its aesthetic experience and creative expressions fully integrated and satisfying. For this, I believe, the tribal musical model is a very good example.

MAN GREATER THAN THEORISTS OF HUMAN SCIENCE

ANTHROPOLOGY OF SURAJIT CHANDRA SINHA

P. K. Misra

Introduction

Initiation in Anthropology

Surajit Chandra Sinha (b. 1926), who now prefers a shorter version of his name as Surajit Sinha, has a brilliant academic record. He graduated in Chemistry, Mathematics and Geology with honours (B.Sc. 1947), and wanted to do his M.Sc. in Physics but too much of Mathematics prevented him from doing that course. Circumstances prompted him to join Anthropology. While doing B.Sc. he had gone to Chaibasha (Singhbhum, Bihar) on one of his vacations. There he visited some of the Ho tribal settlements. This was his first exposure to the tribal world. He liked their simple and down-to-earth lifestyle. In September 1946, when educational institutions were closed on account of wide spread disturbances, following Indian Independence movement, he took his father's permission to travel in Santal region. The inspiration came to him from his uncle who then had just returned from Deogarh (Santal Pargana, Bihar). His uncle was a guest of William Archer, the famous British administrator, who had by then compiled valuable notes on the life of the Santal. So when he returned to Calcutta he had a lot of stories to tell to his nephew and other members of the family. His uncle had made some sketches of the Santal way of life.

Surajit Sinha's father readily permitted him to travel to the Santal area but advised him to carry a gun for his safety. So a gun in one hand, and sketch book and pencil in the other, he travelled through the tribal area.

Surajit Sinha enjoyed his visit to the Santal area very much. He collected Santal songs and made sketches of their life. These sketches were later exhibited in Calcutta and were reasonably well-received. Stella Kramrisch, the well-known art critic, who was then at Calcutta commended his sketches. During this visit Boddings' book on the Santal was presented to him by a missionary. These were the early impressions which slowly grew into him a life-long interest in people.

After obtaining B.Sc. degree in first class, scoring a high percentage of marks, Sinha approached K.P. Chattopadhya, then Professor of Anthropology at Calcutta University for advice. Chattopadhya told him that the track record of Geology students joining the Master degree course in Anthropology had been very good (Dharni Sen and Nirmal Kumar Bose, for examples).

Sinha followed Chattopadhya's advice and obtained an M.Sc. degree in Anthropology in 1949. In his fieldreport paper, he got the highest marks which has been a record at the Department of Anthropology, Calcutta University. N.K. Bose was his examiner. This performance not only enabled Sinha to get a scholarship of Rs.100 but also earned a life-long goodwill of Bose.

Research career in Anthropology

For his doctoral work Bose wanted Sinha to study the Juang, but T.C. Das, who was known as an excellent teacher and trainer in fieldwork, encouraged him to study the Bhumij. Das favoured study of the Bhumij because this community had been studied earlier by scholars such as Dalton and Risley, and he thought that the base-line data would be available to find out what changes had taken place in the community. Das advised him to select a village for intensive study.

Sinha took the advice of Das. Bhumij became his life-long interest, though soon he was to realize that it was not enough to study a village, or a series of villages, to understand the social formation among the Bhumij. During his life-long association with Bhumij he carried out both intensive and extensive fieldwork in the region. Data on almost all aspects of anthropological study were collected first by himself and later with the assistance of his colleagues in the Anthropological Survey of India.

Assignment from the West Bengal Government

While doing his Ph.D. work among the Bhumij, Sinha had a brief assignment from the West Bengal Government to study the problem of the Bengali settlers in the Andaman Islands. He visited the Islands and prepared a report based on the data he collected there. The visit enabled him to get acquainted with the problems of the primitives. At that time, there were at least two populations in the Andamans which had no contact whatsoever with the civilization, and the Ongee were in the process of being settled. This experience, though brief, was valuable. Much later Sinha was to contrast these populations with food-gatherers and hunters of other regions under the pressure of the expanding civilization in terms of primary and secondary primitives.

Sinha was awarded a Fulbright Fellowship to do Ph.D. at the North-Western University, USA (1953-56). The topic of his Ph.D dissertation was "The acculturation of the Bhumij of Manbhum : a study in social class formation and ethnic integration".

In the USA, Sinha came in contact with several eminent scholars such as Robert Redfield, Milton Singer and McKim Marriot, to name only a few. Recommendations of Alfred Kroeber enabled him to get a brief assignment at the University of California, Berkeley. These years in the USA and his association with the American scholars interested in India, particularly Robert Redfield, proved extremely beneficial in the pursuance and development of his interests in Anthropology.

Formative period in ASI

On Robert Redfield's recommendations, Sinha got some funds from Ford Foundation to study State formation in Manbhum. He returned to India and started collecting data. Meanwhile there was an advertisement for the post of Anthropologist in the Anthropological Survey of India (ASI) (then known as the Department of Anthropology). He applied for the post and was selected. He was posted at Nagpur and later he became officer-in-charge of the Central India Station of the ASI. Sinha's association with ASI from 1957 to 1961 marks an important phase in his anthropological career. He supervised a variety of research programmes, two most important being socio-cultural, linguistic and biological studies of the people of Bastar, and all-India material trait survey. We will come to the material trait survey a little later. Along with these programmes, he also carried out fieldwork in Manbhum region with the assistance of some of his colleagues in ASI. His work on the Bhumij resulted in a series of landmark publications on Indian anthropology: Bhumij-Kshatriya social movement in south Manbhum (1959b), State formation and Rajput myth in tribal central India (1962), levels of economic initiative and ethnic groups in Pargana Barabhum (1963), and tribe-caste and tribe-peasant continua in central India (1965b). These papers have been widely cited in the anthropological literature.

In his paper on Bhumij-Kshatriya movement (1959b), Sinha identifies the urge of the Bhumij to move away from the tribal base to acquire a Kshatriya status. Sinha made a significant observation that while the Bhumij aspired for Kshatriya status, the secular movements, the pan-Adivasi movement, the world of Bengali upper caste Hindus, the State and Central Governments, the various political parties had all substantially remained external to the Bhumij world; and in 1951when the Bhumij were labelled as one of the scheduled tribes of the region, they were shocked and protested against it.

In his paper on State formation (1962) Sinha found that the State formation among the tribes of central India was an indigenous effort, but the same, he added, could not be considered in isolation from the overall Hindu milieu. This was a significant departure from the existing idea that the tribes were an isolated people. His ideas about Indian civilization and tribes which he had elaborated in several other publications (1957a, 1958b, 1965) are also reflected in this paper. He observed, "the diffusion of the Rajput model of State as also indigenous development process could gain ground only among those tribal groups like Bhumij, Munda, Gond, or Bhuiyan who had attained the technological level of settled agriculture" (1962: 174). However, he indicated that the Ho and the Santal have been an exception to this rule. He further observed that although the tribals had the Rajput States as model, there were significant differences between the two. The final validation of the tribal States was in terms of kinship, marriage and ritual symbols, suggesting that the tribes retain their identity in the Indian context.

His paper on levels of economic initiative (1963) is extremely important for those who are interested in social development and planning. Sinha observed that different communities in Pargana Barabhum show different levels of economic initiative in spite of the fact that the people of different communities had been interacting with each other for a long time. In other words, there cannot be a uniform policy of development.

In 'Tribe-caste and tribe-peasant continua' (1965) Sinha has systematized his ideas about the tribe, seen in the overall context of the

Hindu castes on the one hand and technological development leading to settled plough cultivation on the other. However, he cautioned that technological evolution, population growth and increase in settlement size by themselves did not generate caste system among the tribes (p.78). As for the data on Manbhum, publication like 'Agriculture crafts and weekly markets of south Manbhum' (1961c) and "Ethnic groups, villages and towns of Pargana Barabhum" (1966c) indicate how extensively the area was surveyed by him.

His supervision of the work in Bastar, a typical tribal region, helped him to further sharpen his ideas about the tribes in India.

All-India material trait survey

When Nirmal Kumar Bose joined as Director of the Anthropological Survey of India he wanted to test his hypothesis of the culture zones of India. Sinha was entrusted with the responsibility of carrying out the material trait survey.

A preliminary schedule for a pilot study in sixteen contiguous districts in Madhya Pradesh (Jabalpur division) and Maharashtra (Vidarbha division) was drawn up in March 1959. Sixteen workers were engaged for this work and the results of the pilot programme were evaluated and later the project was launched in 1959. Data were collected from 311 out of 322 districts of India during October 1959 to March 1961. Altogether 430 villages were studied. In selecting the villages, urban centres and typical isolated tribal villages were avoided. The data so collected were transferred on cards. Altogether data on 41 different material traits were available. After the data were transferred on cards, the same were arranged traitwise for the entire country. The research workers were then asked to write reports on the selected traits on an all-India basis. A preliminary report on eleven items was published by the ASI in 1961 under the title *Peasant life in India : a study in Indian unity and diversity*.

This was a stupendous task. While the project provided a significant picture of the distribution of some material traits for the whole country, it trained young research workers in accurate observation, recording, classification and analysis. Sinha was the man behind all this. While he would not allow any let up in the target set for collection of data, writing of reports, etc., the young researchers working with him had all the freedom to think independently and argue out their points of views. Sinha's leadership was democratic, liberal and humane to the core. He encouraged and inspired the young researchers to develop their own interests. Sinha was quick in discovering a new idea or a point in the young researchers deliberations which he would refer to in his talks, discussions, letters and papers. This had a tremendous effect on the young researchers. They were transformed into persons having ideas. This stimulated them to no end and led them to work with a zeal which hitherto was unknown in a government research organization.

Thus, his contribution to this project was not only in terms of getting the whole work done and a report published but training and enthusing a band of young researchers, who later on became scholars on their own right.

Sinha, who already was trying to see things of the local level in an all-India perspective, got the opportunity to further develop these ideas, owing to his intensive involvement in the all-India material trait survey. He also had the benefit of interacting with so many young research workers from different regions of the country. The impact of this project on him and the spirit of collegium that he had created among the young scholars in the Anthropological Survey of India get fully reflected in the programme of research that was adopted when he had a second stint with the ASI.

Second trip to USA

In 1961, Sinha left the Anthropological Survey India and joined the University of Chicago as a Visiting Fellow. This trip was quite different from the previous one. He was already an established professional anthropologist. He not only had done intensive field investigation in the region inhabited by the Bhumij but had been closely associated with other research projects of the ASI. In 1962-63, he was at Duke University, USA. He spent the summer of 1963 in studying an American village which he called as Mapel town. In this study his main concern was to know as to why religion persists in the most technologically advanced country such as America contrary to the expectation. He was also interested in finding out the relationship between the secular and sacred life there. This study was published in *Current Anthropology* (1966a). Besides some very pertinent and incisive observations of the village-life in America, he observed that field conditions are entirely different in America than in the villages of India.

In 1964-65, Sinha moved to the Centre for Behavioural Sciences, Stanford University, USA, where he was a Fellow in Sociology.

He enjoyed his stay in the USA, particularly the interaction with fellow intellectuals. No doubt the interaction was of the higher order but he felt it was 'too much cerebration' and he was missing interaction with the people closer to life.

In 1965, he returned to India and joined Palli Siksa Sadan at Santiniketan. From there, in 1966 he moved on to the Institute of Management as Professor.

His research interest in tribe-caste relations continued. In his paper 'Caste in modern India: its essential pattern of socio-cultural integration' (1967a), he tried to examine the basic principles which guide the patterns of interaction between the ethnic groups within the caste system in India. His interest in religion also continued and he published a few papers on this topic (1966a, b).

Second stint at ASI

At the time when Sinha joined the ASI for the second time (1967-75), most of the research programmes that were taken up after the all-India material trait survey were nearing completion, such as potters and their pottery, fishermen and their craft, nomads, and caste *panchayats*. The impact of Christianity, industrialization on tribes and various mobility movements among various populations were also studied in detail. Although Sinha himself with N.K. Bose was responsible for initiating these research programmes he realized that there was an element of ad-hocism in selecting the topics for research. He felt that there should be a little more debate to systematize the ideas and programmes. Perhaps the time was ripe for such an exercise.

Therefore, the first thing that he did was to initiate a dialogue within the ASI as to what should be the programme of research for the next 10 years. It may be worthwhile to recall that he had already done some thinking on this subject. In a paper on 'Urgent research in social anthropology' (1968b) he had given a broad idea of what was to be taken up for research. In his scheme, study of dwindling groups, and problems which give the totality of Indian society and national integration should have priority. These ideas were expressed more elaborately and systematically in the exercise that he initiated at the ASI.

Seminar on research programme

In September 1967, Sinha organized a seminar at the ASI, Calcutta, entitled 'Research programmes on cultural anthropology and allied disciplines'. It was inaugurated by N.K. Bose. Proceedings of the seminar were published under the same title in 1970(c); with the following eleven themes:

1. Tribal solidarity movement.
2. Comparative study of the fisherfolk.
3. Complex religious institutions.
4. Comparative study of the nomads.
5. Impact of industrialization and urbanization on tribes.
6. Ethnographic research.
7. Area studies.
8. Ethnomusicology.
9. Psychology.
10. Linguistics.
11. Photography and cinematography.

Introducing the seminar Sinha highlighted the point that the success of the research programmes albeit the success of the Survey itself would depend upon rigorous and detailed planning. This exercise, he said, would reflect the range of interest of the Survey. Giving a brief history of the Survey, he said that so far the approach for understanding the reality of India had been through fringe, like the study of tribes, peasants, fisherfolk, nomads, etc., but the core too should be focused. He wanted civilizational centres and associated networks also to be studied; and the transformation of the Indian society owing to industrialization and urbanization to be adequately covered. These were new research focuses for the ASI and new emphasis for anthropology in general.

Soon after the seminar, the work got started on different research projects. However, for a variety of reasons, pace and enthusiasm could not be sustained on all the research projects.

Weaker section study

Towards the end of the '60s and early part of the '70s there was a tremendous focus on the poor in the country. Removal of poverty became a national objective. Various research organizations of the country had a variety of research and applied programmes on the poor. For the ASI, being a government organization, it became a thrust area of research.

In 1972, Sinha organized a seminar on the weaker sections of Indian population and it was decided to study a village intensively in each State. Unfortunately before final reports could be prepared, Sinha left the ASI and the weaker sections study was left in the lurch.

Two other important research programmes initiated during the tenure of Sinha were the border area study and bio-anthropological study of the Indian population.

Collegium of young scholars

Apart from these, the most significant change that Sinha brought into the ASI was a sense of freedom, participation and dignity among the research staff in spite of its built-in bureaucratic hierarchy. To further loosen the organization from the bureaucratic hold, he promoted the policy of recruiting research fellows from various disciplines and encouraging them to develop a collegium of concerned scholars. *Impromptu colloquiums* and continuous stress on dialogue generated much-needed stimulation for research and self-confidence in the minds of young scholars. Sinha's idea was that the young minds would not only provide the future leadership but also would be able to draw out the regular staff of the ASI from the bureaucratic shell and create an atmosphere conducive to research, dialogue and generation of new ideas.

Widening horizon

In studying Indian civilization, while he continued to approach the subject through the traditional path by focusing researches on religion, its organization, institutions, etc., (1970d, g, 1972c), he added other dimensions too. He initiated the study of scientists and their occupation (1970a, b), the modern hinge groups or cultural brokers. He entered into the arena of urban studies: organized a seminar on Calcutta (1972a) where the attempt was to mop up whatever information one can get through the existing specialists and their ideas about such a conglomeration as Calcutta; and promoted similar efforts at other places, namely, Mysore by P.K. Misra in 1973 and Shillong by B.B.

Goswami in 1979. Sinha (1972b) thought that although urban studies were truly the domain of other social scientists, there was room for qualitative data in them, the speciality of the anthropologist. He indicated that there were numerous points of entry to understand the urban conglomeration.

In *Anthropology of Nirmal Kumar Bose* (1972e, 1986a) one can easily discern the powerful influence Bose had on Sinha. Sinha was much impressed by Bose's varied and chequered career. Bose's insistence on detailed observation has been like a *guru mantra* for Sinha. Sinha has extensively quoted Bose in his own writings. Bose's *Hindu Samajer Gadan* (1949), 'Hindu method of tribal absorption', (1941) and *Paribrajaker Diary* (the diary of a wanderer) had been the favourites of Sinha. Sinha himself floated an organization in 1980 called '*Paribrajak Mandali*', the association of wanderers, to promote communication between urban and rural learning. Both Bose and Sinha value human encounters and feel very strongly against one-way communication system in the modern world. Both felt that the creative urges of the common people have no place in the modern world. Both thought that sensitive intellectuals could become a link in communication of the ideas of common man to the wider world. While Bose extensively wrote about such encounters, Sinha wrote much less but has been consistently communicating such experiences in his informal get-togethers in a true Bengali *adda* style.

Is there an Indian tradition in Anthropology?

In 1968, Sinha wrote a paper entitled 'Is there an Indian tradition in social/cultural anthropology : retrospect and prospect', a theme which was further elaborated in 1971. Here one can easily discern a certain degree of Sinha's restlessness, perhaps arising from his exposure to the anthropology of North America, his concern for the roots of Indian anthropology, and from his association with Nirmal Kumar Bose, the only professional anthropologist who was actively involved in the national struggle for Independence and was also a close associate of Gandhi and quite independent and original in his thinking. Sinha noted that some anthropological writings of Indians in the constructive phase were influenced by national interest but earlier in the formative phase it was the colonial interest. In the current phase, Sinha observed, researchers in anthropology were more or less imitative of what happened in North America. lacking in vigour and independent exploration. He however felt that the new generation showed some promise and social commitment.

These concerns induced him to organize a seminar on fieldwork on the people of India in 1972, the proceedings of which were published in 1978(c). This seminar was unique in the sense that it was an attempt to bring the young Indian scholars together to reflect on what happens in the field.

Search for roots

Sinha left the ASI in 1975 and joined Visva-Bharati, Santiniketan, as its Vice-Chancellor (1975–80). The duties of the Vice-Chancellor leave one with very little time and energy for active research. As Vice-Chancellor Sinha had the benefit of interacting with numerous scholars, perceptive creative writers, painters, sculptors, scientists, etc. Santiniketan is unique in many ways. It carries the halo of Rabindranath Tagore. It has attracted people from all over the world. It is ironic that though Tagore and all those who have been associated with Santiniketan built an intensive humanistic concern there, Santal, an indigenous population of the region on whose idyllic condition Santiniketan was based, were not adequately noticed and appreciated. In fact Santal who love music, poetry and art provide an ideal backdrop to the atmosphere of Santiniketan.

Sinha and his associates realized this and took initiative so that communication between the indigenous Santal and the cultivated gentry of Santiniketan could be established. The Paribrajak Mandali came into being. This is the period when he started rethinking about tribes and Indian civilization (1978b, 1980, 1981, 1982).

In 1980, Sinha came back to active research by joining the Centre for Studies in Social Sciences, Calcutta. He look up his pet theme, State formation among the tribes (1987), and wrote on the development of the tribes (1983), growth of scientific temper in rural context (1984), and on social and ecological contexts of rice cultivation in India (1985).

Themes and issues

Change and individual

Some of the research themes have remained consistent with Sinha, for example the phenomena of change. His concern in the '50s was the tribal transformation. In his paper 'Evolution reconsidered' (1955b), apart from changes due to evolution and culture contact, he considers the role of an individual important in bringing about changes. He believes that the individuals have changed the course of history, and often cites Lenin, Gandhi and Tagore as examples. This idea has remained close to him. He is always on the look-out for interesting and creative individuals, a search which led him to form the Paribrajak Mandali.

Tribe and non-tribe relations

Sinha has been trying to look at the phenomena of change from both theoretical and practical angles. This concern unfolds itself stage by stage as he got involved with the study of the Bhumij.

In his first reconnoitre of the Bhumij area in June-July 1950, he went to select a village for study, and came back with several questions as to why the Bhumij were obsessed about their status in caste hierarchy and at the same time try to maintain an egalitarian stance; why they play down their tribal customs and try to project the Sanskritized version of their customs. He also felt that the Bhumij were like any other caste of the region.

As Sinha got immersed in the field (from August 1950 to August 1951), with the above questions in his mind, his universe of investigation as well as discourse kept on enlarging. He began his study of the Bhumij by concentrating at village-level. Since he was interested in acculturation the bench-mark data were acquired through the memories of old people. In order to find out how the Bhumij in different places have responded to change, he selected a series of villages in a belt, the axis of which was from west to east – the Bhumij were supposed to have a Mundaric base and had moved from Chota Nagpur towards east.

The intensive field investigations made him realize that the satisfactory answers to the questions he had in mind could be got only when he enlarged the context both in time and in space. The 'present' predicament of the Bhumij should be related to the fact that after all the Bhumij were once the ruling group in the region. This led him to examine the Bhumij in the frame of former chieftaincy of Barabhum, covering an area of 635 square miles and 596 revenue villages and their interaction with 64 other ethnic groups. This was done from

October 1956 to December 1957 and again from 1957 to 1960. During this period a formidable amount of field data were collected on the nature of the Bhumij State, its internal administrative divisions and its external inter-connection and the model it had before itself (1962), technology and the nature of interaction with other ethnic groups (1961c, 1965b, 1966b).

Much later Sinha reflecting on his fieldwork observed, "I have tried to convey how systematic perusal of recurrent impression of status anxiety and identity-anomaly among the Bhumij led me to widen the context of space, time and ethnicity in my enquiry on cultural transmission among the Bhumij tribe" (1978c: 155).

This expansion in space and time helped him to discover a wider network and structures leading to all-India Rajpur-Kshatriya linkages (1959b), paving the way for a yet wider frame, namely, Indian civilization (1958b, 1965b, 1970f. His ideas about tribe and Indian civilization get fully elaborated in 1980.

Evolutionary and historic perspectives

In his papers on 'Co-existence of multiple scales and network of civilization: India' (1978a) and 'Rethinking about tribes and Indian civilization'(1978b), Sinha seems to be caught up in the dilemma of evolutionary and historic frame of references. This dilemma is real for any serious scholar working within the framework of an ancient civilization. A scientist cannot throw away the fact of evolution but how to accommodate it into different styles of life. This Sinha did by conceiving an ideal tribe in contrast to ideal caste/peasant placed in continuum. In 1965, he was viewing tribe as a system of social relations as well as a state of mind and cultural tradition, characterized by isolation and lack of stratification, and the caste-pole was characterized by heterogeneity, role specialization, formation of elite classes, enlargement and diversification of territorial network, cultural and social heterogeneity, greater systematization and connectedness with the centres of civilization. In a classical evolutionary frame of reference he conceived that tribes were continuously moving towards caste-pole. This formulation appeared to have resolved the problem of the people at different stages, within the framework of an ancient civilization. But the immersion in the field brought another dimension, that some communities were quite advanced in terms of technology, social and political organization than expected of their tribal status.

The Bhumij had managed a feudal State and were now considered backward with the status of tribe. Sinha had called 'tribe as a system of social relations as well as a state of mind'. How can a feudal aristocracy become backward? Sinha repeatedly felt that the Bhumij were out of sorts. This was expressed in several ways: the Bhumij suffered from 'loss of nerves', were 'somewhat shaky', 'have not been able to handle confidently the hangover of the aristocratic past', and so on. He had tried to put these valuable impressions, in the evolutionary scheme.

In 1978, he appears to be taking a more historical position. He concedes that movement from tribe to caste/peasant is not unidirectional, and is intervened by historical circumstances. He also finds cases where the evolution was in the operation in reverse. He however does not go into theoretical debate that if evolution was a process from simple to complex, from primitive to civilized, from underdeveloped to developed, how it could operate the other way round also. Instead he proposes the distinction between primary and secondary primitives and takes the help of civilization to resolve the apparent contradiction. He observes: Indian civilization maintains multiple scales and networks. It preserves the unique in the presence of universalistic norms. Numerous castes and sub-castes and diverse levels of productive technologies and associate scales co-exist. They operate under the super-arching networks of the civilization (1978a). Although tribe and civilization appear to be too distant from each other to be related, to resolve this he takes the idea of tribe as a dependent historic structure as proposed by Kroeber in his famous Huxley memorial lecture on Ancient Oikoumene (see Sinha, 1982). Sinha writes, 'A return to this perspective of tribe as dependent historic structures which I had once rejected in my earlier evolutionary formulation (1958) clarifies many of the apparently anomalous observations in the tribal transformation scene in India. It not only gives a perspective to the role of State formation in integration of hitherto isolated ethnic groups in regional caste/peasant patterns but makes the development of caste analogous inter-ethnic clusterings in tribal areas meaningful. . . . However, I still retain my predilections for looking at "tribes" as quality of socio-cultural integration' (1978b). The scientist in Sinha cannot discard this predilection. To me, it appears, the problem cannot be resolved in terms of evolution or historical approaches but by conceding that all human societies organize their lifepatterns in two realms. One is technical, based on causal relation, and the other is traditional, integrally linked with the culture. These two realms are not guided by the same law of development.

Tribes and Indian -civilization

As indicated, very early in his fieldwork, Sinha was able to realize that to understand the tribes in India, one has to put them in a wider perspective. He wrote a number of papers on this theme. In his review of the tribal situation in the context of Indian civilization (1982), he says that it was the British scholars who felt that the tribes were outside the frame of *varna-jati* system. The tribes themselves presented a wide spectrum of relationship with the plough cultivators from complete isolation to close interaction. He also analyses the mutually adaptive strategies of Indian civilization *vis-a-vis* tribal cultures. The civilization absorbed the tribes but maintained their identity, and also determined their isolation. Sinha writes, 'It may be speculated that perhaps the core plain regions of Indian civilization deliberately preserved enclaved and frontier zones as Atabika Janas, not merely for preserving a reservoir of human resources adapted to forest ecology or as political "buffer zones", the centres of civilization periodically sought nourishment by coming in contact with vigour of the primordial worldview in the tribal regions (p.13).

'In modern India, the stance of the civilization has significantly changed. Increase in population, industrialization, etc., are creating entirely new conditions. The conscious stance of the modern nation State is to make tribes fully participate as equals in the emerging civic order of the nation. In practice the tribal people, particularly the primitive groups, continuously lose command over the vital resources. The tribal population have reacted in a variety of ways. One of the ways is to take an aggressive stance. Such groups have tried to mobilize their population on dissatisfaction. But ethnic-based political movements are accompanied by creative cultural movements too which accentuate the distinctive "boundary marking" traits. These attempts also try to recreate and universalize the tribal traditions. In order to make them authentic and prestigious, borrowing is often from the Hindu and the Christian traditions' (p. 34).

The range of movements launched by the tribal people cover a wide spectrum from cessation to seeking some economic and educational support.

As for north-east India, he says, sea changes have taken place in the social, cultural, political, economic life of the people. The attempt should be to bring a new synthesis. He feels that the tribal people 'still preserve the image of man not alienated from society, nature and a shared moral order' (p.49). Sinha hopes that in the emerging India, 'ways will have to be found to make it possible to preserve the primordial essence of a "social civilization" while we work out the optimum pace for participation in the universal endeavour of modern man in the exploration of science, technology and global human values' (p. 52).

Tribe-caste distinction

In a number of papers Sinha has been trying to establish tribe-caste distinction, but the paper written in 1985 and entitled 'Social and ecological context of rice cultivation in India' is of a different genre and from the point of view of methodology a new experiment. This paper was based on UNESCO initiated multi-national research for comparative study of 'civilization related to rice cultivation in Asia'. This programme was based on the assumption that the rice cultivation is crucial as it has been the staple diet for millions and must have shaped their technology, social organization, worldview, rituals, etc. For this study Sinha chose one tribal hill village, a multi-ethnic peasant village and a multi-caste village in the plains of West Bengal. He found that although there was considerable similarity in the technology in the three villages, there were essential differences: 'In the hill village Puniyasasan, rice cultivation addresses itself to tribal social formation operating within the framework of emphasis on solidarity of the ethnic group, village, family, lineage and household. Although with the growth of wet rice cultivation there was an incipient tendency towards class formation . . . the dominant ethos remained uni-ethnic, inward looking and egalitarian. . . . Thus, the incipient tendency for class formation had to operate within a tribal style. In the two plain villages . . . the population was significantly divided into two essential classes those who own and supervise the land and those who do the manual work. It was observed that these binary agrarian class divisions operated in caste style' (p. 92). He concludes by saying 'tentatively we may describe the two situations as representing tribal and caste modes of productive organization of rice cultivation' (p. 92).

State formation

Sinha's interest in the political formation among the Bhumij was a logical extension of the kind of questions that came up from field-work. There was something more to it. He was the eldest son of Maharaja Bhupendra Chandra Sinha of Susanga. Although it is another matter that under normal circumstances he would have inherited the title of Maharaja and the right to rule the State, he had 'felt' and 'heard' about it in the process of growing up. Susanga State though located at the fringe of Indian society had a varied population from tribe to the highest caste and other communities. This background of Sinha cannot be stressed beyond a point, but nevertheless it provides an angle to understand his ideas, an insider's perspective so to say. As a scientist his predilection is for evolutionary frame of reference but both his insider's knowledge and his data among the Bhumij force him to enlarge his time and space perspective and accommodate in it the groups referred to as tribes. In the process of enlargement the points hitherto considered minor both in terms of space and time too get enlarged and cannot be easily explained by uni-directional evolutionary perspective and hence his attempt to look at the tribe as a dependent structure.

In his paper on State formation and Rajput myth in tribal central India (1962) Sinha finds some correspondence between technological level for settled cultivation and State formation. He writes, 'as a matter of fact, it is hard to find any settled agriculturist tribe of importance in the entire belt of Central India, with the possible exception of the Santal, which has not been substantially affected by long-standing connection with feudalistic State organization' (p.152). Sinha finds that the political evolution in Barabhum was not through sudden invasion and conquest of the region by an aggressive militant immigrant group. The growth of the State appears rather as a reconstruction of traditional socio-political units of the Bhumij, but the model they kept before them was Rajput-Kshatriya. On account of extreme sensitivity to one's rank and perpetual drive for higher status and also to generate more surplus, Brahmins and peasantry were invited to settle in their areas. Brahmins were given villages as gifts. Gorgeous religious festivals were celebrated and the Bhumij aristocracy set the 'highest standard' of cultural style. The historical circumstances changed rapidly after the Britishers came and the Bhumij became tribes.

In 1987, Sinha sums up his earlier works. He still holds on to his evolutionary framework but is fully aware of the various formations particularly from north-east India which make the field complicated. He writes, 'We are therefore dealing with complex interacting fields of secondary primitive hunters and gatherers, secondary tribesmen and chiefdoms and secondary pre-modern principalities and States, overlain by colonial rule and later formations of modern multi-State sovereign federal political formation since independence'(p.xi). He reiterates that caste structure and civilization framework provide a very important dimension to the tribal principalities. Tribals are drawn to it and react in a variety of ways. He observes that the structure of the caste system as a confederation of ethnic groups provides a natural framework for accommodating the tribal ethnic groups which are well adapted in the environment of the forest principalities (xii). This is indeed one of the keys by which the complexity owing to the coexistence of numerous castes and tribes in a general field of Indian civilization becomes understandable. In this paper he introduces some new ideas too. He proposes that there are two types of formation, one is eastern India type and the other is north-eastern India type. In the former tribe-caste/peasant is correlated and there is continuity between hill, plateau and plains, while in north-eastern India there is contrast in tribe-peasant/caste socio-political formation and also there is contrast in the ecology of plains and hills.

The 'stimulus diffusion' for the formation of the States in central and eastern India has come from Kshatriya-Rajput kingdoms, whereas in South-East Asia it is Ahom-Metei State model; Sikkim was influenced by the Tibetan-Bhotiya model. The Khasi-Jaintia case, he thinks, is unique in many ways and needs more systematic probing.

He finds a significant correlation between degree of surplus extraction through appropriate technological innovation and the level of functional differentiation, stratification and centralization of polity. The Ahom could form a State but the Mizo could not as they neither could generate any surplus in their rugged hills, nor extract it.

On the question as to why the kingship was needed in the tribal regions, Sinha opines that the small principalities needed large kingdoms for their safety and the large kingdoms needed principalities for preservation of their States in outlying forest and hill areas. The principalities played the role of either a buffer or a mediator between tribes and also between tribes and kingdoms.

He observes 'while the States withered away the microregional pattern of socio-cultural interaction and participatory, genuine regional folk culture which had been generated within the framework of the earlier States persisted' (xx). This was a crucial finding which led him to the conclusion that the State formation generated multi-ethnic local regional culture synthesizing and universalizing the tribal and caste customs. He thus moved far away from the idea of tribe as an isolate.

Caste studies

Sinha's interest in caste developed as a result of his Bhumij studies. In the process of expanding the universe of study for appropriate understanding of the Bhumij he had to include the study of numerous ethnic groups and the way they interacted with each other, and the kind of model they presented to the Bhumij for emulation (1966c, 1969b, c). He did a number of papers on the Hindu-Bhumij relations (1957a, 1959b, 1965b).

In his major paper on 'Caste in India, its essential pattern of socio-cultural integration'(1967a), Sinha tries to examine the basic principle which guides the patterns of interaction between ethnic groups within the framework of the caste system in India. Sinha believes that the caste system cannot be considered either as a cultural or socio-structural system. Both need to be combined. He disagrees with Dumont that there is a binary opposition and mutual repulsion between castes on 'pure and impure' axis. He agrees that while the concept of purity *vis-a-vis* impurity underlies the hierarchy of occupations and corporate caste statuses, it cannot be said that mutual repulsion is the primary principle in social interaction among the castes. He argues, 'reality lies in the fact that the *jati* groups within a caste system are committed to the maintenance of internal boundaries in the caste system as well as to organic inter-caste solidarity' (p.95).

Residual tensions in the caste system, Sinha opines, are resolved partly by group mobility built into the system and partly by the coercive force of the upper castes.

He however holds the position that the caste system is vastly different from the race relations in the United States. The racial hierarchy is an aberrant adjunct to the open-class American society, whereas the multi-segmented and intricately ranked grouping of castes is the central principle in the organization of the Hindu civilization. Inter-caste tensions do not intend to break the system, but focus around caste *britti*, culture and relative status. Sinha writes, 'Thus while the Hindu caste system generates a multiplicity of stabilized hereditary craft and ritual traditions and styles of life, racial stratification has no feel for such micro-stylization. The two social systems aim at qualitatively distinct cultural tasks' (p.99).

He further elaborates the distinction by comparing the Hindu method of tribal integration with the pattern of integration of the Negro in American life. A tribe in India after prolonged contact ends up by becoming another caste with specific economic functions and corporate social rank. This cannot happen at the corporate level in American society. However, Sinha makes a very important observation when he says 'even at its final phase of integration with the Hindu society, the tribe tends to preserve its corporate identity and cultural uniqueness' (p.99). In American society the Negro is supposed to 'melt'. In Hindu caste system upward mobility is possible by playing the game of the caste system maintaining the group identity; in the USA the mobility, if at all, is by 'passing'.

As regards the caste in the context of recent changes in India, Sinha after reviewing the various observations made by Bose, Srinivas, Lloyd and Susanne Rudolf, Morris D. Morris and Martin Orans opines that the forces of politics will consolidate caste interests while an increasing pace of industrialization will break the barrier between the castes (p.103).

In another interesting paper, Sinha along with Ranjit Bhattacharya (1969b) highlights the significance of *bhadralok* and *chhotolok* categories within the caste system. They observe that these categories are deep-rooted and include blocks of castes. This is born out of compromise between the long-range historical stream of *varna*-based hierarchy and the concrete situational context.

Study of religion

Sinha's interest in the field of religion developed as a result of his focus on acculturation. One of his early papers is on the changes in Bhumij religion (1953). His probings into Hindu-Bhumij relations led him to discover the kind of influence Vaishnavism had on the Bhumij (1961a, 1966b). He observed, the Vaishnava impact on the Bhumij represents a special kind of acculturation within the general context of the study of emergence, persistence and spread of civilization. The Vaishnavas are one of the many "hinge groups" or "cultural brokers" that mediate between the Hindu civilization and the tribal society' (1966b, 1987).

As he entered into the general arena of Indian civilizational study he realized that the core institutions and organization should also be studied anthropologically (1970d). He proposed the study of complex religious institutions (1970f, i) also. His interest was basically to locate the network and media of communication between different sects and ethnic groups and interpenetration of secular and sacred. He proposed that the Sankaracharya *mathas*, Shakta *pithas* along with temples, *akhadas*, sects, organization of *sadhus* and association of learned Brahmin, and Vaishnava *maths* and other seats of Sanskritic learning be studied in detail. These, he believed, would provide a profile of the Indian civilization and establish a communication with textual scholars. However his pull is towards anthropology; his emphasis is contextual. He along with Baidyanath Saraswati proposed the study of Kashi (1978), as a civilizational centre. The thrust of their proposal was to delineate the complex network of relationship which connected its varied sacred institutions with other centres and regions. Before these proposals were made he along with other associates had completed a study of Kalighat (1967d). In a paper on 'Kali temple' (1972c) Sinha observed that in spite of numerous changes around Kali temple, it continued to attract the attention of a growing number of devotees. Yet in the midst of stubborn persistence of the sacred centre everything had not remained the same. He felt that for a large number of people, 'Kalighat today plays the role of cultural monument' (p.71).

His review paper 'Sociology of religion' (1974) takes into account all the major works on the religion of the people of India. He also identified the gaps in the study of religion in Indian society and proposed that secularization of Hindu religion and its political linkages should receive some attention.

In his study of religion in an American village (1966a) apart from the main objective, Sinha was also interested in finding what were the essential differences between Hinduism and the religious organization there. He found that in American society there was less reliance on divine intervention in daily life. There was no stress on denial of pleasure but at the same time the religious system there did not allow any freedom for spiritual quest.

He also referred to the difference in field experiences in two situations. In India he found that there was hardly any concern by the investigator in encroaching the privacy of the subjects but it was not possible there. There the social distance between the investigator and the investigated was much less. The respondents could give data and also participate in discussion to analyse it. These observations are valuable both in terms of evaluation of the role of Anthropology in different contexts and in dealing with the ethical questions on fieldwork.

Urban studies

As stated, Sinha made an important breakthrough by organizing a seminar on Calcutta (1972a) and promoting similar exercise elsewhere. For Calcutta seminar he was able to involve medical practitioners, historians, linguists, anthropologists, artists, film makers, police officers, etc. Besides the formal seminar he organized two informal get-togethers in the style of *adda* at his home.

In his brief summing-up of the Calcutta seminar, Sinha observed that Calcutta provided a number of contradictory pictures. Urban milieu of Calcutta had allowed the existence of primordial social identities of castes, of religious groups and of languages. Diverse religious practices too have persisted. Social world of executives was alienated from the masses. On the one side the creative artists have tried to assert the universality of their approach, on the other, social domains rested on primordial relations. Rich and poor continuously jostled with each other. Urbanity of Calcutta was based on rural surroundings.

In his paper on 'Scope of urban Anthropology and the city of Calcutta' (1972f) he made out a case that conventional tools of anthropology could be used to study the urban conglomeration. He outlined a variety of entry points that were available in the study of urban conglomeration. He felt that qualitative studies besides quantitative could be made use of with good results. He, however, stressed that anthropologists would require appropriate orientation and training for urban studies. He added a word of caution, 'It is much easier to cross the cultural norms of one's society while studying the remote tribal groups about whom one does not have an immediate stake. It is quite another thing to overcome the barrier of stereotypes and prejudices in the case of studying people whose activities have social relevance in our immediate surroundings'.

Study of scientists

In taking up the study of Indian scientist (1970b) and editing a volume entitled 'Science, technology and culture' (1970a) Sinha made a significant departure from the beaten track. The study of scientist not only broadened the horizon of anthropology but in this there was an effort to integrate the modern science with society. He noted that the Indian scientist generally belonged to the Bhadralok class and was dissatisfied with the general organizational set-up. He also noted that there was little coordination between science and industry.

Development studies

The period immediately after Independence was rife with the theme of development. Community development, tribal development, industrial development were in the air. This period incidentally coincided with Sinha's formative and most productive phases in anthropological career, yet interestingly he did not write much on this theme. This becomes a little intriguing because he was closely associated with the Government and various other bodies supported by the Government such as ICSSR, UGC, etc.

However, along with B.D. Sharma, the then Joint Secretary, Tribal Development, Ministry of Home Affairs, Sinha organized a workshop-seminar for developing the strategy for research-cum-action programme on the basis of a few diagnostic case studies. The proceedings of the workshop-seminar were published under the title, *The primitive tribes: the first step* (1977d). In his brief paper (1977a) Sinha highlighted the importance of appropriate definition of primitive people. This was necessary if the benefits of development were to flow to them. He made a distinction between the primitive archaic and 'secondary primitives' who had been living under the pressure of Indian civilization. The latter group may be primitive in terms of technology but had a long-standing dependent symbiotic socio-economic articulation with the surrounding dominant peasants. He wrote, 'Unlike the archaic primitives, the secondary primitive tribes have learned to accommodate the pressures of the encroaching civilization, and, at the same time, to carve out an area of relative autonomy in ecological niches outside the adaptive reaches of the larger society' (p.18). He noted that the planners did not take the indigents into serious consideration for evolving a plan for development. He said that the strategy for development of the primitive tribes should strengthen their resource base in their characteristic habitat, provide them a functional literacy and try to extend their adaptive capacity beyond their ecological niche into the larger arena of the region and the nation.

For the researchers his advice was that they would have to be conscious of the insider's perspective. He felt that Patric Gedde's famous dictum 'development through conservation' should guide the development programmes. The task of genuine humane development of the primitive tribes was very important, 'for a nation will be judged within itself and also outside, in a very important manner, not only by the development of the majority but by the informed tenderness with which we deal with the problems of the weakest elements' (p.2). After this, in the 1980s , only a few papers on the development: theme appeared. In 1981, he wrote 'Perspective for rural development: some observations' in an edited volume. In 1983, he did another paper, 'Tribal societies in India : case for development through conservation'. The idea of development through conservation had been with him for a long time. This idea had impressed Bose who had borrowed it from Patric Geddes. Sinha argued that since man belonged to a single species it is possible to establish communication across cultures, provided people have sympathetic disposition. In this essay he cited the example of the tribes of Andaman Islands, Jenu Kuruba of Karnataka, Garo of Meghalaya and Santal. The tribes of Andaman Islands had been overwhelmed in a variety of ways including the so-called development; the Jenu Kuruba had been denied their natural right over forest. In Garo area land-man ratio had been disturbed. Same was the case with the Santal and added to that, their rights over forest had also been taken away. In such a situation he asked how development could work. As in 1977 he advocated a policy of development through conservation which he says will be in tune with the Indian tradition. He said, 'I plead for patiently working out programmes through which primary hunters . . . peasantized tribals can participate in full vigour in giving shape to the emergent "composite culture of India" from a secure and vigorously participant base. Indian sub-continent had worked out over the millenia the experiment of conservation of cultures in the pre-colonial and pre-industrial period with an extraordinary skill and imagination within an unambiguous framework of inter-ethnic interdependence in a hierarchic order' (1977a, p.25).

In another brief paper (1984), he argued that whether it was the tribals of the hills or the rural folks of the plains, they were not ignorant masses on whom anything can be dumped. He pointed out that the rural folks looked for appropriate technologies, they did make empirical observations and in their context they were as much rational as anybody could be. His anthropological training and intense humanistic bias come to the fore when he writes, 'The lores, rituals and supernatural beliefs which are often associated with their technological activities do not operate as substitutes for their carefully cultivated, empirical observation based skills. Often the lores and rituals have an underlying core of rationality and serve to enliven the spirit of the rural technologists to pursue their vocation with zeal' (1984; 1986b).

Biography

Sinha has by now done three major writings on Nirmal Kumar Bose. The first came out in 1972(e) in *festschrift* volume in honour of Bose's 69th birthday which was brought out by the N.K. Bose Memorial Foundation, Varanasi (1973a), under the "Builders of Indian Anthropology Series". For the benefit of general reader, he did another piece on N.K. Bose (1986a). Sinha says he is further enlarging the book. Bose was a prolific writer and an extraordinary person. The fact that Sinha feels he has not been able to adequately cover all the dimensions of Bose's life and his works indeed speaks volumes about the man but it also suggests that Sinha was not only deeply attached to Bose but was greatly influenced by him. Though Sinha has neither written as much as Bose nor on so many topics, there is a clear indication that he has been continuously drawing inspiration and ideas from Bose's writings. Tribe, caste, Indian civilization, culture trait distributional studies, science and modern India are some of the common themes treated by *guru* and *shishya*. The wanderer in Bose attracted Sinha most and so he formed a Paribrajak Mandali of which the focus is human encounter.

Sinha in a personal communication from Santiniketan outlines the programme of work he has chalked out for himself. He would do a book on the Bhumij, (who trained him to become an anthropologist), a full biography on Professor Nirmal Kumar Bose and a book on tribes, civilization and nation-building. Besides, he would apply his mind to develop the Paribrajak Mandali. He writes, 'the sole aim of the forum (Mandali) would be to involve some genuine persons, from the villages and urban centres to explore the creative power of the people (also their predicaments) in rural, particularly tribal, India'.

WORKS OF SURAJIT SINHA

Sinha, Surajit, 1950. A village in Singbhum, *Geographical Review of India,* April-June pp24-42.

Sinha, Surajit, 1951. The weekly market at Bamni, a village in south Manbhum, *Geographical Review of India*, Oct-Dec. pp. 21-36.

Sinha, Surajit, 1952(a). A scheme for organization at museum of rural arts and crafts, *Eastern Educationist* (Patna) January, pp. 24-26.

Sinha, Surajit, 1952(b). Types of human adaptation in the Andamans, *Geographical Review of India*, July-Sept., pp. 9-24.

Sinha, Surajit, 1952 (c), Book Review: *The development of behaviour* by Dawy, Richard & Humber, W.J.; The Macmillian, New York, 1951 (pp. 762 + vii), *Man in India*, 32(3): 184-185.

Sinha, Surajit, 1952 (d). Book Review: *Land and society in Malabar* Adrain C. Mayer, Oxford University Press, 1952, *Man in India*, 32(4), 264-265.

Sinha, Surajit, 1952(e). Book Review: *Notes and queries on Anthropology*, Sixth edition, revised and rewritten by "A Committee of the Royal Anthropological Institution of Great Britain and Ireland", *Man in India*, 32(4), 265-266.

Sinha, Surajit, 1953. Some aspects of changes in Bhumij religion in south Manbhum, *Man in India* 33(2), pp. 148-164.

Sinha, Surajit, 1954. Symposium on Indian village, *Man in India*, 34(4); 315-317.

Sinha, Surajit, 1955 (a). *Resettlement of East Pakistan refugees in Andaman Islands: report on survey of further possibilities of resettlement*, Jan-May, Superintendant, Govt. Printing, W.B. Press, Alipore, W.B.

Sinha, Surajit, 1955 (b). Evolution reconsidered, *Man in India*, 35(1).

Sinha, Surajit, 1956 (a). *The acculturation of the Bhumij of Manbhum: a study in social class formation and ethnic integration*, Unpublished Ph.D. dissertation, North-Western University, Evanston, Illinois, USA.

Sinha, Surajit, 1956 (b). Book Review: *Alluring hypothesis on feudalism, feudalism in History*, Edt. by Rushton Coulborn, Princeton, New Jersey, The Princeton University Press, 439 pp. $ 8.50, *Literature of Race and Culture, The Atlanta University Review of Race and Culture*, 17(4), pp. 403-404.

Sinha, Surajit, 1957(a). The media and nature of Hindu-Bhumij interaction, *Journal of Asiatic Society of Bengal: Letters and Sciences*, 23(1), pp. 22-37.

Sinha, Surajit, 1957 (b). Expression of sentiments in the songs associated with the Karam festival of rural Manbhum (Bihar, India), *Man in India* 37(1): 34-49. The paper was read at the Annual Meeting of the Mid Western section of the American Folklore Society, held at Bloomington, Indiana, in May 1955.

Sinha, Surajit, 1957 (c). Tribal cultures of India as a dimension of little tradition in the study of Indian civilization: a preliminary statement, *Man in India*, 37(2): 93-118.

Sinha, Surajit, 1957 (d). Book Review: *Culture in crisis: a study of the Hopi Indians* with a Foreword by John Collier and a chapter from the writings of Benjamin Lee Whorf, by Laura Thompson Harper and Brother, Publishers, New York, *Man in India*, 37(1): 85-87.

Sinha, Surajit, 1957 (e). Book Review: *Sociology* by Emory S. Bogardus, Fourth Edition, pp. 616, The Macmillan Company, New York, *Man in India*, 37(1): 877-88.

Sinha, Surajit, 1957 (f). Book Review: *The Yao village: a study in the social structure of a Nyasaland tribe* by J. Clyde Mitchell, Published on behalf of the Rhodes Living Stone Institute, Northern Rhodesia by Manchester University Press, 1956, 235 pages, *Man in India*, 37(4): 309-310.

Sinha, Surajit, 1958 (a). Changes in the cycle of festivals in a Bhumij village, *Journal of Social Research*, Ranchi, 1(1).

Sinha, Surajit, 1958 (b). Tribal cultures of peninsular India as dimension of little tradition in the study of civilisation: a preliminary statement, *Journal of American Folklore*, 71, 28.

Sinha, Surajit, 1958 (c). Training of a Bhumij medicine man, *Man India*, 38(2): 111-128.

Sinha, Surajit, 1958 (d). Some palaeolithic finds in Old Delhi, *Man in India* 38(2): 151-153.

Sinha, Surajit, 1959 (a). Tribal culture of peninsular India as a dimension of the little tradition in the study of Indian-civilisation: a preliminary statement, In *Traditional India: structure and change*, Milton B. Singer (Ed.), 298-312.,

Sinha, Surajit, 1959 (b). Bhumij - Kshatriya social movement in south Manbhum, *Bulletin of the Department of Anthropology*, Government of India, Calcutta, 8(2): 9-32.

Sinha, Surajit, 1961 (a). A note on the concept of union for spiritual qcquest among the Vaishnava preachers in the Bhumij belt of Purulia and Singbhum, *The Eastern Anthropologist*, 2.

Sinha, Surajit, 1961 (b). Comment on 'Integration of culture: a review of concept' by Elizabeth, E. Hoyt. in *Current Anthropology*. 2, (5) pp. 423-424.

Sinha, Surajit, 1962. State formation and Rajput myth in tribal central India, *Man in India*, 42 (1).

Sinha, Surajit, 1963. Levels of economic initiative and ethnic groups in Pargana Barabhum, *The Eastern Anthropologist*, 16(2).

Sinha, Surajit, 1965 (a). Rituals and social organization of deer-hunting in a Bhumij village, *Bull. of the Bihar Tribal Welfare Research Institute*, Ranchi, 7(1) pp. 1-4.

Sinha, Surajit, 1965. Tribe-caste and tribe-peasant continua in central India, *Man in India*, 45(1).

Sinha, Surajit, 1966 (a). Religion in an affluent society, *Current Anthropology*, 7(1), pp. 189-195.

Sinha, Surajit, 1966 (b). Vaishnava influence on a tribal culture. In *Krishna: myths rites and attitudes*, Edited by Milton B. Singer, pp. 64-89. East West Centre Press, Honolulu.

Sinha, Surajit, 1967 (a). Caste in modern India, its essential pattern of social-cultural integration. In *Caste and race: comparative approaches*, Edited by A.V.S. de Reuk & J. Knight J.C.A. Churchill Ltd., London.

Sinha, Surajit, 1967 (b). Involvement in social change, *Economic and Political Weekly*, Sept. 16, 1707-1710.

Sinha, Surajit, 1967 (c). Social integration of the hill tribes and the plainsmen, (speech). In *A common perspective for North-East India*. Rathin Mittra and Barun Das Gupta (Ed.), 4-16, Calcutta.

Sinha, Surajit, 1968 (a). Is there an Indian tradition in Social/Cultural Anthropology: retrospect/prospect (Abstract). Conference on the *Nature and functions of Anthropological traditions*, Wenner-Gren Foundation for Anthropological Research, New York.

Sinha, Surajit, 1968 (b). Urgent problems for research in Social and Cultural Anthropology : perspective and suggestion. In *Urgent research in Social Anthropology*. Edited by Behari L. Abbi and Satish Saberwal. Indian Institute of Advanced Study, Simla.

Sinha, Surajit, 1968 (c). Deer-hunting in a Bhumij village, *Man in India*, 48 (2): 183-186.

Sinha, Surajit, 1968 (d). Tribal solidarity and messianic movements: a review article, *Contributions to Indian Sociology*, New Series. II, 1968.

Sinha, Surajit, 1969 (a). Modernization and religion in India, *Seminar on problems of modernization of underdeveloped societies*, November 1-6, 1969 Golden Jubilee: Department of Sociology, University of Bombay.

Sinha, Surajit, 1970 (a), (Ed.). *Science, technology and culture : a study of cultural traditions and institutions of India and Ceylon in relation to science and technology*, Research Council for Cultural Studies, India International Centre, New Delhi.

Sinha, Surajit, 1970 (b). Indian scientists: the socio-cultural and organisational context of their professional environment. In *Science, technology and culture*, Edited by S. Sinha, Research Council for Cultural Studies. India International Centre, New Delhi,

Sinha, Surajit, 1970 (c), (Ed.). *Research programmes on Cultural Anthropology and allied disciplines*. Anthropological Survey of India, Calcutta.

Sinha, Surajit, 1970 (d). Introducing the seminar. In *Research programmes on Cultural Anthropology and allied disciplines*, Edited by Surajit Sinha. Anthropological Survey of India, Calcutta.

Sinha, Surajit, 1970 (e). Complex religious institutions and the study of Indian civilisation : preliminary statement. In *Research programmes on Cultural Anthropology and allied disciplines*, Edited by Surajit Sinha, Anthropological Survey of India, Calcutta.

Sinha, Surajit, 1970 (f). Study of solidarity movements : general propositions. In *Research programmes on Cultural Anthropology and allied disciplines*, Edited by Surajit Sinha, Anthropological Survey of India, Calcutta.

Sinha, Surajit, 1970(g). Complex religious institutions: study of sects in Hinduism. In *Research programmes on Cultural Anthropology and allied disciplines*, Edited by Surajit Sinha, Anthropological Survey of India, Calcutta.

Sinha, Surajit, 1970 (h). An encounter with Adivasis, *Times of India*, Sunday, February, 15: 1970.

Sinha, Surajit 1971 (a). Is there an Indian tradition in Social/Cultural Anthropology: retrospect and prospect, *Journal of the Indian Anthropological Society*, Calcutta. 6: 1-14.

Sinha, Surajit, 1971 (b). The Indian caste system and modern times: three points of view and a fourth one, *Souvenir*, Re-Union, Department of Anthropology, Calcutta University.

Sinha, Surajit 1972 (a). *Cultural profile of Calcutta*. Indian Anthropological Society, Calcutta.

Sinha, Surajit, 1972 (b). Introducing the seminar. In *Cultural profile of Calcutta*, Edited by Surajit Sinha, Indian Anthropological Society, Calcutta.

Sinha, Surajit, 1972 (c). Kali temple at Kalighat and the city of Calcutta. In *Cultural profile of Calcutta*, Edited by Surajit Sinha, Indian Anthropological Society, Calcutta.

Sinha, Surajit, 1972 (d). *Aspects of Indian culture and society*. Indian Anthropological Society, Calcutta.

Sinha, Surajit, 1972 (e). Anthropology of Nirmal Kumar Bose. In *Aspects of Indian culture and society*, Edited by Surajit Sinha, Indian Anthropological Society, Calcutta.

Sinha, Surajit, 1972 (f). Scope of urban Anthropology and the city of Calcutta. In *Aspects of Indian culture and society*, Edited by Surajit Sinha, Indian Anthropological society, Calcutta.

Sinha, Surajit, 1972 (g). Wenner Gren symposium on scale and social organization: news and views, *J. Indian Anthrop. Soc.*, 7: 99-100.

Sinha, Surajit, 1972 (h). Ethnicity, space and time in studying tribal transformation: the Bhumij of Barabhum, Paper prepared in advance for participants in "Prof. T.C. Das memorial lecture and seminar on Anthropological feild studies on the people of India.

Sinha, Surajit, 1972 (i). Talk before the entire staff of the Anthropological Survey of Indian on April 7, 1972, *News Letter*, 1(1): 10-15, Mar-Apr, '72, Anthrop, Survey of Ind., Calcutta.

Sinha, Surajit, 1972 (j). Tribal solidarity movements in India: a review, in *Tribal situation in India* Edt. by K.S. Singh, 13, pp. 410-423, Indian Institute of Adv. Study, Simla.

Sinha, Surajit, 1972 (k). Obituary: Nirmal Kumar Bose 1901-1972, *Newsletter* 1(4), Anthropological Survey of India. The Indian Anthropological Society & Max Muller Bhawan, Calcutta, March, 1972.

Sinha, Surajit, 1973 (a). *Anthropology of Nirmal Kumar Bose*, N.K. Bose Memorial Foundation, Varanasi.

Sinha, Surajit, 1973 (b). Primitive hunters, shifting cultivators, *Times of India*, Annual Number.

Sinha, Surajit, 1973 (c). The late Rama Prasad Chanda as an Anthropologist, *Lecture* delivered on Sept. 21, at the Centenary Celebration of R.P. Chanda, Organized by the Asiatic Society of Bengal, Calcutta.

Sinha, Surajit, 1974. Sociology of religion. In *A survey of research in Sociology and Social Anthropology*, 2, Indian Council of Social Science Research, Popular Prakashan, Bombay.

Sinha, Surajit, 1975 (a). Expansion of the social base of culture in modern Inida. *Presidential Address*, the Indian Anthropological Society, Calcutta (This is primarily based on data on ethnic groups in Purulia district, West Bengal).

Sinha, Surajit, 1975 (b). Implication of a cultural policy for social equality. In Satish Saberwal (Ed.) *Towards a cultural policy*, Vikas Publishing House Pvt. Ltd. Delhi, pp. 76-81.

Sinha, Surajit, 1976. 'Rabindranath Tagore's ideas about the structure and essence of Indian-civilization, *Presidential Address*, Indian Anthropological Society, Calcutta.

Sinha, Surajit, 1977 (a). Problems of diagnostic research and the strategy of development of pre-agricultural 'primitive communities, In *Primitive tribes: the first step*, Edited by Surajit Sinha & B.D. Sharma, Government of India, Ministry of Home Affairs, New Delhi.

Sinha, Surajit, 1977 (b). 'Varma-jati model and the rural poor in India today', *Presidential Address*, Indian Anthropological Society, Calcutta.

Sinha, Surajit, 1977 (c). Structure of Indian civilization: continuity and change, *Lecture* delivered at the Aurobindo Centre, Calcutta.

Sinha, Surajit, 1978 (a). Coexistence of multiple scales and networks of a civilisation: India. In *Scale and social organization*, Edited by Fredrik Barth Universitetsforlaget, Oslo.

Sinha, Surajit, 1978 (b). Rethinking about tribes and Indian civilisation, *Journal of Anthropological Society*, 8(2).

Sinha, Surajit, 1978 (c), (Ed.). *Field studies on the people of India: methods and perspectives*, Indian Anthropological Society, Calcutta.

Sinha, Surajit, 1978 (d). Introducing the seminar, In *Field studies on the people of India: methods and perspectives*, Edited by Surajit Sinha, Indian Anthropological Society, Calcutta.

Sinha, Surajit, 1978 (e). Space, time and ethnicity: fieldwork among the Bhumij of Barabhum. In *Field studies on the people of India:*

methods and perspectives, Edited by Surajit Sinha, Indian Anthropological Society, Calcutta.

Sinha, Surajit, 1979. What we have learnt from the seminar. In *Cultural profile of Shillong*. Edited by B.B. Goswami, Anthropological Survey of India, Calcutta.

Sinha, Surajit, 1386 (Beng.). *Rarh Parikalpana O Visva-Bharati Samaj* (in Beng.) Visva-Bharati Gabeshana Prakashan Samiti.

Sinha, Surajit, 1980. Tribe and Indian civilisation: a perspective, *Man in India*, 60(1).

Sinha Surajit, 1981 (a). Perspective for rural development: some observations. *In Rural development, action and management*, Edited by Madhu S. Mishra, Indian Institute of Management, Calcutta (vii-xi).

Sinha Surajit, 1981 (b). Tribes and Indian civilization: transformaion processes in modern India, *Man in India*, 61, (2).

Sinha Surajit, 1982. *Tribes and Indian civilization: structure and transformation*, N.K. Bose Memorial Foundation, Varanasi.

Sinha, Surajit, 1983. Tribal societies in India: case for development through conservation. In *Proceedings of the seminar on conservation of nature: a tribute to Alexander von Humboldt*, Edited by Sibdas Ghosh and Manju Mukherjee. Humbold Club, Calcutta.

Sinha Surajit, 1984. Growth of scientific temper: rural context. In *Science and technology policy in 1980s and beyond*, Edited by Michael Gibbons, Phillip Gummelt and B.M. Vadgaonkar.

Sinha Surajit, 1985. Social and ecological context of rice cultivation in India, *East Asian Cultural Studies* (TOKYO), 24, (1-4), March.

Sinha, Surajit, 1986 (a). *Nirmal Kumar Bose: scholar wanderer*, National Book Turst of India, New Delhi.

Sinha, Surajit, 1986 (b). Bharatbarsher, Samajik Sabhyata *Siksha-Niketan Patrika: Naba Paryaya*, pp. 42-44. Emphasing 'social civilization' in tribal cultures.

Sinha, Surjit, 1987 (a), (Ed.). *Tribal Politics and State Systems in pre-colonial eastern and north-eastern India*. K.P. Bagchi & Co., Calcutta.

Sinha, Surajit, 1987 (b). Introduction, In *Tribal politics and state systems in pre-colonial eastern and north-eastern India*, Edited by S.C. Sinha, K.P. Bagchi & Co., Calcutta.

Sinha, Surajit, B.K. Das Gupta and H.N. Banerjee, 1961(c). Agriculture crafts and weekly markets of south Manbhum, *Bulletin of the Anthropological Survey of India*, 10(1).

Sinha, Surajit, B.K. Das Gupta and H.N. Bannerjee, 1966 (c). *Ethnic groups, villages and towns of Pargana Barabhum: report of a survey*, Anthropological Survey of India, Calcutta. Memoir No. 14.

Sinha, Surajit, Baidyanath Saraswati, Deepali Ghosh, and Sriparna Ray, 1967. *Report on the sacred complex of Kalighat,*, Unpublished report, Anthropological Survey of India, Calcutta.

Sinha, Surajit and Ranjit Bhattacharya, 1969 (b). Bhadralok and chhotolok in rural areas of West Bengal, *Sociological Bulletin*, 18(1).

Sinha, Surajit, Jyoti Sen, and Sudhir Panchbhai, 1969 (c). The concept of diku among the tribes of Chota Nagpur, *Man in India*, 49, (2) pp. 121-138.

Sinha, Surajit, and Baidynath Saraswati, 1970 (i). Study of the sacred complex of Kashi. In *Research programmes on Cultural Anthropology and allied disciplines*, Edited by Surajit Sinha, Anthropological Survey of India, Calcutta.

Sinha, Surajit, and Purnima Sinha, 1970 (j), Science in India today: a symposium, *Samatat Prakashan*, 2(2).

Sinha, Surajit and B.D. Sharma, 1977 (d), (Eds.). *Primitive tribes : the first step*, Government of India, Ministry of Home Affairs, New Delhi.

Sinha, Surajit and Baidyanath Saraswati, 1978 (f). *Ascetics of Kashi*, N.K. Bose Memorial Foundation, Varanasi.

THE IMPLICIT PHILOSOPHY AND WORLDVIEW

1

TRIBAL COSMOGONY: PRIMAL VISION OF MAN AND COSMOS

Baidyanath Saraswati

Introduction

There is nothing in Indian thought structure, nor in the traditional organization of Indian society, that may correspond to the western evolutionary notion of tribe as a vestige of savagery and barbarism. Yet, tribe exists in India as a political category created by the British Raj, intellectualized by the colonial anthropologists, and sanctified by the Constitution of modern India. These so-called pre-cultural groups, properly speaking, are the people of Oral Culture.[1] This essay in honour of Professor Surajit Chandra Sinha attempts to explore their philosophy and vision of man and the cosmos. In so doing, it examines the cosmogonic myths of the North-East India tribes.

Myth[2] may be defined as a body of revelatory knowledge of the unseen reality that flows eternally in time and space. As a self-reflective and self-validating statement of the true nature of the phenomenal world, it is founded in the faith that supports all knowledge, and formed in the style of a narrative that makes all intricate theory understandable. It is usually stated in the past tense because it describes the reality that has already been seen. But, then, it is not just a history, the event of the past; it is the past, the present and the future – the truth of life unfolding itself everywhere and every moment of the existence. It is not an ideational construct; it is an experiential reality. It is not an empirical description of the natural phenomena; it is an expression of the experience of the mystery of existence. Myth is not a moral code; it is a treatise on the divine cosmology. For a traditional man, it is the wisdom of the ancients that remains all-time new.

Since myth is concerned with matters of transcendental reality, its linguistic construction is translucent. As a primary presentation of the unseen and unmanifest, it is articulated in a poetic, or metaphorical, form with multiple possibilities of interpretation and reformation. But, viewed comparatively, all such successive presentations are regressive in character. This is what the tribal myths speak of paradigmatically: at first there was a common language for the gods, men and animals; God wrote all wisdom on pieces of skin and gave one to the tribe, but the hungry tribesmen roasted that piece of skin and ate it up.[3]

This discourse confesses its limitations arising from the author's inexperience of the myth that he deals with. As stated, myth is an expression of a revelatory experience. Though experience and its expression are not unrelated,[4] the latter is only a partial manifestation of the former. Moreover, unless myth is lived from inside, one cannot comprehend it fully. The tribals follow their myths without interpretation; the purity of a revelatory knowledge is lost the moment it is manipulated. To them the true meaning, or value, of a myth lies in its intuitive realization through ritual action rather than in its intellectualization. The present analysis may not, therefore, fully convey the kind of meaning which the tribes themselves attach to their myths.

The Supreme Principle

The text of the tribal myths is varied and complex because of its primordial simplicity. Its translation into another language, or mode of transmission, is problematic. The only way to have some understanding of it is to follow the text faithfully. To explore its implicit philosophy we may consider the creation myths under three moments:[5] (a) solitude, (b) sacrifice and (c) integration.

Solitude

The tribal cosmogonic myths[6] agree that at first there was nothing, nothing, nothing at all; neither earth nor sky. Most of the myths speak that in the beginning all was water. The Singpho myth[7] describes that there were only clouds and mist. The Hrusso Aka myth[8] tells us of two great eggs which shone like gold. In the Panggi belief,[9] the world was wrapped around by darkness. All these imply radical solitude. The primeval ocean, cloud and mist, the golden egg, and darkness are a concrete representation of the unspeakable mystery that shrouds the cosmos.

The mystery deepens further as the 'life' emerges and the original unity is broken. The earliest form of life comes from things incomprehensible: woman in the form of cloud; moving soft rocks; revolving soft golden eggs, and the like. The woman cloud gave birth to a pair of male and female snow. From the rocks a female rock was born; from her another female rock which united with a male rock. The eggs broke open; from one came the Earth, from the other the Sky, her husband. From the union of these two the other things and creatures.

The first principle of the cosmos is, then, 'one-two-and many'.

Sacrifice

There are myths of creation by sacrifice, the divine transformation. The Apa Tani myth[10] reveals that Kujum-Chantu (the Mother Earth) died of her own accord for the sake of the world; and every part of her body became the part of the world; her eyes turned into the Sun and Moon. According to the Bori,[11] at first there were two spirits, one of whom had the form of a *mithun* (*bos frontalis*) and the other the form of an elephant, who fought and killed each other, and from their flesh and bones the world was formed. The Hill Miris[12] speak of the original tree, which grew out of the sea and fell to the ground; its bark became the skin of the world, the trunk turned into rocks and the branches into hills.

The sacrifice of the Mother Earth was the indicator of the primordial love that binds all the creatures of the world. What had provoked the spirits to sacrifice themselves is again a pointer to beings' worldly attachment. The primordial energy becomes manifest with the sacrifice of the tree and other great personage.

Thus, what sets the cosmos into motion is the sacrifice.

Integration

The myths describe how the creatures played an important part in the construction of the world. The Gallongs[13] say that at first when everything was water the prawn collected a great pile of rubbish on the surface, the crab dug a pit below to drain off the water, and thus the earth emerged. The Hill Miris[14] describe how an enormous tree grew out of the sea and worms ate the wood until, by the constant falling of the dust into the water, the world was formed. In Minyong tradition[15] a great *mithun* dug a pit into which the waters poured and allowed the dry earth to appear. The Sherdukpens[16] believe that two heavenly brothers threw a lotus down on to the surface of the ocean, whereupon it was covered with flowers, over which the four winds blew clouds of dusts, until the earth was formed. A Taraon Mishmi tale[17] describes how there was a lot of mud below the waters and a god created in it a pillar up which a swarm of white ants climbed with their mouths filled with earth. The Kaman Mishmis tell[18] of two powerful spirits who do not actually create the world but come down from the sky and make the hills and mountains.

A creature born miraculously[19] becomes the creator of another creature. The Bugun Khowa myth[20] says that two sons of Zongma (a god) were formless. They made the Earth and the Sky. The Earth and the Sky made love and every kind of creature came into being. In a Bugun story,[21] Apuphulwa, an elderly man, married a hideous creature. From their union the first rock was born and from it flew the first rivers. Then she bore a son who went into the Sky and made the thunder and lighting, and another who went below the Earth to cause the earthquake. A fourth son was a rain-maker, the fifth originated the four winds and the sixth caused the rainbow. Other children were snakes, poisonous insects and demons of disease. The last born was the pathetic child of Death who unknowingly killed his own parents and then, in search for them, goes on killing everyone he meets.

In these myths the creation of the world is not attributed to a Supreme Being. The distinction between the creature and the creator is unclear. The early phase of creation is characterized by total integration of all that came into being. Everything that has been created has its own life, and hence no ontological difference between the man and the mountain.

Thus, what makes the cosmos the One undifferentiated reality is the supreme principle of non-duality.

The Unity of All Experience

The truth of the unity of all experience is expressed in the tribal eschateological belief.[22]

> The Apa Tanis believe that the soul, Yalo, of all those who die a natural death go to the Neli, the place of the dead, which looks like

> an Apa Tani village with long rows of houses. At the entrance of the Neli, they are met by Nelkiri, the guardian spirit who questions all newcomers about the exploits of their earthly life. He inquires how many enemies and wild animals they have slain, how many slaves they have bought and how much land they have owned. As Apa Tani lived on this earth so will he live in Neli: a rich man will find the cattle he has sacrificed during his lifetime, but those animals which have passed to his heirs are for ever lost to him. Every woman returns to her first husband, but those who died unmarried may there marry and beget children. Life in Neli is similar to life on this earth; people cultivate and work, and ultimately they die once more and go to another Land of the Dead.

The Khasis also believe in a continued existence of man's life in blissful conditions.[23] Nothing is so pleasant and entertaining to a Khasi as 'betel-nut eating' in his earthly career. Hence, after this life on the earth when he goes back to the House of God, it is believed, he would be eating betel-nuts in the company of his dear and near ones who have all assembled there.

The belief in the continued existence is demonstrated in practice:[24]

> When a Wancho Chief dies, his body is bathed, wrapped in cloth, and laid on a mat. A special kind of basket is placed by his head. His relatives and subjects come one by one and each puts a little bark, betel and tobacco in it saying, 'This is for you, to save you from trouble.' Sometimes a friend may add a piece of cloth and says, 'This is for you; this is for you to wear.' All the dead man's possessions, his *dao*, gun, spear, ornaments, bags are put by him, and later are hung on the tomb, which quickly becomes a most desirable museum. For, the deceased must take these things below; in the Land of the Dead he will have to build a house, so he will need his *dao*; he will go head-hunting so he will need his gun; there will be swiddens to cultivate. If these things are not given, the ghost says, 'I have no cloth, I shiver with cold; I have no gun, how can I hunt? I have no *dao*, how can I clear the path? They won't give me anything, so I will not give them good crops.' If the dead man had owned a tree, a little of the bark or a twig is brought, for otherwise he might worry about it. Then the mourners kill an animal, a pig or fowl, and place its head by the corpse saying, 'we give you this so that you will not be hungry'. The head is later hung by the tomb.

The belief in continued existence is a support to the tribal perception of death as beneficient. According to the Hill Miri,[25] before the death came, the world was so full of people that there was not enough land to give them food, and they were hungry and unhappy. Most miserable of all were the old: they became dry as sticks, there was no blood in them, they had nothing to do. For they got older and older and did not die. Death was then brought to men by Abo-Tani for their benefit. When life in earthly existence loses the savour of youth and becomes a burden, death comes to man as a boon and takes him on to the heavenly existence. A Wancho tale[26] describes how at first men did not die but changed their form, just as the caterpillar and silkworm do, with the result that the world got too full of human beings who gave a lot of trouble to the birds and animals. Death came to the world, not in this case as an act of mercy to men (who did not grow old and miserable, but constantly renewed their youth) but out of pity for the animals and birds.

The ontological experience of life and death is the same. For, death brings to man only a new existence. The errant self moves on in the cosmos between the earth and the sky through an unending cycle of birth and death on this earth, also in the other world, from one abode to another.

The Harmony of All Existence

The tribal myths deny the uniqueness of man insofar as his origin is concerned. The Dhammai Miji[27] myth describes how from the union of the Earth and Sky a male and a female frog were born first and when they mated they had human children. In another type of myth, the first human beings are described as emerging from various material things. The Moklums[28] describe how the daughters of Rang, the Lord of the Sky, gave birth to a lump of flesh which was neither dead nor living. She dried it by fire and presently it burst open and bits of it scattered about the world and turned into human beings. A Khampti story[29] tells us that in the beginning there was a great tree, from the berry of which there grew a flower; out of this flower came a pair of human beings, the first man and woman. In one Singpho story[30] the great spirits who lived at the dawn of the world left three children, one of whom was human, the second a rock and the third a gourd. As the children were playing together the rock-child broke open the gourd and many little people came out of it: these are the first human beings. A Taraon

Mishmi story[31] also describes how many of the first men and women came out of the magic tusk of an elephant.

Man and animal are close kins. There are many stories of marriage of human beings with gods, spirits, animals (real animals, not human beings in disguise, or under enchantment) as well as leaves, trees, and even fire. A Sherdukpen tale[32] describes how a woman gave birth to a human child, and then to snake, monkey, tiger, cow and dog. Monkeys, in a Nocte story,[33] were originally men. In a Hrusso tale,[34] a woman turned into an animal to avoid incest with her brother to whom she had been forcibly married. A man turns into a tiger, a woman gives birth to twins, of whom one is human and the other a tiger.[35] There is a Minyong story[36] of two brothers, one of whom turns into a cat and the other into a tiger. A Wancho story[37] describes how men and tigers exchange their teeth. Animals talk and also often behave like men.[38] Indeed, in those early days, there does not seem to have been any real distinction between man, animal and spirit.

Man is not unique even in the possession of knowledge. Primordial knowledge came to him from birds and animals. In a Hill Miri story[39] god sends two birds to the first man and woman (who were innocent of any knowledge about the facts of life) to people the world. In a Bugun story,[40] after the first couple have come into being, a god excites them to intercourse. In another version,[41] a boy and a girl are fertilized almost as flowers are fertilized by bees. There is an excellent Singpho story[42] describing how the first man learnt to make the pillars of a house from the legs of an elephant, the poles from the body of a snake, the roof from the skeleton of the buffalo, and the thatch from a fish's scales. Another tribal myth[43] describes how at a time when all men lived naked, the growing of cotton and the art of weaving was taught to men by the gods, in a dream. The Singpho story[44] tells how from the spider, a girl learnt how to weave. According to Wanchos,[45] from the first rat who fell down from the sky man learnt how to cultivate. The Singphos[46] believe that man's knowledge of iron is a gift from goddess Lepchan. Men got fire from various animals.[47] A bird brings water to mankind.[48] Men learnt from birds how to weep.[49]

Like men, the gods and spirits are also not unique; the myths about them follow the same pattern. As stated, from the union of an elderly man and a hideous creature were born the god of death, the god of water, the god of rain, the god of lightning, and the god of earthquake. At first there was only one man in the whole world. He united with the god Yang's daughter; from her many children were born. Of the two brothers, one became the ancestor of men and the other the ancestor of the spirits. Following a fight between the two brothers, the sphere of influence of men and spirits was divided. When the land was divided between man and spirits, the fathers of mankind got the best land from the ancestors of the spirits.[50] The Khasis[51] believe that in the beginning god was walking hand in hand with man. At that time there was a tree which served as a ladder to the original sixteen families of human beings for their communication between heaven and earth.

The statement that neither man nor god is unique implies that every creature is an organic part of the cosmos. Nobody reigns supreme; one is only different from the other. Every creature performs the same paradigmatic act of (a) creation, (b) preservation and (c) destruction. The cosmic order is maintained by the harmonious functioning of each one of them. The tribal myths present an example of the early age.

Creation

As stated, a creature becomes the creator of another creature. It is through this process that the intrinsic difference between man, animal and god is totally eliminated. The ontological meaning and significance of creation is conveyed by the myth of incest. At the beginning of the world the first brother and sister came together to produce the human race. In an Idu Mishmi story[52] the parents of the first boy and girl decide that since there are no other people in the world, they will have to marry each other. The girl tries to escape, but in the end she is compelled to marry her brother and, in due course, gives birth to a tiger and a god in human form. The shadow of incest lies across many of the stories of creation. But all these myths have only one message: that the act of creation is paramount, higher than human morals.

Preservation

Every creature, howsoever small and insignificant it may appear, plays the role of the preserver. In a Nocte tradition[53] the cock claims to be the Chief of men and animals because even the Sun and the Moon come into the Sky at his command. In a Singpho tale[54] the cock crows to tell men when the first waters have subsided that they can come to occupy the earth. In a Kaman Mishmi tale,[55] a bird seeing great gods levelling the mountains becomes frightened that his nest will be destroyed, and brings them a message that their wives are sick and their parents dead, thus saving the hills and mountains for the world. In a Singpho tale[56] a parrot warns men to escape from the power of a dangerous demon. In a Tagin tradition[57] a little bird persuades men and animals to act in a way that saves them.

Destruction

As mentioned, death is brought for the benefit of the world. Before it came life in the world was miserable. Death eventually serves as a leaven for rejuvenation and preservation of life. The eschatological beliefs of the tribes show that beneath this tragic world the eternal life flows; the soul changes its body to acquire a new body for a better existence. According to the Wanchos,[58] death came to human beings for the preservation of the birds and animals. For they not only killed them but took away their food. One day a crane caught a fish and was about to eat it, when a man came by and snatched it from its beak and ate it instead. The crane lost its temper and cursed him saying that he would soon die. Another day a crow got a mouthful of meat and was about to eat it when a man snatched it from its beak and ate it. The crow exclaimed: 'If men live for ever, we birds will surely die.' The god Tatchak Namlong heard the crow and declared that men should henceforth begin to die. In a Singpho story[59] seven suns destroy mankind for its inequity. The first men were destroyed by fire and flood, and only one man and woman were saved: from them modern humanity has descended. In a Wancho tale[60] the world is destroyed by flood and the tribe is descended from a girl who was impregnated by the wind. In the same way, many traditions hold that the first race of men was destroyed and a new race created.

Man as a Ritual Being

As the cosmos was created by a primordial sacrifice, all creatures, in essence, become ritual beings. Man is not unique in respect of ritual, he is only more expressive than the other creatures. As a ritual being he demonstrates his paradigmatic role, communicates with others, protects himself from the unseen forces of destruction, and becomes the beneficiary of the benevolent powers.

Priestcraft

The Dafla myth[61] reveals that ritual is the ontological need of every being, and hence there are priests of men, priests of the earth, priests of gods and spirits, and priests of tigers and all animals. Tarngum Sung-Sung was the ancestor of all the priests in the world. The Sherdukpen myth[62] describes how the great god Lopung-Chungba created the Jiji priest and sent him to teach mankind to sacrifice to the gods and spirits so as to be saved from distress. In the Singpho tradition[63] when sorcery began and as a result people fell sick and died god's help was sought. Four gods help the Tumsawa priest who fights against evil spirits. One god watches over them from the sky while three other gods go about the world making men priests, and teaching them what to do.

The priest brings the desired harmony between the creatures confronting inequality of 'power'. The celestial creatures are described as more powerful than the terrestrial creatures, and even within each of these categories all are not equally powerful. Then, there are also benevolent and malevolent forces. To maintain equilibrium in the world order these forces have to be harnessed. In the tribal tradition neither spirits nor gods are omniscient and omnipotent. All beings and all powers subsist in sacrifice. Hence the priests were born to transmit the ritual knowledge not only to mankind but to all creatures. Man's priestcraft is, however, more manifest and far more complex than that of the other creatures.

Recreating the cosmos

As the cosmos originates from sacrifice, ritual becomes the strongest ligament that binds together the temporal and the eternal, the creature and the creator. Aware of this reality, the tribesmen perform ritual not only for their personal well-being, or private destiny, but also, and pre-eminently, for the maintenance of the cosmic order. Fertility rites and the sorcery rites of destruction are known to mankind. The cosmic drama is enacted in a grand ritual where the priests of man perform his paradigmatic role in the cosmic creation. The entire community celebrates this occasion of man's greatest performance as creator of the cosmos. The *Lai Haroba* ritual dance of the Meiteis is an apt example. Vatsyayan[64] has interpreted its symbolic meaning and significance with remarkable clarity:

The *Lai Haroba* is a collective ritual in which all members of the (Meitei) community participate. It is conducted by hereditary priest (*maiba*) and priestess (*maibi*). The *maibas* and *maibis* are selected for life. . . . When a person shows special signs, i.e. of any kind of supernatural powers, whether a child or an adult, male or female, he or she can be identified to be a *maiba* or a *maibi*.

The *Lai Haroba* is a recreation of the cosmos. It lasts like the *yajna* for ten to fifteen days. As elsewhere the universe is ritually created and ritually destroyed. The festival begins with an important ritual invoking the deities which lie in the waters. A procession is led by a *maiba* and a *maibi* from the centre of the village to a stream outside the village. Dressed in immaculate white, an impressive austere procession arrives at the stream. Now the nine gods, who are believed to have brought earth from heaven and the seven goddesses who took the earth and threw into the waters are invoked. This is done through music and dance. Ritually two leaves are placed in the waters – one facing upwards and the other downwards. These two symbolically represent the female and the male principle. The seed is symbolically within the leaves. The first part is called *Lai Ekauba* and the second *Lai Themba*. These leaves are placed on two water pots which have also been carried to the stream empty. Now they are full of the energies of creation. The procession solemnly walks back to a temporary shrine which has been constructed for the festival. Two earthen pitchers are placed near the shrine. The deities in the shrine can be made of cane, wood or mud; in short, all ephemeral material which will be destroyed at the end of the festival. Once the earthen pitchers are placed near the shrine, symbolically and ritually, creation takes place, the human being is born. As in the case of other festivals in other parts of India for this time and duration, a new universe has been created. It is essential therefore also to invoke the deities of the four directions. These are *Wangbaren*, the deity of the South; *Thangjing*, the Lord of Moirang tribe, who protects the South-West; *Marjing*, the Lord of the horses, protects the North; and *Koubru*, the mountain guardian of the North-West. Having invoked the directions, the stage is ready for recreating the life-cycle of the human being. First there is the birth of a child. This sequence is called *Laipou*. Now a procession moves in two rows and the whole growth of a human being in various stages is recounted. The *maibi* touches different parts of her body to indicate the making of the human being: as the procession moves, one can almost see how a human being is being formed. Thereafter is the sequence of the human being needing shelter and thus the construction of a house. There is the need of human being for sowing and for harvest. Each function of the life-cycle is recreated day after day in a beautiful moving procession and movements accompanied by equally fascinating strains of music to the sole accompaniment of that unique string instrument called *pena.* The *Pam Yanba* and the *Phi Shaba* recreate the different phases of cultivation, harvesting of lashing (cotton plant) and the weaving of textiles. Movements of the loom called *Khuthek* are typical of these sequences. In each phase the choreographical pattern is that of an intertwined serpent. There are other beautiful and vibrant sequences. . . .

On the concluding day of the *Lai Haroba* festival, many martial dances are performed. They are known by the generic terms *Thang Haiba* and *Takshaw Saiba* or *Ta-Khoushaba.* The mood of quiet austerity is replaced by a virile fierceness; daggers, spears, swords, shields, maces are held. Movements are quick, swift and sharp. Crisp hops and extensive open movements with spear attacking the ground are dominant in some phases: the art of attack and defence strongly reminiscent of fencing techniques is characteristic of others. . . .

As has been mentioned above, the whole festival is a recreation of the cosmos – the movement of the universe from the beginning, i.e. *Shrishti* (creation) to *Samhar* (destruction) – is presented. It moves from the most esoteric to the exoteric.

Communication with divinity

Through ritual man communicates with the divinity. In this act he is helped by other creatures. There are myths concerning the creation of birds for sacrifice. In a Minyong myth,[65] the cock is one of the animals who goes to find the Sun who has hidden in fear and sorrow. He acts as a messenger to tell mankind what must be done to persuade her to return and crows triumphantly when appears. Fowls are specially suitable for sacrifice to the gods. An Idu myth[66] describes in detail the process of transforming a small round stone into a fowl for this purpose. A Hrusso myth[67] explains the dilemma of a man who is told to sacrifice a domestic fowl and pig for the relief of his sick children, and how he manages to create them.

Ritual serves as a bridge between man and god. During the performance of a ritual the Meitei[68] priest and priestess usually fall into a trance and speak in unintelligible syllables which are interpreted as the answer of the god. The Khasis[69] make a divine consultation through the medium of an egg, or a fowl, or any other animal judging the divine response from the signs that he asks for. When, for instance, the sacrifice for a sick person is done with a cock-sacrificing ritual, after ripping open the intestines to find out the answer, the performer asks the god to give the cause of sickness.[70] From the position of the intestine the signs are read and the cause is found. This having been done, god's grace for the recovery of the patient is asked and a word of satisfaction from god comes forth.[71]

Such methods of communication with the divine being are adopted on all important events in tribal life.

The Foundation of Tribal Thought

Evolutionary interpretations[72] of the tribal mind may be summarized in such epithetic terms as prelogical, prescientific, irrational, savage mind. A more sympathetic interpretation would allow logical but not scientific understanding of the 'savage'. For instance, the Khasi method of finding out the cause of sickness by cock-sacrificing ritual may be considered logical but unscientific. Such considerations have led many a scholar to conclude that the savages are natural philosophers,[73] that the savage mind puts the philosophy of the finite into practice,[74] or that the savages too are rational creatures but their mode of rationality is different from our mode of rationality.[75] No anthropologist, nor even a philosopher, would, however, grant conceptual and abstract thinking to the tribal mind.

Without contesting all these racial prejudices, or prejudgements, we may straightaway approach the foundation of the tribal thought.

In the tribal worldview, myth is entry into the unthought and unthinkable; ritual is an act that leads into direct contact with the reality. Myth and ritual are, therefore, inseparable in tribal cultures. Myth, as an expression of the ultimate experience, stands for the reality, but in itself is not the reality. It represents a symbolic reality, the indirect message of the transcendence; but the transcendental reality is not the symbolic reality. The knowledge of ritual is revelatory. The priests of all creatures were born at the beginning of the creation. Man is not unique in the possession of knowledge;

primordial knowledge came to him from birds and animals. The implication of this belief is that the universal knowability lies with the transcendence, the unthought, the unthinkable, the unknowable, the unmanifest, and not with man, god, or the other creatures.

In such a perception of human faculty, it is no wonder why the intellectual construct of knowledge has been given no pride of place in the tribal cultures. It is also true that modern scientific thinking – rational, logical, conceptual and abstract thinking – as cognitive part of man cannot decrease the space of the unknown, the infinite. For, man's faculty is limited and regressive. The only tool of grasping the unknowable, which is available to man, is the ritual. Hence, the Khasi cock-sacrificing ritual is not only logical but also the most perfect way of knowing the unknowable cause of sickness. The only language in which the unthinkable, and the unknowable, can be thought and spoken of, even partly, is the symbolic language of the sacred myth. In the tribal thought structure, myth is more intelligible and acceptable than any other mode of knowing the reality. Hence, it places itself above philosophy.

The fact that the thought comes from the unthought is borne by the tribal cosmogonic myths. We have seen how in the primordial time, or no-time, the manifest comes from the unmanifest. The unmanifest remains unnamed, unqualified, expressed only symbolically in terms of primeval ocean, darkness, or the self-effulgent light. From the water comes the lotus, the symbol of the manifest. The manifest is named and qualified. Hence, all named gods, spirits, men and animals are creatures and creators of the second order. In the tribal perception, none of them is omniscient and omnipotent. The first principle of the universe is: One-and-many. Hence, the tribesmen think of non-duality at all levels of existence. This is contrary to the modern anthropological interpretation of human understanding in terms of binary opposition.[76]

Obviously, one's understanding of the universe depends on how he interprets the reality, or what he calls the reality. Modern man's formulation of existence is based on his personal aspirations and interest in the temporal world; for him that alone is real, the ultimate. Traditional man's vision of existence and well-being is based on a much wider horizon, the transcendence, where his true and complete identity is undifferentiated from the other beings.

Such reflection of human understanding is found not only in the tribal thought structure but also in the traditional organization of the tribal life and culture.

NOTES

1. In 1970, I had suggested a classification of cultures in terms of three principal modes of transmission of knowledge: oral, textual and transcendental. This was further developed in 1986. From the evolutionists' point of view writing is the hallmark of civilization. Hence the preliterate tribals are a precultural group. My contention is that writing is another mode of transmission of knowledge and in no way superior to the oral (Saraswati 1988).
2. Raimundo Panikkar, one of the leading religious thinkers of our time, has set standard for hermeneutic interpretation of myth. My own initial understanding of myth has come largely from his works: but he is in no way responsible for any unclarity that one may find in the present formulation which I have tried independently.
3. This story, in various versions, has been recorded from Gallongs, Noctes, Panggi, Adis, Taraon Mishmis and Wanchos, and is known to many other tribes (Elwin 1968: 107).
4. For a comprehensive philosophical analysis of human experience, see Panikkar (1983:292-308).
5. Panikkar has analysed the Hindu myth of Prajapati under these three levels *(Ibid,* 70-78). The present interpretation follows this format but not the contents.
6. See Appendix.
7. *Ibid.*
8. *Ibid.* The Vedic Risis had revealed the creative energy of *Hranyagarbha*, the Golden Germ, which caused heaven and earth, waters and all that lives (*Rig Veda* X).
9. *Ibid.*
10. *Ibid.* This idea of creation by sacrifice echoes the famous *Purusa Sukta* of the *Rig Veda* (X). For philosophical interpretation, see Panikkar (*op. cit.*, 70-86).
11. *Ibid.*
12. *Ibid.*
13. *Ibid.*
14. *Ibid.*
15. *Ibid.*
16. *Ibid.*
17. *Ibid.*
18. *Ibid.*
19. *Ibid.*
20. Elwin, *op. cit.*, 9-10.
21. *Ibid.*, 10-14
22. Furer-Haimendorf (1953), cf. *Ibid.*, 299-300. The truth of unity of all experience was visualized by the Upanisadic Risis:

    Whatever is here, that is there,
    What is there, that again is here.
    He who sees any difference here
    Goes from death to death. (*Katha Upanisada* II.1.10)

23. See Mawrie (1981: 29-32).

24. Elwin, *op. cit.*, 308-309.
25. *Ibid.*, 317-318.
26. *Ibid.*, 329.
27. *Ibid.*, 103.
28. *Ibid.*, 104.
29. *Ibid.*, 105.
30. *Ibid.*
31. *Ibid.*
32. *Ibid.*, 390.
33. *Ibid.*, 393. The myth reverses the modern ideas of evolution.
34. *Ibid.*, 390.
35. *Ibid.*, 104.
36. *Ibid.*, 394.
37. *Ibid.*
38. *Ibid.*, 103.
39. *Ibid.*, 105.
40. *Ibid.*
41. *Ibid.*
42. *Ibid.*, 213.
43. *Ibid.*
44. *Ibid.*, 219.
45. *Ibid.*
46. *Ibid.*, 227.
47. *Ibid.*, 251.
48. *Ibid.*, 377.
49. *Ibid.*, 319.
50. *Ibid.*, 154.
51. Mawrie, *op. cit.*, 33.
52. Elwin, *op. cit.*, 106.
53. *Ibid.*, 376.
54. *Ibid.*
55. *Ibid.*, 376.
56. *Ibid.*
57. *Ibid.*
58. *Ibid.*, 329.
59. *Ibid.*, 105.
60. *Ibid.*
61. *Ibid.*, 76.
62. *Ibid.*, 269.
63. *Ibid.*, 282.
64. Vatsyayan (1987:132-35), the internationally known aesthetist, has made excellent analysis of the tribal ritual dance from different parts of India.
65. Elwin, *op. cit.*, 376.
66. *Ibid.*
67. *Ibid.*
68. Parratt, (1981: 57).
69. Mawrie, *op. cit.*, 28.
70. *Ibid.*, 31.

71. *Ibid.*, 35.
72. For instance, Levi-Bruhl's and Sartre's interpretations. See Chandra (1988).
73. Evans-pritchard (1935).
74. Levi-Strauss (1966).
75. For a critique of anthropological and philosophical interpretations of the savage mind, see Chandra (1988).
76. Durkheim (1965), and many of his followers. See Saraswati (1984: 3-7).

REFERENCES

Chandra, Suresh 1988. Evans-Pritchard on persons and their cattle-clocks: a note on the anthropological account of man, Paper presented at the National Seminar on *Philosophy, Anthropology and Tribal Societies* (North-Eastern Hill University, Shillong, June 7-8, 1988).

Durkheim, Emile 1965 (1912). *The elementary forms of the religious life*, New York.

Elwin, Verrier 1968. *Myths of the north-east frontier of India*, Shillong.

Evans-Pritchard, E.E. 1935. *Science and sentiment*, University of Egypt, quoted by Peter Winch in *Ethics and Action*, London 1972, p.11.

Furer-Haimendorf, C. von 1953. The after-life in Indian belief, *Journal of the Royal Anthropological Institute*, LXXIII, p.37.

Levi-Strauss, Claude 1966. *The savage mind*, Chicago.

Mawrie, H.O. 1981. *The Khasi milieu*, New Delhi.

Panikkar, R. 1983. *Myth, faith and hermeneutics: cross-cultural studies*, Bangalore.

Parratt, Saroj Nalini 1980. *The religion of Manipur*, Calcutta.

Saraswati, Baidyanath 1984. *The spectrum of the sacred: essays on the religious traditions of India*, New Delhi.

Saraswati, Baidyanath 1986. Thinking about tradition, *Man in India* 66(3).

Saraswati, Baidyanath 1988. Textualizing tribal tradition, Paper presented at the National Seminar on *Philosophy, Anthropology and Tribal Societies* (North-Eastern Hill University, Shillong, June 7-8, 1988).

Vatsyayan, Kapila 1987. *Traditions of Indian folk-dance*, New Delhi.

APPENDIX

The following myths have been recorded by Elwin (1968):

1. At first Kujum-Chantu, the earth, was like a human being; she had a head, and arms and legs, and an enormous fat belly. The original human beings lived on the surface of her belly.

   One day it occurred to Kujum-Chantu that if she ever got up and walked about, everyone would fall off and be killed, so she herself died of her own accord. Her head became the snow-covered mountains; the bones of her back turned into smaller hills, her chest was the valley where the Apa Tanis live. From her neck came the north country of the Tagins. Her buttocks turned into the Assam plain. For just as the buttocks are full of fat, Assam has fat rich soil. Kujum-Chantu's eyes became the Sun and Moon. From her mouth was born Kujum-Popi who sent the Sun and Moon to shine in the sky (Apa Tani).
2. At first there was nothing but water. There were two brothers, Poling the elder and Terring the younger. They lived separately in the water and neither of them knew that the other existed. Terring had the form of a *mithun* and Poling had the form of an elephant. Each thought he was the only creature living in the world.

   But after many years had passed, as they moved about the lonely ancient waters, they met each other, and Poling said, 'Who are you and where do you come from?' Terring asked, 'Who are *you* and where *you* come from?' Though there were only these two in all the world, they did not make friends; each accused the other of invading his territory, they quarrelled and in the fight that followed they killed each other.

   From the flesh of Terring, the earth was formed, from his bones came the trees and from his hair the grass. From Poling's bones came the rocks and from his flesh the mountains (Bori).
3. In the sky were the old man Puk and his woman Yuk. At that time the earth was covered with water. The prawn and the crab tried to dry it up. The prawn used his antennae to collect the rubbish, leaves, grass and bits of wood that were floating on the surface and the crab dug a deep pit down below. The water poured into the pit and the earth appeared. The prawn's pile of rubbish turned into mountains.

But the earth was very soft at first. Then the Sun and the Moon came up and hardened it by their heat (Gallong).

4. Everything was water, water as far as the eye could see. But above the water rose the tree Teri-Ramula. As time passed a worm was born in the tree and it began to eat the wood. The dust fell into the water, year after year, until slowly the world was formed.

   And then at last the tree fell to the ground. The bark on the lower side of the trunk became the skin of the world; the bark of the upper side became the skin of the sky. The trunk itself turned into rock. The branches became the hills (Hill Miri).

5. Long ago, before the world was made, the Wiyu Chungum-Irum was living with his wife Chingum-Erum. One day when this woman was lying asleep, a little water fell and flowed into her. She woke up and felt bitterly cold inside. She looked everywhere to see what had made her so cold, but there was nothing. She told her husband about it, how she was shivering with the cold thing that had entered her body but he too could not make out what it was.

   Twenty days later, Chingum-Erum laid an egg. Husband and wife looked at it in wonder and put it carefully aside. After six months it broke open of its own accord, and out of it came Sichi, the earth, Togle the great mountains and Togji the little hill (Hill Miri).

6. At first there was no earth and sky; there were only two great eggs. But they were not ordinary eggs, for they were soft and shone like gold. They did not stay in one place, but went round and round. At last, as they went round, they collided and both the eggs broke open. From one came the Earth, from the other the Sky, her husband.

   Now the Earth was too big for the Sky to hold in his arms and he said, 'Though you are my wife you are greater than I and I cannot take you. Make yourself smaller.'

   The Earth accordingly made herself pliable and the mountains and valleys were formed, and she became small and the Sky was able to go to her in love.

   When the Sky made love to the Earth, every kind of tree and all living creatures came into being (Hrusso Aka).

7. Long long ago there were two powerful spirits named Draku and Supaideng. They were strong and powerful but rather lazy and

spent their days in a free and happy way.

One day Draku met Supaideng on the bank of a river and said, 'Look brother, let us do some real work which will remain on earth in token of our strength and power.' Supaideng agreed and after some discussion they decided to level down the hills and make the surface of the earth equal. They each went to opposite corners of the earth and crushed the hills and mountains to sand and dust (Kaman Mishmi).

8. At first there was nothing, nothing at all, but rocks and water. The first living beings were the rocks, but they were not as rocks are now: they were soft and they could move about. From the rocks, a female rock Eling-Litung-Tune was born and from her another female rock Peddong-Nane was born. When Peddong-Nane grew up she was ashamed, for she was naked. She married another rock, Eling-Limuk-Muktum, and her first child was the fish; it went to live in a mountain stream. Then she gave birth to the big frog and then to Etut-Tigling, the little frog, and then to the land-frog. After that she gave birth to the insect Kungung-Pangam, which lives in water, and then to another fish.

   But now Peddong-Nane left her husband and went to the sky village Engo-Takar among the stars, where she married Karba-Bojong. By him she had many children – Ninur-Botte, Lomang-Botte, Doini-Nibu and Darro-Rabbo – and when she had borne them all she died. Doini-Nibu and Darro-Rabbo prepared rice beer for her funeral. When the millet was ready and they poured water over it, a great cloud arose, and from the cloud was born Polung-Sabbo, the *mithun*.

   They held a Kebang to discuss how to make an earth. 'There is nothing but water. Who will dry it up and let the earth appear?' 'I can do it', said Polung-Sabbo and forthwith he dug a great pit with his horns and when the water had poured into the pit, the dry land appeared. After this the rocks became hard as they are today (Minyong).

9. It was night. There was no day. There were Wiyus in the world, but not yet men (Panggi).

10. Before the earth was made everything was water. There were two brothers who were supreme in the sky. The elder was Lopong-Rimbuche and the younger was Chom-Dande. One day they said to each other, 'When men are created, how will they live if there is nothing but water in the world?' There was lotus

flower growing in the sky. The brothers threw this down and immediately the water was covered with flowers. Then they called the winds from the four quarters. The east wind brought white dust and scattered it on the flowers. The west wind blew yellow dust, the south wind red dust and the north wind black dust. The wind blew the dust round and round and mixed it up together until the earth was formed. This is why the earth is of different colours (Sherdukpen).

11. At first there was no earth nor sky, but only cloud and mist. From it a woman called Khupning-Knam was born, and since she came from the mist she was a sort of cloud. In time, she gave birth to a girl called Ningon-Chinum and a boy called Tung-Kam-Waisun. They had the appearance of snow. When they grew up they married each other and from them were born a girl called *Inga* (Earth) and a son called *Mu* (Sky). *Inga* was mud and *Mu*, a cloud. These two also married and had a boy called Imbung, the Wind. When he was born he blew so strongly that he raised the cloud, his father, into the sky and dried up his mother, the mud. In this way heaven and earth were made (Singpho).

12. At first there was nothing but water in the world. Below the water there lived the god Techimdum. He came up to the surface and saw nothing but water.

    Now below the water there was a lot of mud and in this Techimdum erected a great pillar. White ants swarmed round and crawled up to the top with their mouths full of earth, which they spread over it. When it was dry, the wind blew the earth all over the surface of the water.

    Techimdum said to the ants, 'I will put up four more pillars and you must help to bring the earth up from the bottom of the ocean.' He put one pillar in each corner of the world and the ants became very busy carrying earth up above the surface of the water. Along with the earth they brought the seeds of flowers and trees. In some places they put too much earth and there were hills and mountains (Taraon Mishmi).

2

TRIBAL COSMOLOGY: DISPLACING AND REPLACING PROCESSES IN ANDAMANESE PLACES

Vishvajit Pandya

Introduction

Ethnographies of different parts of the world depict people's ideas of production and consumption which articulate relations of exchange. Analyses of these ideas have emphasized either the value which is involved in the process of exchange or the value of exchange itself. In both cases analysts have tended to find hierarchical relations endured over a period of time in terms leading to formation of certain values and ideology which creates and generates social relations between givers and takers, or those who receive and those who reciprocate (Dumont, 1980).

May it be Dumont's Indian ethnography (Dumont, 1970) or Malinowski's account of Trobriand Islanders (Malinowski, 1922), exchange can be seen as functioning on a number of levels and frequently on temporal and hierarchical dimensions simultaneously. It is often presupposed that production and reproduction of value at the social and cosmological levels bring together individuals, groups, neighbours, clans, spirits, ancestors and visitors (Kapferer, 1976; Strathern, 1971). Value is always seen as 'intrinsic' and 'instrumental' with a hierarchical objectification within a total system of exchange relations within a culture (Stanner, 1985; Ernest, 1985). As a consequence the daughters are prescribed to be given away within the Indian caste system, or the bride price is paid for, a recurrent theme in the ethnographic depiction of African tribal and nomadic society. Within this way of looking at the event of marriage or any other occasion we have created a perhaps dominant idea of value which is not the culture's own construct. We have inherited and imposed the idea of value which is based on the presupposed fact that *X* is different from *Y*, it is either less or greater, and in the process of exchange an equation is set up whereby certain number of *X* equals to *Y* or value of *Y*. The *X* and *Y* could be daughters, cattels, armshells, pigs, or it may involve a group's identity and its hierarchical position. This implicit equation process within the exchange relations has characterized the perspective of value and relations of exchange itself being valued (Brown, 1972, 1974). For instance, identity *X* provides *x* to group *Y* and in turn group *Y* reciprocates by providing *y* to *X*. Since the focus has been on the transaction of *x* and *y* inbetween *X* and *Y* we have seen much of value given to exchange of valuables and production of value for exchange (Meillassoux, 1972, Munn, 1986). Ever since the writings of Mauss (1954) we have seldom gone beyond a frame of exchange. Analysis has always been constricted by the presupposition that because relations of exchange exist (Levi-Strauss, 1963) value as an idea and ideal emerges affecting the whole ideology within a given culture.

Negrito hunters and gatherers of the Andaman Islands and the Andamanese culture present a different premise for analysis of exchange and value. For the Andamanese value's existence precedes from the formation of social relations including relations of exchange. For the Andamanese value is an idea and ideal pertaining to objects in an allocated place which generates the exchange system as well as expresses the value through the movement of the valuables known as *gobolagnane* from one place to other bringing together a totality of relations. This totality of relations is hierarchically differentiated and includes hunting and gathering islanders, hunted animals, gathered plants and spirits (formed out of dead human beings) who hunt and gather all that is on the island.

In the course of my fieldwork and research among the Ongee hunters and gatherers, one of the surviving groups of Andaman Islanders,[1] I found that the relations among the spirits, humans, and animals are articulated and expressed in terms of every activity constituting a phenomenon involving all three of the hierarchy (spirits, humans and animals/plants) and has a particular specified place. The interaction between the three in terms of hunting and the hunted has to take place in a particular place and in a particular procedure, and in doing so the value emerges. Because of this concern within the very

Ongee worldview, as I will show in this paper, every relation and phenomenon has a place and every place has a particular relation and phenomenon to it. This principle of maintaining hierarchy is not only generative of social relations but also unites the social with the mythological and conceptual schemes within the Andamanese culture itself.

Value for the Andamanese and Ongees specifically, emerges from replacing that which is displaced within the scheme of place (social as well as cosmological). Value for the Ongees is an idea pertaining to the process, emphasizing on act of replacing whereby order emerges. This order is not just a balance or equation within the hierarchical structure involving different places but also the very process is an ordering principle for the hierarchy and related places. Relations are based not on just giving and taking, or transacting detachable commodities *per se*, but on keeping the value of placement as a prime concern while continuing to displace from one place to replacing it in another. This makes the Ongee worldview devoid of typical exchange ideas where values are exchanged and exchange is valued. Every effort made and represented in Ongee relations founded on the principle of replacing the displaced, embodies aspects analogous to our notion of having a savings account and using only the interest to live on while leaving the principal of the savings intact.

It is in the light of this particular idea about exchange as the Ongees see that the Pan-Andamanese mythological theme (recorded by earlier ethnographers also) should be reconsidered.

> The future life will be but a repetition of the
> present, but all will then remain in the prime
> of life, sickness and death will be unknown,
> and there will be no more marrying or giving in marriage.
>
> (Man 1883 : 94-95; Pandya 1987)

It is often quoted (Levi-Strauss, 1969: 457) and has been seen as the negation of exchange in the sense of patterned transference of items, both material (shells, food, labour) and immaterial (status, power) between individuals and groups creating an isolated and insulated social man (Levi-Strauss, 1969: 497). For the Andamanese, and Ongees specifically, I will show that the very absence of exchange relations as we understand is a valued idea.

Spirits and Principle of Placement

Solely dependent on hunting and gathering activities, the Ongees undertake seasonal translocation. From November to February, the Ongees live in the coastal area and hunt turtles and dugongs. During the wet season, from April to September, the Ongees set up their residential camps in the forest and hunt pigs. Not dependent on anything or any outsider, Ongee life has continued to be relatively isolated and insulated and solely dependent on the tropical island of Little Andamans which provides all that the Ongees need. All that is on the island, in terms of resources, is available to all the Ongees. It is only the factor of skill and chance that differentiates the Ongees in terms of who has what resources, and how much of it.

Each evening when the men return to the camp with the kill of their hunt and women return with what they have gathered, all the food is placed in the middle of the camp ground at the communal cooking place. All the Ongees are expected to just go and pick up a portion of whatever food is there, irrelevant of who brought it and who is related to the person who either hunted or gathered it. As the Ongees explain,

> No one gives food *(choge)* and tools *(maonale)* since they are never taken away. They are always there for use. It is only spirits who take away and not return.

The Ongee language demonstrates the egalitarian attitude which underlies Ongee notions of giving and taking. The term *ka* which means 'where' also implies 'to give'. The term *ma* which means 'not here' also implies a refusal to give something. However *ka* and *ma* are never used for requesting or refusing *choge* or *maonale*. The words *ma* and *ka* are appropriately used only for substances and objects referred to as *gobolagnane*. *Gobolagnane* is a collective term referring to fire and clay paints (applied on the body), but the prime form of it is the ancestral bones (mainly the lower jawbone) made into ornaments. The bone *gobolagnane* of a dead relative are ceremonially acquired by the living relatives. On the first Full Moon after the burial of the *gegi*, corpse, the son or son-in-law of the dead person digs up the burial site with a digging stick. All the bones, particularly the *ibeedange*, lower jawbone, are removed and the soil is replaced in the grave. Once the bones are removed the body is believed to rapidly change into a spirit and leave the island to live either in the sky or in the sea with other good spirits. The *geebaroye-tomya*, good spirits, are regarded to be blind, formless, or lightweight, and to be without the capacity to masticate food since they do not have lower jawbones. Though the Ongees and spirits are related, they live separately and depend on the same island for food since spirits return to the island to eat.

The bones of the dead ancestor are wraped with dried orchid skin and strung with beads and fibrous cord and are made into ornaments. Generally, the ornaments are wraped up and kept in a closed basket, so that it is not easily visible and exposed to heat and winds. Within the Ongee conception of bodies the bones are the hardest and coolest part as well as the most internal part of any living thing and are nothing else but hardened *kwayabe* smell. Since bones are internal to all living things, they constantly release smell in the form of various body fluids such as sweat, tears and blood. The bones on being exposed to heat and winds start disintegrating due to the loss of smell. The smell of the bones, carried by the winds, attracts the ancestral spirits back to the island to the living descendant who holds or owns the bones. The ancestral spirits who are attracted to the bones give help to and protect the Ongees from *geebeteeye-tomya*, malevolent spirits, who are also attracted to the smell released from the body of the living Ongees. Benevolent ancestral spirits and malevolent spirits are alike in several respects : they both are capable of moving anywhere and everywhere and they are always attracted to a place from which smell is being emitted. The distinction between the two kinds of spirits is based on the possession of a lower jawbone by the malevolent spirits. Bad spirits are created from corpse whose lower jawbones are not retained by the Ongees and made into *goblagnane*.[2] The bad spirits, therefore, are known to be extremely hungry and will even eat living Ongee bodies.

When bad spirits are attracted to the living Ongees, 'they come and take away the Ongees'. This act is known as death caused by *enegetebe* (to be embraced and taken away). It is an embrace due to the coinciding of the spirit's movement, smell's movement, and the Ongee's location. To avoid such an encounter, the Ongees try to create, through the smell released from the *gobolagnane*, a conjunction of their own body's and smell's movement with that of the good-protective spirits. When both forms of spirits are attracted to the place where the Ongee and *gobolagnane* are, a situation is created in which the spirits negotiate among themselves, just as the Ongees negotiate marriage and child adoption among themselves. In dav-to-day life, an Ongee may not ask for food from any or every family, since the food is always given without being asked for, but the Ongees never feel any hesitation to demand *gobolagnane*. It is this attitude regarding the bones made into *gobolagnane* which makes the very term *gobolagnane* a verb in Ongee language, meaning an instrument that makes possible 'giving and taking' or 'to go and bring'. The underlying logic here is the fact that the ancestral bones release smell which makes it possible for the living Ongee to return without having an *enegetebe*. Excluding the items under the category of *gobolagnane*, every other thing is and can be given away but may not be expected or demanded back. The *gobolagnane* are owned by each family. If an individual outside of the family asks to use a family's ancestral bones, they are shared but the bones must be returned to the owners. It is in the returning of the shared bones that the Ongees can continue to live on the island and not get transformed by the spirits through the process of *enegetebe* and into a dead individual living in the sky or sea. *Gobolagnane* and the relations formed through and around it thereby make it possible for the Ongees to remain in a place, the island.

Both kinds of spirit also share food and tools among themselves. Since good spirits do not have lower jawbones, they depend on the Ongees to provide them with food. During negotiation, the good spirits convince the bad ones to let the Ongees live so that they may provide a continuous supply of food which all spirits may share. Bad spirits agree to the negotiation since the good spirits provide them with *maonale,* which good spirits alone are capable of making them or directing the Ongees in making them. This relationship between spirits and Ongees is also the basis for seasonal translocation among the Ongees. Since the spirits and the Ongees depend on the island for food the potential encounter with spirits who can cause death makes it necessary for Ongees and spirits to be on the island but in different parts. Ongees explain:

> In each season spirits along with winds come from a particular direction. When they leave other spirits come in from a different side and it is a different season. When spirits come to the sea, then we move to the forest for hunting pigs. When spirits come to the forest we all go to the sea for hunting turtle. Spirits and Ongees both have to be on this island, sky, and sea around. But the place where spirits are feeding is the place in which Ongees should not hunt and gather. If the two are in the same place then all the Ongees

> will be taken away by the spirits to the sky and sea . . . by letting the spirits in a place in a season we get more plants, more animals, and more children . . . also spirits will hunt and gather all of us if we are all at the same place so Ongees and spirits hunt and gather in the same *injube*, space, but in different *nanchugey*, place. Many *nanchugey* in the land, sea, and sky make one big *injube* in which we along with animals, plants, and spirits live.

The idea that Ongees should be present where spirits are absent is the Ongee principle of placement. If this principle is not maintained, displacement in the form of *enegetebe* occurs.

Given this worldview in which value is attached to placement, replacement and displacement, Radcliffe-Brown in his accounts of the Andaman Islanders (1922 [1964]) also noticed the use of ancestral bones (1964:126, 184, 292) and regarded them to be 'social valuables' (1964: 264) since they appeared to be constantly exchanged (*Ibid.* : 113) among the islanders.[3] However in Radcliffe-Brown's analysis ornaments made of bones are worn in order to express the personal value of the individual who has died in the community as well as for the sake of protection from spirits and misfortune.

The ancestral bones, known as *gobolagnane*, are rightly to be regarded as social valuables but the value is not in exchange of the bones itself generating a relationship of interdependence and security. For the Ongees the value of the bones is in the fact that it is an object and form to be kept and saved for the content of smell in it. It is not the bones that are valued but the smell within it. The smell itself is the medium of interaction between the living and the spirit world, transaction of smell itself leading to negotiations and interactions keep the living Ongees on the island and the spirits in the sky and sea. Since the lack of the smell from being given off from the bones and received by the bad spirits ensures the continuity of life both for the Ongees, against the bad spirits, it is shared among all the Ongees for collective perpetuation of life. Ongees believe that death, hunting, birth and regeneration are the result of not giving or losing *kwayabe*, smell. By the release of smell life form changes but in controlling and retaining it the life forms grow. However the loss of smell from life forms is a natural process. The Ongee explanation for this loss being natural is embodied in the fact that all that is living not only has hard bone inside it but on being cut or subjected to heat gives away blood, sweat and tears which are also forms of smell. Ongees describe this movement of smell from its hardest bone form to liquid form, being subject to cutting and heating and consequently affecting the form of life as :

> Smell is like the water of the sea and the tides nobody knows or affects the water coming to land and rising and then going back. It happens always. Smell also like the tide waters comes and goes from all that is living, but just like the tides change the land at the coast the loss of smell changes the form that is living. If the smell is not kept, there is no life, if the tide's water does not go back to the sea then there is no land and no sea.

The smell itself is not 'given or taken' among the Ongees but it is used to keep themselves in a place and keep the spirits in their place. For the Ongees the bones are the most condensed form of smell which can be used to cause either the replacement or displacement of smells of spirits and Ongees, whereby spirits and Ongees remain in their respective places. Bone ornaments are means of control. Ornaments being held and covered control the loss of smell from it and makes possible the manipulation of smell. By focusing on the use of bones, *gobolagnane*, I intend to show that the Ongees do not exchange anything in the traditional sense of the term Exchange.

Displacement and Replacement

Within the Ongee cosmology, human beings and animals have limited movement potential, and are restricted to move along the horizontal axis of space to places like the forest and sea. In relation to this, birds and ritual specialists known as *torale* (spirit communicator) are different. They, along with animals such as the monitor lizard and civet cat are forms of life that can move across land, into water, and also upwards. Within this classification of various elements of Ongee cosmology, based on the elements' capacity to move, all humans and animals are in a lower position compared to the hierarchical position of the spirits, and winds. Spirits and winds have a significant position since they can move any and everywhere within Ongee space. Within this system of hierarchy of movements, a certain amount of flexibility and change of position is attributed to each element and is visible through the emission of smells, which are carried, by the winds, to the spirits who are the prime absorbers and receivers of smell. This movement of smell and wind sets up the possibility of equality within the hierarchical system. This equality is evident in the outcome of the *enegetebe*, whereby the spirits causing death of an Ongee also create a spirit. This equation is brought about by the movement of smell and affects the hierarchically differentiated spirits and humans in terms of their place of existence and movement. The movement of smell sets up the basic quality of dynamics and distinction within the hierarchy of elements such as humans, spirits and animals.

Spirits, humans and animals are distinguished from one another on the basis of their differing moving capacities and body conditions. They are in a hierarchical relationship with one another in which body which has smell and a body which does not have smell are 'encompassed' elements. Bodies that move on both vertical and horizontal axes and bodies that move only on one axis or the other, outlining different places, are the 'encompassing' features of the hierarchical system. This structures (Dumont, 1970) the Ongee cosmology with a fundamental opposition between men and spirits, and between men and animals.

The relative position of the elements within the hierarchy depends on the characteristic opposition of smell-absorbers and smell-emitors. Each element characterized as living limits its dispersal of smell. Loss of smell transforms living elements into dead elements not capable of emitting smell but only of absorbing smell. However, all living elements by the loss of smell are capable of becoming non-living/dead elements. This makes it possible for the elements within the hierarchical system to change their relative position depending on whether smell is kept, dispersed, or completely lost, upholding the Ongee cosmological foundation of necessary hierarchical coexistence of spirits, men, and animals, where the 'encompassed' becomes the 'encompassing'. It is because of this interrelationship of elements within the hierarchy that the Ongee worldview is expressed as :

> Spirits hunt and gather in our forest and sea around it. If we are not hunted and gathered by the spirits then the animals get hunted and gathered by us!

Ongees believe that although spirits, men and animals share a common space (that is collection of different places such as sea and forest constituting space), it is through their different capacities of movement within places that each remains alive within different places of a space. It not only is the Ongee justification for seasonal translocation but also an explanation for the very process of *gitekwetebe*, hunting. Spirits hunt Ongees and displace them by killing and taking them away (*enegetebe*) from the island to the sky or the sea. Human beings, like the spirits, hunt animals and take them away from the forest or sea. Hence the process of *gitekwetebe* and *enegetebe* makes the cosmological structure and hierarchical relation within the elements of the system not just apparently static but consistently dynamic and inter-reflective. Cosmological construct for the Ongees is therefore not based only on the idea of nature but also on how nature is related to the social. The recognition of this relationship between nature, where things move in place, and society where things are accordingly moved from place to place, leads to the emergence of real value of smell and movement. Smell and movement directly do not create or sustain the relationship between the hunter and the hunted but they uphold the hierarchical and dynamic relationship between the spirits, humans and animals.

Replacing the Displaced

Hunting of animals by the Ongees, *gitekwetebe*, may it be out in the sea or in the forest is regarded to be just like the *enegetebe* whereby spirits hunt Ongees and take them away. In fact when an Ongee hunter first locates an animal and succeeds in attacking it, it is glossed as 'an animals *enegetebe*'!; it is only after the killing of the animal is completed that the whole act is glossed as *gitekwetebe*. Ongees believe that hunting and killing of an animal cause the release of the hunted animal's body fluids (blood) and ultimately smells, due to the 'cut' made by the hunter on the living body of the animal. Other animals smell the killed animal due to the smell from the hunted animal (after the act of 'cut') carried by winds. Winds carry the smell of hunted animals from the place of hunt to the other places where the animals are living. Ongees therefore are very particular about cutting up the *gitey*, hunted animal, at the edge of the forest or at the coastal area, and only bringing back to the residential camp grounds the *gereebo*, meat of the hunted animal. *Gereebo* is distinguished from *gitey* as the bones and flesh of animal from which blood is not dripping. In fact I have seen that often the Ongees would walk out of the camp ground after the *gereebo* has been brought in to make sure that no trail of blood drops is left behind. By this procedure what the Ongees ensure is that the act of killing and the feeling of an animal being dead (for the living related animals) is restricted to the sea or forest. The Ongees regard it important to deceive the animals so that the hunter of the animal is regarded to be in the forest and not in the Ongee residential camp. This deception is also regarded by the Ongees as an insurance for the future when they are out in the same location of hunting in a place they will again have an *enegetebe*, since the living animals would be in that very place smelling the smell of the lost animal. The Ongees regard this also as the major difference from the animals *vis-a-vis* the spirits who hunt both humans and animals and say :

> We Ongees are different from animals. When one of us is hunted by the spirits we leave and move to a different camp ground so that the spirits may not come to our homes and hunt all of us. Animals when they are hunted could also cause the living animals to follow the blood and come to our home. We will have to kill all of them or get killed by them. So we keep the smell and blood of the hunted animal near or in the forest and sea, so that on next hunt we may find more animals to hunt in the place where the previous hunting was done.

The concept of smell sets up the basic Ongee relationship involving spirits and animals even within the act of hunting and gathering. The Ongees hunt and gather plants and animals from the various places and so do the spirits but the spirits particularly the bad ones also hunt and gather the Ongees. What is taken away by the spirits from the island becomes dead. What is dead in the context of the living world of the island becomes living in the context of the spirit world. Bad spirits who succeed in *enegetebe* transform the Ongee body into a formless spirit which has jawbones along with other bones. An Ongee believes that the body taken away by the spirits also becomes the spouse for the bad spirits and results in creation of children within the community of bad spirits. Just like the hunting of animals by the Ongees is a means to sustain themselves and continue living, they regard that the spirits hunting them are also a means for them to ensure their continuity.

Good spirits however do not multiply like the bad spirits. In part they are formed due to the Ongees' processing the dead human body and retaining the bones, particularly the lower jawbones to make the *gobolagnane*. However, the good spirits are responsible for the multiplication of humans, animals, and plants. Since the good spirits do not have lower jawbones as a consequence they have to enter animals and plants substance to satisfy their hunger. This indirectly causes the multiplication or 'swelling up', Ongee metaphor for regeneration and reproduction of animals, plants, and also humans. Humans like the bad spirits have lower jawbones, they too hunt and gather like all the spirits but humans can only cause death (and if overdone results in a subtraction) not multiplication or addition. Animals, like humans, hunt, eat and gather plants but do not add anything to the total system of elements within the dynamic hierarchical cosmological structure.

This hierarchy of spirits, Ongees, animals and plants is not only based on the life-taking activity of hunting, the prime form of displacement, but also on the principle of things being in a particular place. Value is maintained by being in a place where no Ongee is hunted and gathered but animals and plants are hunted and gathered by humans and spirits. This is only possible through restraining and confining the dispersal of smell, resulting in a minimal amount of displacement so that life continues as a balance between who hunts and gathers and who gets hunted and gathered.

Each season good and bad spirits move in and out of the Ongee's island. The danger of being displaced by spirits is always present and consequently is the prime concern of all and for all the Ongees. Though every counter-measure is taken *enegetebe* (death) can happen. To avoid *enegetebe* the Ongees use the good spirits for protection and minimize the possible creation of bad spirits by properly processing dead bodies and retaining the lower jawbones of the dead.

Keeping the lower jawbones of the dead not only protects the living Ongee, but also indirectly causes the multiplication and addition of children to Ongee society. Good spirits without lower jawbones must enter the food they wish to eat in order to satisfy their hunger. Because of this honeycombs and *cicada grubies* are the preferred food items of the good spirits since these foods are soft and juicy and easy to eat. In between two seasons, while the wind directions are changing and spirits for alternate days (duration from month of February to June) the Ongees leave out honeycombs and *cicada grubies* on a wooden scaffold in the coast and forest areas for the spirits to eat during the night. Next day in the morning the leftover food is then ceremoniously eaten by the Ongees, particularly the women. When women eat this spirit food (*tanja*, honeycombs and *tombowage, cicada grubies*) they are believed to become pregnant. The ancestral spirit trapped inside the food and consumed by a women is in due course transformed from spirit to fetus. The Ongees believe that women become pregnant and deliver children as a result of *talabuka*, created conjunction and *enegetebe*. Childbirth, an addition to the community of living Ongees, occurs by displacing the good spirits from the spirit world and into the human world. This displacement is simultaneously a replacement (*utokwobay*) of one dead Ongee (existing as good spirit) with one living Ongee child. Just as bad spirits displace Ongees so too do Ongees displace good spirits. The idea that one death in a place is birth in another place sets up a symmetrical self-reciprocating relationship. Every displacement leads to a replacement whereby the elements in the different places, that is, spirits in the sky and sea and the Ongees on the island, remain alive.

Bones which mark displacement also cause replacement. When the bones of the dead are taken by the Ongees, the jawless ancestral spirit must depend on the Ongees for food. This starts the transformational process by which the boneless body becomes a child's body.[4] The bones of the dead here complete the replacement of what was displaced. Therefore the Ongees say :

> For every living Ongee on the island there is one spirit who has died. For every living spirit in the sky and sea there is one Ongee who has been taken away from us. To keep it this way we do not give food and tools among ourselves but give and take only with spirits. We take bones of the spirits and give food so that we can have children. For children to come with bones and stay with us we take the bones of the dead person.

The bones of dead animals (those hunted and killed by the Ongees) operate in the same manner as human bones, since bones of all living things are the most condensed form of smell. Consequently, the skulls and lower jawbones of pigs, turtles and dugongs are carefully preserved by the Ongees and kept in their homes. At the end of each hunt and after cooking, the skulls of the hunted animals are carefully preserved with cane strips tied around them to form a containing basket like casket. The animal skulls are stored above the cooking areas of the camp or individual home's cooking area, and are believed to release the smell of hunted animals. The ongoing fire at the cooking place is regarded to provide heat for the bones to exude smell. The canework done on the skulls is a means to slow down the dispersal of smell from the animal bones. The Ongees say that the smell of the dead animal's skull is dispersed from the place of cooking and causes living animals in the forest and sea to be :

> Attracted to the place from where the smell is originating, the smell from the skulls of the hunted animals makes the animals to be hunted to remain in the place where the previous animals were hunted. It makes the living animals know that the animal which cannot be seen is still somewhere in the *injube* because of the smell from our fireplace also makes it possible for the hunter to go and hunt again in the place from where the previous meat was brought back. If the skulls of the hunted animals are not kept then the living animals realize the death of animal because the smell is not found . . . and they would leave the places from where we had hunted them previously.

If for any reason the bones cannot be kept near the cooking place where the heat of fire induces further release of smell to be carried by smoke and winds to animals which are still alive the bones are covered in red clay paint known as *alame*. The dispersal of smell of the dead animals is aided by painting the skulls with red clay paint, mixed with fat of the animals hunted. *Alame* is regarded to be conducive to release of smell because of its heating quality. This makes it possible for the Ongees to carry the bones of the hunted animals in course of translocating as well as when they go out hunting they carry some along to ensure success of having an *enegetebe* with the animal.

In the Ongee economy the bones of the dead are 'socially valuable' since they aid in transforming spirits into living beings and ensure that hunted animals are hunted again. The bones represent a relationship of life, food and fertility. Bones detached from the body, an outcome of death, are circulated for their smell value. It is the circulation of smell from the circulated bones that within the Ongee economy and politics involving the spirits, humans and animals the value of food, life and fertility for all within the cosmology of the Ongees is expressed for each other. The value is not only created within the original hierarchical relationship between the spirits, humans and animals through the bones and smell but the bones and smell also set up the possible circulation of the elements of the hierarchical system through manipulation of smell and retention of bones, the very source of smell. In this Ongee economy nothing is ever really lost or gained, there is no transaction because the smell as embodied and objectified in bones is kept as the 'principal savings'. In keeping the bones as 'principal savings' the generated 'interest' is the smell through which the relationship between all forms of hunter and hunted are maintained in a constantly self-reciprocating relationship. Thus by taking away the body but keeping the bones makes it possible to get another body. In every giving of body may it be hunter's to the spirits or the animal's to the Ongee the bones make it possible to get another body.

Placement, Displacement and Replacement

The hierarchical relation among spirits, Ongees, animals and plants is only temporally subject to displacement. However, each displacement has its self-reciprocated replacement, so that everything has a place and there is a place for everything. Because of this the hierarchical relations within the Ongee cosmology are never subverted in the politics of the hunter and the hunted. Because of the smell economy, embodied in the 'circulating currency' of bones only the particular elements of hierarchy (which are also made up of smells and bones) circulate through a relative change of their position in places within the Ongee space. The world of Ongee and the political economy of smell within it where both hunter and hunted have a self-reciprocating relationship can be best illustrated by children playing on a see-saw. As long as two children are positioned on the two ends of the see-saw, the see-saw continues to move. If one child falls off, that is, displaced, then another child, a replacement, is required for the see-saw's motion to continue.

In 1790, the British had succeeded in setting up a small fort at Port Blair (Middle Andamans), but they faced the hostility of the Andaman Islanders who would periodically emerge from the thick tropical forests and attack with bows and arrows. Till 1858 this hostility continued (Portman, 1899; Mouat, 1863) and it was decided that the very hostility of the Andaman islanders could be used for keeping the convicts within the penal settlement which was set up in the Andaman Islands. In this duration (1790-1858) and even in later years particularly in the region of South and Little Andamans the British colonizers tried to subdue the Andamanese hostility by loading the Andamanese with gifts such as glass beads, tobacco, grains, glass, small scraps of iron and cutting blades. The gift of metal from the colonists did not pacify the Andamanese. Metal was made into arrowpoints and returned to the colonists and, in turn, colonists would display their fire power (Colebrook, 1795; Portman, 1899; Majumdar,

1975; Mathur, 1968; 1985). The various confrontations were bloody and did not aid in the erasing of native's memory of earlier visitors such as the Malayans, Burmese and Chinese who visited the island for not only bird's nest and ambergris but also the Andamanese themselves for the slave market in courts of Siam and Achen (Portman, 1899; Tarling, 1960). Despite attempts to engage in interaction with the Andamanese the British met with frustrating failure. It was expected that the Andamanese would return the gift as friendship and let the colonial rule prevail. But British gift-giving failed to secure the desired results (Portman, 1899: 188-89). In fact the Ongees of Little Andamans resisted the British forces till 1867 (Portman, 1899: 716, 768, 771, 778, 795, 808). The Sentinelese (Northwest of Little Andaman island)[5] till this day have not let the outsiders land on the island without bloodshed (Singh, 1978; Planning Commission of India, 1976).

The British also tried to introduce agriculture to the Andamanese in 1865 (Portman, 1899: 497), not only as a means of increasing island's food resources but more for turning the hunters and gatherers into settled agriculturists so that the traditional translocation pattern would cut down making the colonial administration easier. The British who regarded the islanders to be 'savage' assumed that agriculture would domesticate and civilize the natives (Homfry and Ford, *Annual report of Andamans settlement*, 1868). The British experiment in agriculture was also a failure.

Today the islands are subject to the Indian Government. The Indian Government has been no more successful than the British in dealing with the Andamanese. The islanders still have neither given up their resentment towards outsiders nor have they taken up agriculture. In the 1950s, the Italian anthropologist, L. Cipriani, gave seeds to the Ongees and tried to explain to them the process of multiplying plants, and fruits (Cipriani, 1966). He, too, failed to make them understand and concluded that the Ongees have no sensibility or sympathy for cultivation and agriculture.[6] In 1983-84 during my stay with the Ongees of Little Andamans, I found out why the British and their gift-giving and the introduction of agriculture both had failed. The reasons are rooted in the Ongee notions of displacement and replacement. The outsider, his gifts and his agriculture do not have a 'place' within the Ongee worldview. These notions may best be understood in the context of digging for tubers and in the fate of outsiders and escaped convicts in the past.

Men with young boys and women with young girls go to collect *gegi*, tubers (also the term for corpse) with a digging stick. In the dense forest, upon spotting the right foilage people start digging around the main stem of the *gegi*. Carefully, gently and in silence all the smaller tubers surrounding the main large tuber are removed. The dug-up soil is again put back on the spot. When I asked why not take the big central tuber, I was told :

British in bloody encounters. They would then cut up the bodies and burn them till the bones turned into ashes. The intensity of this act and sight often lead to misleading earlier reports of Andaman islanders being cannibals (Portman, 1899; Singh, 1978; Mouat, 1863). Nothing from the outsider's body was retained. The complete destruction was necessary to guarantee that the outsider could not enter the Ongee hierarchical and cosmological system. The complete destruction of the outsider's body and his bones, like the outsider's notion of agriculture, has no place in the Ongee world in which there is a place for everything and for everything there is a place. There is no place for the Ongees who would multiply plants through agriculture. There is no place for the bones of the outsiders since the spirits originating from it are outside the scheme of Andamanese places and hierarchy of spirits, humans and animals. It is not just that the Ongees and other Andaman islanders had no place, but that to make a place would make it a permanent part of the system, which would throw everything out of a balance maintained by self-reciprocating relationship. It would then be a place and cosmology based on a model of a see-saw where on the one side there would be more children leading to complete absence of movement of the see-saw itself.

NOTES

1. Fieldwork among the Ongees of Little Andamans was conducted during 1983-1984 and was supported by research fellowship from the American Institute for Indian Studies and grants from the Committee on Southern Asian Studies at University of Chicago. The study was also made possible due to kindness of the Government of India and Andaman and Nicobar administration.

   I am also grateful to all the panel members and participants of the 85th A.A.A. meetings held in December 1986 where the earlier version of this paper was first presented in the session 'Beyond Exchange'.

2. When an Ongee dies accidentally and the living relatives are unable to locate the dead body, the consequent inability to conduct proper burial of the corpse leads to formation of a bad spirit. Since the ceremonial recovery of the bones is not carried out the dead person transformed into spirit retains the lower jawbone.
3. Radcliffe-Brown in his account of the Andaman Islanders (1964) regards things like fire as protective power and socially valuable. It is through things like fire that the individual, according to Radcliffe-Brown, feels his dependence upon society. Social valuables are believed to have 'protective power'. Radcliffe-Brown adds further, 'by social value of anything I mean the way in which that thing affects or is capable of affecting the social life. Value may be either positive or negative, positive value being possessed by anything that contributes to the well-being of the society . . . negative value . . . anything that can adversely affect that well-being' (Radcliffe-Brown 1964:264). Given this outline, in Radcliffe-Brown's ethnographic account and analysis fire is not the only thing having protective power; ornaments of bones (*Ibid.*:257) and clay paints (*Ibid.*:255) also have magical and protective power.
4. Within the Ongee worldview child and spirit are regarded to share common characteristics. For the Ongees the child is transformed spirit since both the child and spirit are without teeth and depend on liquids (in case of child, mother's breast). Because of this common identity between the child and the spirit Ongees never refer to a dead person by name and wait for the child to have the first set of teeth when a name is given to him.
5. Sentinel Islands, northwest of Little Andamans, in olden days used to be visited by the Ongees. According to many Ongees their fathers as young boys had accompanied their fathers to visit Sentinels in order to bring metal for making arrow points.
6. The only exception is the occasional caretaking Ongees extend to the coconut plantation started by Cipriani in mid-1950s and now being managed by the Andaman Administration, specially through the organization of the Andaman Adim Janjati Vikas Samiti. However, it is important to note that the only work the Ongees prefer to be involved in is collection of fallen coconuts and clearing of the ground around the trees.

REFERENCES

Brown, P. 1972. *The Chimbu: A Study of Change in the New Guinea Highlands*, Cambridge Mass.: Schenkman Publications.

Brown, P. 1974. Mediators in social change, new roles for big men, *Ocenia* 9(3):224-230.

Cipriani, L. 1966. *The Andaman Islanders*. New York: Weidenfeld and Nicholson.

Colebrooke, R. 1795. On the Andaman Islands, *Asiatik Researches* IV:385-94.

Dumont, L.1970. *Homo Hierarchicus*, Chicago: University of Chicago Press.

Dumont, L.1980. On value (Radcliffe-Brown Lecture), *Proceedings of British Academy* 66:207-41.

Ernest, T. 1985. Radcliffe-Brown, individualism and transactionalism, *Social Analysis* 17 (Aug):135-37.

Kapferer, B.1976. "Introduction", B. Kapferer (ed): *Transaction and meaning*, Philadelphia: I.S.H.I.

Levi-Strauss, C. 1963. *Structural Anthropology*, New York: Basic Books.

Levi-Strauss, C. 1969. *The elementary structures of kinship*, Boston: Becon Press.

Man, E.H. 1882. *On the aboriginal inhabitants of the Andaman Islands*, London: Royal Anthropological Institute Publications.

Mathur, L.P. 1968. *History of Andamans and Nicobars*, Delhi: Sterling Publications.

Mathur, L.P. 1985. *Kala pani: history of the Andaman Islands*, Delhi: Sterling Publications.

Majumdar, R.C. 1975. *Penal settlement in Andamans*, Delhi: Department of Education & Culture.

Malinowski, B.1922. *Argonauts of the western Pacific*, London: RKP.

Mauss, M.1954. *The gift*, London: Cohen and West.

Meillassoux, C. 1972. From reproduction to production, *Economy and Society*, 1, (1):93-105.

Mouat, F.J. 1863. *Adventures and researches among the Andaman Islanders*, London.

Munn, N. 1986. *The fame of Gawa*, Cambridge: Cambridge University Press.

Pandya, V. 1987. *Above the forest: a study of Andamanese ethnoanemology, cosmology and the power of ritual*. (Unpublished dissertation) Deptt. of Anthropology, University of Chicago.

Planning Commission of India, 1976. *Yojna* (Special volume on Andamans and Nicobars) 20(13), New Delhi: Govt. of India Publications.

Portman, M.V. 1899. *A history of our relations with Andamanese*, Calcutta: Government Printing Press.

Radcliffe-Brown, A.R. 1964 (1922). *The Andaman Islanders*, Illinois: Free Press.

Singh, I. 1978. *The Andaman story*, Delhi: Vikas Publications.

Stanner, W. 1985. Radcliffe-Brown's ideas on social value, *Social Analysis* 17 (Aug):113-25.

Strathern, A.J. 1971. *The rope of Moka*, Cambridge: Cambridge University Press.

Tarling, N. 1960. Pirates and convicts: British interests in the Andaman and Nicobar Islands in the mid-19th century, *Journal of Indian History*, V.38:505-28.

3

THE TRIBAL WORLDVIEW : CHANGING PERSPECTIVE

Ashim Kumar Adhikary

Introduction

Study of worldview and philosophic endeavours among the preliterate people is yet to gain adequate currency in anthropology, though its importance has been felt even by the early evolutionary thinkers. Evolutionary scholars like Tylor and Frazer were also found to be concerned, among other things, with the study of the mode of thought of the preliterate people and their nature of relations to the natural and supernatural phenomena. The foundations for a worldview study were, however, laid by Emile Durkheim and his nephew Marcel Mauss in 1903, when they established *Annee Sociologigue* school in France. The scholars of this school devoted their attention to the study of ideas of peoples about themselves and the world around them, as well as the study of their *representative collectives*. In the concluding chapter of their book *Primitive-classification*, Durkheim and Mauss (1963:81) observe that the object of primitive classifications 'is not to facilitate action, but to advance understanding, to make intelligible the relations which exist between things . . . such classifications are thus intended, above all, to connect ideas, to unify knowledge; as such they may be said . . . to constitute a first philosophy of nature". Unlike the English scholars Tylor and Frazer who dealt with isolated customs of preliterate peoples, these French scholars were interested in their whole complexes of ideas, beliefs and meanings. Though they differed in conceptual and analytical framework, all these early scholars were interested primarily in the archaic, or primitive, nature of human thinking. The name of Luden Levi-Bruhl may also be mentioned in this connection. He described the thought of 'primitive' man as 'prelogical' and 'mystical', 'symbolic' and 'allusive'.

In a recent review Michael Kearney (1975), however, identifies four distinct periods in the developmental history of worldview study and theory in anthropology. They are: (i) the *formative* period, (ii) *transitional* period, (iii) *propositional* period, and (iv) the *systematic* period. The *formative* period is exemplified by the Boasian configurationalists who delineate a synthetic pattern from and among the diverse phenomenon of a people's culture. Benedict's *Patterns of culture* (1949) is cited as one of the best examples during this period. The *transitional* period is typified by the ethnographers' explicit and specific concern with 'worldview' *per se* studies. The writings of Sol Tax (1941), Hallowell (1955) and Redfield (1952, 1953, 1955, 1956) fall in this period. The *propositional* period, which is marked by an analytic treatment of worldview, is best exemplified by the writings of Foster (1965), Hoebel (1960), Kearney (1972) and Kluckhohn and Strodtbeck (1961). During the *systematic* period the scholars show concern not only with the exploration of the nature of relationships among the various elements of a particular worldview but also with the nature of relationships of the worldviews with their socio-cultural and geographical environments. Essays of such an integrated holistic approach are apparent in Mary Douglas' (1973) *Natural symbols* and Michael Kearny's (1975) concept of 'logico-structural integration'.

It is, indeed, Daryll Forde (1954) in Britain and Robert Redfield (1952) in America, who initiate among the ethnographers a tradition for the explicit study of worldview of 'non-civilized' peoples. In his *African worlds* (1954), Forde compiles nine articles on the worldview of the people of Africa. His interest is to understand man in relation to his place in nature and society. Redfield is perhaps the first anthropologist who discusses, in great detail, the concept of worldview and tries to explicate the nature of 'primitive' worldview. He also inspired a number of scholars (E.M. Mendelson, 1956; Charles M. Leslie, 1960; Calixta Guiteras-Holmes, 1961) to undertake systematic and explicit study of worldview of particular cultures and individuals. Redfield conceptually differentiates 'worldview' from 'culture', 'ethos', 'mode of thought' and 'national character', and defines it as 'the picture the members of a society have of the properties and characters upon their stage of action'. He says that 'worldview attends especially to the way a man, in a particular society, sees himself in relation to all else. It is the properties of existence as distinguished from and related to the self' (Redfield, 1962: 270). Based on the available ethnographic literature on preliterate peoples and ancient civilizations. Redfield further postulates certain universal elements of worldview, and the nature of their integration in the 'primary worldview'. Broadly these elements are man, nature and God. He observes that 'the separation of God from nature and of these two together from man is . . . made in some degree and in some sense in every worldview' but in the 'primitive worldview' the man-nature-supernature relationship tends to be 'unitary' and 'morally significant', (*Ibid.*:271). In his subsequent works Redfield (1953, 1955, 1956), however, becomes interested in the dynamics of worldview and the nature of its transformation in the context of modernization. In an endeavour to study the impact of 'technological and urban revolution on primary worldview' he (1953) observes that the man-nature-supernature relationship which is unitary in 'primary worldview' gets dissociated with the change of economy.

Tribal Worldview Studies in India

With this purposive introduction on the conceptualization and nature of worldview and philosophic endeavours among the preliterate people we may now move on to the study of the tribal worldview in India. As per the 1971 Census there are as many as 427 distinct tribal communities constituting about seven per cent of India's total population. In terms of language, numerical strength and levels of economy these tribal groups exhibit a wide range of diversities among themselves, though in contrast to the non-tribal people they appear to be perpetuating a distinct outlook on life. Though mostly concentrated in the hilly and forested regions of India, they can no longer be found in their ideal situation of 'habitat, economy and society'. Many of them are now in perpetual contact with their neighbouring non-tribal communities, and are variously exposed to the forces of modernisation. There are some communities who maintain regular economic symbiosis with the dominant Hindu caste-peasant groups but move about at the periphery of the village society. There are also groups who are found to consciously assert their tribal identity through various kinds of revivalistic movements in the context of their confrontation with the socio-political forces of the larger society.

The tribal groups in India are, no longer, stationary, nor is their worldview static. With the passage of time they have come across various kinds of faiths, categories of people and their customs and institutions. In fact, there have been tremendous changes in the life-situations of the people, and with these, the elements of their worldview are also undergoing changes. The tribal people are, however, found to constantly adjust with the changing situations, trying to weave their new experiences with the old ones in a meaningful way, thereby perpetuating a 'characteristic outlook' on life. Their worldview is, indeed, 'constantly in process: a fluctuating assemblage of more or less connected ideas that change as to focus, affective coloring perhaps the content and choice of connection and emphasis' (Redfield, 1962b : 281). In the present paper my purpose is, therefore, to grasp the dynamics of the tribal worldview in India. I intend to understand their perceptions of the changing universe and the way they confront it in the context of their present-day life-situation. My approach will be not merely to describe the normal state of their ideas and beliefs relating to the nature, other men and the super-natural phenomena but to bring into relief the 'focus' of their 'total view' as reflected from their thought and action. For this purpose I will depend primarily on my empirical study of the worldview of a specific tribal group, the Birhor, as well as on my observations on a few other Mundari groups of tribes in central-eastern India. Relevant studies and observations on the worldview of Indian tribes will also be used.

There are only a few explicit studies on the worldview of specific tribal groups in India, though there are some observations on the nature of their religious philosophy. Scattered materials on the aspects of tribal worldview are, however, not rare, but they are embedded mostly into the general ethnographic descriptions on the people. Based on the information available in the ethnographic reports, Mehra (1977) makes an attempt to explicate the aspects of tribal worldview in India. He describes the worldview of the tribal groups in terms of 'origin and creation', 'man-supernature' relation, 'man-nature' relationship and 'man-man' relationship. The worldview of the tribal people is depicted here in terms of their place 'in nature and society'; it gives us more or less 'a stable and abstract picture' of their universe. Subsequently, little attention is given to the nature of the people's perceptions of, and relations with, their changing universe. The pioneer among the Indian anthropologists in this order of analysis of worldview and philosophic endeavours of the tribal people is Prof. Surajit Chandra Sinha. Unlike his predecessors whose primary interest was to describe the 'fossilized persistence of an idealized archaic worldview', Sinha is deeply concerned to understand the changing perspective of tribal worldview in the actual contexts of their life-situations. Precisely speaking, he is found to look at tribal life as 'a quality of socio-cultural integration' as well as a 'state of mind'.

Mention may be made here of Nirmal Kumar Bose who in the broad context of the 'tribal life in India', points out that there is, in every human group, 'a constellation of ideas and emotions' forming the core of its culture, and that a community builds up its worldview by weaving immediate experiences with those of the past; to these are added the hopes and fears for the future. The worldview of a people is, therefore, not a static phenomenon. It changes with the changes in the qualities of its elements, or with the changes in the perceptions of the people (Bose, 1971). Bose further makes a conceptual distinction between the worldview based on sense perception and logical construction of immediate experience and the worldview based on extra-sensory perception. He thinks it important to consider both these pragmatic and transcendental aspects for a proper understanding of the dynamics of people's worldview. Recently, Mahapatra (1983) brings out certain methodological issues for the study of worldview among the 'non-civilized' peoples. He says, "If the concept of worldview is to be made viable, there should be some conscious effort to bring about some coherence, convergence and integration of thought and action: conceptualization, speculation and thought on the one hand, concerns and behaviour in the work-a-day life on the other. The thinker and man of the world should find their place in the anthropologists' integral view of his people's worldview" (*Ibid*).

Though Sinha does not make any conceptual discourse on worldview, in many of his studies and observations on the tribal culture of India he makes use of the concept explicitly and analytically. In an endeavour to understand the nature of tribal cultures *vis-a-vis* the little tradition of Indian civilization, Sinha (1958) makes a critical assessment of the aspects of worldview of some of the tribal groups in Peninsular India. He studies the tribal groups in the context of their habitat, economy and social structure, and then analyses their worldview in terms of their conceptualization of, and relations with, nature, other men and the supernatural phenomena.

He observes that though the 'tribal cultures of Peninsular India do share certain characteristics common to primitive cultures all over the world', there are 'certain specific items' among them that are not 'universally shared by the primitive tribes in other parts of the world'. Of these specific items he mentions 'the existence of a hierarchic pantheon with the Sun God at the top; and belief in reincarnation and transmigration of the soul' (*Ibid*). He, however conceptualizes the tribal worldview as characterized by a 'non-puritanical', 'this worldly', 'hedonistic' attitude towards life, and living for today having no thought for tomorrow. He also brings out the divergences and similarities between the worldview of the tribal people and that of the Hindu peasantry in Peninsular India and points out that though there are some transitional elements in the economy and social structure of the tribal cultures, there are no elements of transition from 'ethically neutral super-naturalism' to 'ethical super-naturalism'. His interest in the nature and quality of tribal worldview in the context of their confrontation with the dominant Hindu worldview is also evident in many of his writings (Sinha, 1953, 1957, 1965).

As regards the nature of religious worldview of the tribal groups in the context of their contacts with Hinduism and other religious faiths in India, Bose (1971) makes an important observation. With specific reference to Hinduism and Buddhism, he points out that the initial encounter of the tribal groups with these religious faiths had been primarily at the sociological level. He notes that though there are Christians, Muslims, Buddhists and even Hindus among the tribal people of India, animism is the dominant faith among them. Inspite of tremendous changes in their religious beliefs and practices there is found, among them, a tendency towards retaining the focus of their worldview. He notices that in the recent years, the tribal groups, irrespective of their religious affiliations, seek their 'tribal identity', therein asserting those aspects of their worldview that seem relevant to them in the context of the present-day lifesituations.

The Birhor Worldview

I made an explicit study on the worldview of the Birhor in the context of their environmental ecology and techno-economic activities (Adhikary, 1984). The Birhor of Sundargarh district in Orissa, among whom I worked during 1971 and 1977, are a small group of people belonging to the Mundari family of tribes. Though broadly branded as hunters and gatherers, they can no longer subsist exclusively on the resources of the jungle ecology. Having specialized in hunting, gathering and jungle-based crafts they perpetuate regular economic interaction with the caste-peasants and market economy of the larger society. The Birhor collect *bauhinja* creepers from jungle, prepare different kinds of ropes and rope-made products, and sell, or barter, them in the neighbouring villages and markets for their day-to-day food and clothing. They appear to have specialized themselves in the profession of rope-making. They are also found to adopt various other occupational strategies like the selling of live monkeys, working as magico-religious experts and selling medicinal herbs and tubers to the neighbouring villagers. The people are, in fact, tagged to the broad framework of agrarian economic structure of the local rural Hindu peasantry, and cannot even optimally operate the clan-lineage-based segmentary social system like other Mundari groups of tribes. The Birhor, however, organize their community by means of their social and cultural norms and perpetuate a distinct socio-cultural identity.

The above-mentioned lifesituations of the Birhor led me to probe into the minds of the people and, subsequently, to understand the meaningful world they live in. I was intrigued not merely to study the ideas and beliefs of the people as regards their natural and super-natural universe but also to grasp their 'total view' of life in the existential context of their lifesituations. Special attention was given to study the meanings of their behaviour from the people themselves.

A probe into the minds of the people reveals that the Birhor distinguish two distinct worlds – one, *disum*, their own territory in the jungle, and the other, *muluk*, the territory dominated by caste-peasants and market economy of the larger society. They also distinguish themselves as *hor* from others as *diku*, thereby denoting the 'men', or the Birhor themselves, and the alien, or the foreigners, respectively. Though they broadly include within the category *diku* all the people other than themselves, they do not look upon all of them in the same manner. In terms of their day-to-day interaction the sharp distinction of 'we' and 'they' becomes lessened. The ethnic groups like the Mundari, Bhuiya, and even the Kurmi Mahato of the locality are often called *horhon,* i.e. they are neither *hor* nor *diku* but more akin to the *hor*. They have also developed adaptive strategies of social interaction in the context of meaning in two sets of environment: a morally ordered *gemeinschaft* in *disum* and a rationalist utilitarian *gesellschaft* in *muluk.*

There is a significant continuity between the human world of the Birhor and the natural and supernatural universe they conceive of. They consider jungles their homes and describe themselves as Birhor i.e. the men of jungle (*Bir*-jungle, and *hor*-man). The different social segments of the Birhor still claim to have their traditional homes on some forest-clad hills or mountains. Manifestation of jungles is found in their settlement pattern and in many other contexts. Every phenomenon of jungle is animated and presided over by some supernatural deity or *bonga*. Though the Birhor seem to have some empirical knowledge about the utility of many plants and animals in jungles and are aware of the regular courses of many natural phenomena, they do not think that they can control and regulate them without any intervention from the supernatural deities concerned. They think that the ultimate power lies with the supernatural deities with whom they maintain a ritual relationship.

The Birhor accord their ancestral spirits or *hapram* a place next to the supernatural deities or *bongas*. The ancestral spirits live in close association with the *bonga*, and are considered to have power to control many natural phenomena. The *hapram* work as intermediaries between the supernatural forces and the living Birhor and often guard their descendants against misfortunes. They get children and prosperity through their *hapram* and *bongas*. The relationships of the Birhor with their ancestral spirits and supernatural deities are basically moral in nature.

In the course of their interaction with the people of the larger society the Birhor have come to know of a number of occupational alternatives like agriculture, basket-making, pottery, blacksmithy, leather work, weaving and three to four types of labourwork. They also know of a number of markets, villages and human categories. A close probe into the minds of the people, however, reveals that the Birhor have little knowledge about the technologies of these occupations and suffer from a social constraint of losing their usual freedom in the midst of an alien social milieu. About agriculture they can talk of different seasonal activities like when the seeds are sown and the crops are raised. They do not have any idea about the important agricultural operations like transplantation, harvesting, threshing and winnowing. They point out that the pursuit of these occupations requires sedentary village life along with other communities. They also feel that almost all these occupations have a social stigma, and most of the people pursuing them are placed low in the local social hierarchy.

In direct confrontation with the socio-cultural environment of the larger society the Birhor have, however, come to learn that they too are looked down upon by the people there and have little grip over their culturally defined meaning of life in the village society. They, therefore, turn back towards their jungle terrain where they feel free and find a meaningful world of their own. Under the changing ecological and economic situations they thus often create myths around their activities and adopt occupational strategies keeping in consonance with their traditional knowledge of, and skills in, jungle ecology.

The villagers consider the Birhor as expert monkey hunters, having exceptional mystic power in supernatural activities. They think that no other people except the Birhor could have been able to lead such an humble life in close association with jungles. The Birhor are well aware of these impressions of the villagers and strategically manipulate them to their ends, reinforcing their articulation with jungle ecology.

It is evident from the preceding pages that in the changing contexts of modernization the techno-economic activities of the Birhor are extended, from their natural universe of jungle ecology, far beyond into the environmental ecology of the market-based larger society, and with these the elements of their worldview have also undergone changes. In the course of their confrontation with the larger society they have gathered much experience but these are not meaningfully integrated into their traditional way of life. Instead, these new experiences help the Birhor reinforce their special relation with the jungle ecology in the context of which the people find their life socially and culturally meaningful. It may be mentioned here that though there have been some significant changes in their nature of dependence on the forest ecology, the Birhor are still found to form a world of their own in which the jungle, the supernatural phenomena and the people themselves are morally bound together.

Other Illustrations

Unlike the Birhor of Orissa who still have an effective ecological base in forest, the Hill Kharia of Purulia district, West Bengal, another Mundari group of tribes, 'find themselves in a situation where their anchorage to the forest economic base has been rudely uprooted and they have been thrown at the doorstep of the peasant societies as landless dependent communities' (D. Sinha, 1984:85-86). The Hill Kharia of this area have experienced, over the years, a gradual decrease of resources in forests, and subsequently, there has occurred an 'erosion of technology and knowledge of ecology' among the people.

In order to cope with the depleted condition of the forest as well as the present situation of contact the Hill Kharia of Purulia have adopted various occupational strategies. They often work as casual agricultural labourers to the caste-peasants, and prepare handicrafts like broomsticks and fish-traps for sale and barter. They are also found to resort to hunting, fishing and gathering in the natural ecology. Mention may be made of their specific adaptation to, and skill in the collection of paddy grains from the rat-holes in the harvested fields of the peasants.

Coming in contact with the caste-peasants and market-economy of the larger society the Hill Kharia are found to suffer not only from a social constraint of being stigmatized as a 'criminal people' but also from a sense of 'relative deprivation'. Though they lead a sedentary village life along with various other castes and communities, they do not belong to the moral order of the village society, and seem to lack a culturally meaningful world of communication.

A careful probe into the existential and cognitive aspects of the life and culture of the Hill Kharia would, however, reveal that they spend much of their time and energy utilizing their traditional skill in, and knowledge of hunting, fishing and gathering in the natural environment with which they have intimate and moral relation. D. Sinha observes, 'although the Hill Kharia realize that the forest resources are more or less exhausted emotionally, they find the forest more easier to adjust with because the supernatural power which reigns over the domain of availability of food can be comprehended with the help of cultural idioms' (*Ibid.*: 52).

Recently, Morris (1981) has shown how the religious worldview of the Hill Pandaram, a hunting and gathering community of South India, is integrated with their jungle habitat and economy in spite of their economic and cultural articulation with the wider Hindu society. He notes the various gods and spirits as conceptualized by the Hill Pandaram and studies their nature of relationship with them. He finds that 'the spiritual agencies recognized by the Hill Pandaram fall into three broad categories: the ancestral ghosts or spirits (*chavu*), the mountain spirits (*mala devi*) and the gods of the Hindu pantheon. The spiritual agencies of this third category – and the myths and rites associated with them have little significance for the Hill Pandaram. The two principal supernaturals of the local villagers, Aiyappan and Karuppaswami, though part of their religious consciousness, have for the Hill Pandaram only a peripheral influence' (*Ibid.*: 204). Though the Hill Pandaram religious system shows some ideological changes, the people make differential treatment to the Hindu supernaturals. The

Hindu deities are looked upon 'as alien spirits who have little concern' for the welfare of the people (*Ibid.*: 214).

It becomes obvious from the preceding pages that many of the tribal groups in the mainland of India living at the level of hunting and gathering economy have now developed a symbiotic relation with the settled Hindu peasantry for their day-to-day subsistence. Subsequently the elements of their worldview have changed, and they have come across a world much wider than before. A careful probe into their worldview reveals that the new experiences of the wider world, though entered into their consciousness, lack meaning in the context of their life and culture and, as a result, do not get their emotional and affective support. The people, therefore, try to perpetuate their socio-cultural identity either by carefully preserving their knowledge of, and relations with, the jungle (as exemplified by the Birhor of Orissa and the Hill Pandaram of South India) or by perpetuating a cover of 'mysticism' around themselves (as in the case of the Hill Kharia of Purulia). It may be mentioned here that the scale of society among these tribal groups hardly exceeds the level of a band, or a small hamlet, comprising a few nuclear families, and lacks any perceptible social differentiation in terms of education, wealth and power. The experiences and meanings are, therefore, shared by all the members of the community concerned.

There are, however, tribal groups who live at a different level of economy and are much intensely enmeshed into the larger society. They pursue agriculture and lead sedentary village life in close association with different castes and communities. Many of these people are even exposed to the forces of modern education, industrial economy and power politics of our State, and, consequently, have got education, employment, and also political party affiliation. These individuals with their new perceptions of, and relations with, the larger society are, in many instances, found to consciously build up a worldview for their respective communities. Orans (1965), based on his empirical study on the Santal in an industrial setting of Jamshedpur, Bihar, observes that the educated, employed and comparatively rich Santals emphasize on works, study and rank-attainment, and discourage their traditional involvement in pleasures or *raska*. A few Santal elites appeared to have been moving towards building up a Great Tradition for their community.

While studying the transformation process of the tribal life in modern India, S.C. Sinha (1981) observes that in the emerging situation of national economic development there has arisen a number of leaders and intelligentsia among the people. They are found to recreate and 'universalize tribal traditions at such a level as to appear authentic as well as prestigious to their own people as well as to the surrounding non-tribal groups in the contemporary situations. In this creative recreation of tribal traditions the tribal intelligentsia and leaders often combine, in an ingenious manner, elements of tribal traditions with those of the Hindus and the Christians[4] (*Ibid.*: 121). Reviewing the tribal situation of Arunachal Pradesh, Sinha points out how the young intelligentsia and leaders of Arunachal Pradesh, in their process of modernization, are consciously weaving their new experiences 'with their age-old traditions' and building up an integrated worldview for the community. Sinha further observes that 'in their search for, and preservation of,. identity in their modern situation some of the tribal intelligentsia are not looking towards either Hindu or Christian model but are creatively universalizing the traditional mythology of 'Sun-Moon god' in a wide social arena' (*Ibid.*: 133).

Changing Perspective

The spectrum of worldview that has been described above is not an integrated picture of the tribal worldview, nor does it cover all the tribal groups in India. An attempt has just been made to bring into relief some aspects of their perceptions of, and relations with, the changing universe in the modern contexts. It, however, becomes evident from the above descriptions that the worldview of the tribal groups in India is not a static picture of their universe nor is it a closed system; it incorporates the changing perspectives of the world(s) which, in turn, guide their day-to-day life and culture.

With the change in the elements of the traditional universe of their jungle habitat and self-sufficient economy there has not only arisen a group of educated and articulate intelligentsia among the tribal people but also occurred an expansion in their cognitive perception of the universe. Based on their experiences the young elites often develop a new outlook on life which, in turn, is placed as a conscious model for their community. Sometimes the leaders of various groups, in direct confrontation with the socio-political forces of the larger society, are found to combine together as a united regional minority group and assert tribal identity. We are, however, yet to know to what extent the specialized experiences of the few educated tribal intelligentsia are articulated with the cumulative experiences of their community and, subsequently, reflect the focus of the people's worldview. It may be pointed out here that the aspect of worldview that the new elites build up in the modern context, besides having an urge for a meaningfully defined area of socio-cultural communication in the modern situation, has a notion of a progressive life in the future.

From our present state of knowledge on the worldview of the Birhor and a few other tribal groups in India we, however, find that the tribal people, regardless of their level of techno-economy and extent of contact with the larger society, perpetuate a 'quality of socio-cultural integration' as well as 'a state of mind' characterized by equality and *representative collectives*. The life and activities of the tribal people are primarily based on their immediate needs and desires. They are basically characterized by a 'this-worldly', 'pragmatic', 'non-puritanical', 'hedonistic' attitude towards life. They are also not loaded by ethical strivings (S.C. Sinha, 1958). 'Although some of the tribes believe in a sequence of lives and others lay great store upon acquisition of social merit which raises the person's status in this life, in none of the tribal societies did we encounter the idea that moral choices affect a person's fate in future existence' (Furer-Haimendorf, 1967:168). A careful study of the day-to-day subsistence activities as well as the concept of good life in economic sphere of the Birhor of Orissa reveals that they are much concerned with the present, and do not have any idea of a future, far away from the present, though they often believe in a golden past. Most of the Birhor desire just two square meals a day, one or two clothes to wear and a little drink. Though the Birhor are aware that the resources of their jungle ecology are not as abundant as they were in the past they do not believe in scarcity of food items in the jungles as a normal state. Even the agricultural activities of a Santal households in the villages of Birbhum, West Bengal, are found to be closely enmeshed into the social and cultural matrix of the village society. The normal security a Santal villager seeks lies in the fulfilment of his immediate needs and desires, in sharing his pleasures with kin and neighbours, and ultimately, in his conforming to the norms and customs of his society (Adhikary, 1983). Personal upliftment of status by accumulating wealth or by attaining political power linkage in the larger society is not encouraged among them. It may be mentioned here that there are some traditional officials, and oldmen among the Santals who are considered, and often referred to, as specialists having more knowledge about nature, supernatural phenomena, and the origin and creation of man and his universe. A careful probe would, however, reveal that these people are simply repositories of their traditional worldview that is integrated into their society and culture.

The Daflas and Apa Tanis of Subansari regions in Arunachal Pradesh, though differ in their level of economy and social structure, also 'subscribe to a worldview which, being basically utilitarian and prudential, is directed towards "this worldly" goal, and lacks a belief in any link between moral and eschatological concepts' (Furer-Haimendorf, 1967 : 82).

That the worldview of a tribal people is not simply a metaphysical, philosophical activity of a few articulate people and that it is directed towards 'this worldly' goal and integrated into the work-a-day life of the people can also be understood from some recent observations on the Koya (Tyler, 1976) and Kota (Mandelbaum, 1961). Tyler studies the conceptual categories of nature, supernatural forces inhabiting the earth and influencing their fate on the earth, land and soil, seasons as well as the relations of these categories with their actual practices of production, and finds that the *podu* cultivation of the Koya is not merely a set of agricultural practices, 'it implies the whole nexus of Koyas' religious belief, self-image and tribal identity' (*Ibid.*: 17). Mandelbaum, in the course of field investigation among the Kota of the Nilgiri Hills in the changing context of modernization, discovers that 'a Kota's main interest' lies 'not in his relations to the gods; not in his necessary dealings with plant and animal and matter but in his relations to other men' (*Ibid.*: 257). However, 'what seems typically to be in the forefront of a Kota's perception – that a man must struggle with man in defence of his social life. Gods are potent but not capricious : they can be dealt with effectively. Nature can be recalcitrant to man's efforts, but is not the centre of interest. The best man is one who does not allow himself to be deprived, one who responds vigorously to any threat of deprivation in social relations' (*Ibid.*: 244).

However, the whole spectrum of tribal worldview that is presented here reveals that the tribal people of India, though incorporate in their worldview the perceptions of the modern universe, seem to lack a meaningful area of social and cultural communication and, ultimately, show resilience to a world of their own in which their positions are socially and culturally defined, and morally ordered. Though most of the tribal groups in the modern contexts cannot perpetuate the economy and the level of socio-cultural integration they had in the past, they retain, or try to retain, an outlook on life as well as a quality of social life which is morally significant and based on the idiom of kinship and sentiments. Altruism and generosity are still valued, and considered as the normative practice of life. The social world of the living is continuous with the world of their dead ancestors, and their relationship with nature and god is more or less unitary and morally significant.

REFERENCES

Adhikary, A.K. 1983. Social and cultural organization of subsistence activities: a preliminary appraisal of the Santhal of West Bengal. *Human Science.*, 32 (2), pp.69-88.

Adhikary, A.K. 1984. *Society and worldview of the Birhor : a nomadic hunting and gathering community of Orissa*. Anthropological Survey of India, Calcutta.

Adhikary, A.K. 1984. *Hunters* and gatherers in India: a preliminary appraisal of their structure and transformation. *Journal of the Indian Anthropological Society*, 19, (1), pp.8-16.

Benedict, Ruth. 1949. *Patterns of culture*. George Routledge & Sons, London.

Bose, N.K. 1971. *Tribal life in India*. National Book Trust of India, New Delhi.

Douglas, Mary 1973. *Natural symbols: explorations in cosmology*. Penguin Books.

Durkheim, Emile and Marcel Maus, 1963 (1903). *Primitive classification*. Cohen and West, London.

Forde, Daryll 1954. *African worlds*. International African Institute, London.

Foster, G.M. 1965. Peasant society and the image of limited good. *American Anthropologist*, 67, pp.293-315.

Furer-Haimendorf, Christoph von. 1953. The after-life in Indian tribal belief, *Journal of the Royal Anthrop. Institute*, 83, pt.1.

Furer-Haimendorf, Christoph von 1969. *Morals and merit: a study of value and social controls in south eastern Asian societies*. Weidenfeld and Nicolson, London.

Guiteras-Holmes, Calixta 1961. *Perils of the soul: the worldview of a Tzotzil Indian*. Free Press, New York.

Kearney, M. 1975. Worldview theory and study. Bernard J. Seigal et al. (Eds.) *Annual Review of Anthropology*, 4, pp.247-72.

Kluckhohn, F. and F.L. Strodtbeck 1961. *Variations in value orientations*. Evanston, Ill., Row, Peterson and Co.

Leslie, Charles, M.1960. *Now we are civilized: a study of the worldview of the Zapotec Indians of Mitla, Oaxaca*. Detroit, Mich.: Wayne Univ. Press.

Levy-Bruhl, L. 1926. *How natives think* (Eng.trans), London.

Mahapatra, L.K. 1983. Worldview, meta-philosophy and Nature. Paper presented at the International Conference on *Man and Environment*, Indian Museum, Calcutta.

Mandelbaum, D.G. 1961. The world and worldview of the Kota. Mckim Marriott (Ed.), *Village India*, Bombay. Asia Publishing House, pp.228-60.

Mehra, J.D. 1977. The worldview of Indian tribes. S.C. Dube (Ed.) *Tribal heritage of India*, 1, pp.58-84. New Delhi: Vikas Publishing House Pvt. Ltd.

Mendelson, E.M. 1956. *Worldview*. Ph.D. Dissertation, Univ. of Chicago.

Mendelson, E.M. 1968. Worldview. David L. Sills (Ed.), *International Encyclopaedia of the Social Sciences*. 16, Macmillan Company.

Morris, Brian 1981. Hill gods and ecstatic cults: notes on the religion of a hunting and gathering people. *Man in India*, 61 (3), pp.203-36.

Redfield, R. 1953. *The primitive world and its transformations*. Ithaca : Cornell Univ. Press.

Redfield, R. 1955. *The little community: viewpoints for the study of a human whole*. Univ. of Chicago Press.

Redfield, R. 1956. *Peasant society and culture : an anthropological approach to civilization*, Univ. of Chicago Press.

Redfield, R. 1962 (a). The primitive worldview. Margaret Park Redfield (Ed.). *Human nature and the study of society: the papers of Robert Redfield*, 1, pp.269-280, Chicago: The Univ. of Chicago Press.

Redfield, R. 1962 (b). Letter to Michael Mendelson. Margaret Park Redfield (Ed.) *Human nature and the study of society: the papers of Robert Redfield*, , pp.280-81. Chicago: the Univ. of Chicago Press.

Roy, S.C. 1914. Magic and witchcraft on the Chota Nagpur Plateau : a study in the philosophy of primitive life. *Journal of the Royal Anthropological Institute*, 44, pp.324-50.

Sinha D. 1984. *The Hill Kharia of Purulia : impact of poverty on a hunting and gathering tribe*. Anthropological Survey of India, Calcutta.

Sinha, S.C. 1953. Some aspects of change in Bhumij religion in south Manbhum, Birhor. *Man in India*, 33, (2), pp.148-64.

Sinha, S.C. 1957. The media and nature of Hindu-Bhumij interaction. *Journal of Asiatic Society of Bengal Letters and Science*. 23, (1), pp.23-37.

Sinha, S.C. 1958. Tribal cultures of Peninsular India as a dimension of little tradition in the study of Indian civilization: a preliminary statement. *Journal of American Folklore*. 71, (281), pp.504-18.

Sinha, S.C. 1965. Tribe-caste and tribe-peasant continua in central India. *Man in India*, 45, (1), pp.57-83.

Sinha, S.C. 1981. Tribes and Indian civilization : transformation processes in modern India, *Man in India*, 61, (2), pp.105-42.

Tax, Sol 1941. Worldview and social relations in Guatemala. *American Anthropologist*, New Series, 43, pp.27-42.

Tyler, Stephen 1974. Fields are for planning: Swidden agriculture among the Koyas of South India. *Journal of the Indian Anthropological Society*, 9, (1), pp.17-38.

4

UNDERSTANDING TRIBAL LORE BY MEANS OF INTENTION THEORY OF MEANING

S. C. Daniel

Introduction

Tribal lore embodies the ancient observations and customs, the notions, beliefs, traditions, value systems and moral laws of a community, or a tribe. Obviously, then, this paper does not endeavour to understand an individual's beliefs, values, etc., but it concerns about only such beliefs, value system, moral law, etc., as are consciously held by a community, or a tribe, taken as a whole.

All the tribal lores convey certain critical values to the listener or the reader. They are like the biblical parables which exhort the listener, or the reader, to follow the moral prescriptions, or codes, that are inherent in them. In this paper, an attempt will be made to outline a philosophical analysis of tribal lores which, I think, would go a long way in interpreting and understanding tribal lores in their proper perspectives – this is not to claim that the philosophical analysis is the one and only way of understanding tribal lores, but to claim that this sort of analysis will help one to understand tribal lores in their entirety.

Meanings of Concepts

My specific philosophical task would be to determine the meanings of concepts that lie hidden in the tribal lores. Philosophers in the West have relied on various theories of meaning such as verification theory, verification principle, denotation theory, intention theory, and so on in their attempt to determine the meanings of social concepts. However, it is the intention theory of meaning that is more efficacious than the others to understand the real significance of tribal lore.

The intention theory of meaning is one of the ideational theories which generally tries to develop the relation between an account of what an expression means, and an account of what a person means by an expression. This view is open to certain difficulties which, I think, are fatal. However, there is another version of the same theory which avoids the difficulties inherent in the version mentioned above which is, namely, this: there is a relation between an account of what an expression means, and an account of what a person means by uttering an expression.

H.P. Grice is a proponent of intention theory of meaning in modern times. He advocates his theory in the articles, 'Meaning' (Grice, 1973) and 'Utterer's meaning and intention' (Grice, 1969). In these two articles, he gives a fresh and highly promising suggestion as to how 'meaning, might be a special case of intending. It is useful to know his views before an endeavour is undertaken to understand tribal lores in terms of intentions.

Grice takes the words 'mean' and 'meaning' in the 'symbol' sense. An example will be helpful to bring out the 'symbol' sense of the words 'mean' and 'meaning'. The Tamil word '*mazhai*' taken in the 'symbol' sense means the same as the English word 'rain', and *vice versa*: this is to say that these two words are locked in the relationship of sense, and not of reference. 'Symbol', therefore, stands for anything that has meaning in the sense explained above. Usually symbols are words. But it is not necessarily the case always, since symbols can also be pictures, gestures, etc. of non-linguistic type of utterances.

Grice makes a distinction between natural meaning and non-natural meaning of utterances. Non-natural meaning is termed as meaning NN so as to distinguish it from natural meaning of utterances. Meaning NN is an abbreviation of non-natural meaning where NN signifies non-natural. Meaning NN must be explicated in terms of intention whereas natural meaning is not related to intention. Natural meaning of utterances is fixed according to rules of language. In the case of natural meaning, '*X* means that *p*', and '*x* meant that *p*', entail '*p*' whereas in the case of meaning NN, there is no such entailment. (Here, *x* stands for any utterance, and *p* stands for any proposition.) In the case of entailment, the meaning of an utterance must remain the same; when there is no entailment, the meaning of an utterance varies and deviates from the standard meaning.

What is necessary for a person to mean something by an utterance is this: he must intend to induce a belief in an audience by an utterance and he must also intend his utterance to be reorganized as so intended. Two intentions are involved here: (1) intention to induce a belief in an audience, and (2) intention to make the hearer to recognize the intention. In other words, the meaning of an utterance is roughly equivalent to the speaker's intention of inducing a belief in an audience or hearer by means of the recognition of his intention by an audience or hearer. These two intentions of the speaker, therefore, are not independent of one another, but, in fact, they are dependent upon one another.

For an audience to have meaning NN, the intended effect must be something which in some sense is within the control of the audience, or that in some sense of reason, the recognition of the intention behind the utterance is for the audience – a reason or ground, and not merely a cause. There is a distinction between cause and reason. The cause of a thing does not give a reason for it, and therefore does not explain it. The cause is merely the mechanism by which a reason explains its consequences. For example, there are different causes for the occurrence of an earthquake, but these causes explain nothing as to why earthquake should occur at all. The logical difference between an event and an action is posed on the logical distinction between a cause and a reason. An event can be explained in terms of causality whereas an action (human) should not be explained in terms of causality – it has to be explained in terms of reason(s). There must be reason(s) for human actions. An action to be action at all, it must be based on reason(s). A cause or an event involves 'brutefactness' which is absent in the case of an action.

The connection between meaning NN and recognition of intention must be explained only in terms of the primary, or original, or primitive intention of the speaker. The intention is primitive in the sense that it is not derived from any other intention. The secondary intention or derivative intention is irrelevant to the connection between meaning NN and the recognition of intention. For example, if I utter *x*, intending, by means of recognition of my intention, to produce an effect (reason) *E* to produce another effect (reason) *F*, only the primary intention *E*, and not the secondary intention *F*, is relevant to the meaning NN of *x*. Moreover, when we try to understand meaning NN of utterance, we are not concerned with what is obvious, and what is deliberately told, but with what is not obvious, and what is not deliberately told. This is to say that only the 'depth meaning' and not the 'simple meaning' is relevant here. Intentions have the following logical fact. If one has an intention, it must be possible for him to describe or envisage the situation in which the intention could be fulfilled. The capacity for this sort of fulfilment can be exercised only within a certain way of life which consists in certain networks of practices (Miri, 1984). Intention is not merely subjective, it is an inter-subjective, inter-personal concept. It has, therefore, an objective element in it.

The explanation of human actions in terms of intentions would necessarily involve the idea of evaluation against certain criteria of propriety/impropriety, right/wrong, correct/incorrect, soon, which exists within different cultures and societies. One of the primary functions of tribal lores is to make moral evaluations in terms of certain criteria.

It is worth reiterating that tribal lores not only embody the cultures and traditions of a people, but also enshrine certain value system which ought to be followed, treasured and preserved for the future generation. Tribal lores must not be treated as ends in themselves: they must be treated as means to achieve certain purpose or end. Therefore, they must be given a teleological account rather than a mere descriptive account. Tribal lores contain certain moral imperatives within them. When the hearer identifies the values as the same values that have been referred to by the speaker of the story, communication is established. Communication can be achieved, when the hearer identifies the intended references of the speaker. A word or two about the speaker's sense of identity and the hearer's sense of identity will not be out of place here. When the hearer fails to identify the values that are being referred to by the speaker, the latter makes only identifying references; he does not identify. But when the hearer identifies the intentions that are being referred so by the speaker, the latter not only makes identifying references, but also identifies. In the case of the hearer, he does not make any identifying references, he only identifies when he recognizes the intention of the speaker as to intended.

The Garo Case

A particular tribal lore of the Garos is given below. An attempt will be made to identify the value(s) that are embedded in the tribal lore by means of the intention theory of meaning.

> In ages long gone when the Achiks were settling in a country, known as 'A'song Saora Chiga Timbra', a man named Asi committed adultery with the daughter of his mother's younger sister. When people suspected openly, he publicly pleaded not guilty and, according to the age-long Achik custom, swore solemnly, biting the blade of a *milam* (two-edged sword) to the effect that if he was guilty, a tiger should kill him outright and devour him. The next day a tiger killed him on account of his first sin of the first false swearing.
>
> At about the same time, another man, named Malja, of the same country, committed adultery with his own niece. When publicly accused of his guilt, Malja denied the charge, and solemnly swore a false oath, biting the blade of a *milam*, pleading that if he was not really innocent, an elephant should surely destroy him outright. The next day he was instantly killed by a rogue elephant solely on account of his sin of the first false swearing.

Ever since, the names of Asi and Malja have become by-words among the Achiks, connoting sin and death due to deliberately sworn lies. The world '*Asimalja*' generally has become surcharged with unsavoury meanings to the Achiks up to this day with reference to any word, thought and action (Rongmuthu, 1960).

Certain things are very obvious, and are told deliberately. It has been already shown that the intention theory of meaning is not concerned with anything that is obvious and deliberate; it only tries to determine the meanings of concept that lie hidden below the surface of language. These concepts are only vaguely hinted at by the speaker. Prior to undertaking this philosophical enterprise, a very brief account of the law of exogamy and some other customary laws of the Garos is necessary.

The Garos are divided into three classes, namely, Sangma, Maraks and Momins. These three classes are exogamous clans. Exogamy consists in the practice of marrying only outside of one's own group or clan. The Garo word for these clans is *katchi*. Members of the same *katchi* cannot marry. For example, a Sangma can marry only a Momin or Marak – he cannot marry a member of the Sangma clan or *katchi*. Levy-Strauss has the following to say about the law of exogamy: "The law of exogamy governs the group at all points and all times. It is based on the values – the women – which are the values *par excellence* both from the biological and social points of view, and without which life is not possible or at any rate is reduced to the worst forms of degradation" (Levi-Strauss, 1958). The Garo exogamy preserves the purity of blood and at the same time avoids the pitfalls of consanguinity. According to Garo custom, a man may marry two sisters but he must marry the elder first. The Garo laws can be classified in three words: *Asimalja, Dakmalja* and *Nima*. These three words defy definition, and there are no equivalent words in other languages. Therefore, a literal translation of them into any other language will fail to bring out the real significance of these words. *Asimalja* represents a moral rather than a legal force. *Dakmalja* is a moral imperative which embodies the Garo's code of honour, comprising moral, civil, criminal and penal laws to match all their actions. *Nima* constitutes the Garo rules of etiquette for about a dozen occasions."

Consider the two kinds of adultery referred to in the above-mentioned tribal lore, namely, (a) *Asi* commits adultery with the daughter of his mother's younger sister, and (b) *Malja* commits adultery with his own niece. In the first case, *Asi* violates his law of exogamy for the following reason. His mother, his mother's younger sister, and the daughter of his mother's younger sister and he himself belong to the same clan or *katchi*. Therefore, he (*Asi*) not only commits adultery, but also degrades his whole community by breaking the long-cherished sacred law of exogamy. It follows from this that the primary intention of the speaker (in this case, the teller of the tribal lore) is to produce this belief (that it is highly degrading for a Garo to go against the law of exogamy) in an audience (hearer) by means of recognition of his intention.

In the second case, *Malja* is guilty of going against a customary law of the Garos by committing another kind of adultery – he commits adultery with his own niece. Niece is a generic term which not only refers to a man's brother's daughter(s) but also to his wife's sister's daughter(s). Here the speaker refers to the latter rather than the former. Committing adultery with one's wife's sister's daughter is much more serious than committing adultery with one's brother's daughter for the following reason. In principle, according to the Garo custom, one's wife's sister's daughter becomes his own daughter (adopted daughter), whether he is married to his wife's younger sister or not, he becomes her adoptive father. Therefore, he commits adultery with his own 'daughter'. There is no need to point out that this kind of adultery is a very serious kind of adultery since it is considered incestuous.

Therefore, the primary intention of the speaker is to point out the seriousness of the violation of a particular moral code.

Undoubtedly adultery is an awful crime according to the laws of the Garos. The unfaithful husband and wives are punished severely by the society. But, there are certain kinds of adultery which are much more serious deserving stronger condemnation. The speaker tries to bring out two kinds of such adultery through this tribal lore.

REFERENCES

Grice, H.P. 1969. Utterer's meaning and intention. *Philosophical Review*, Vol.78.

Grice, H.P. 1973. *Philosophical logic*. Ed. P.F. Strawson, Oxford University Press.

Levi-Strauss, C. 1958. *Les structures elementaires de la parente*. Cf. G. Bertrand, *Secret lands where women reign*. Robert Hace Ltd., London.

Miri, M. 1984. Understanding people and sciences of man. *The North-Eastern Hill University Journal of Social Sciences and Humanities*, 2 (1).

Rongmuthu, D.S. 1960. *The folklore of the Garos*. Gauhati University, Gauhati.

TRIBAL AESTHETICS AND SCIENCE

5

TRIBAL MUSIC : ITS PROPER CONTEXT

Onkar Prasad

Introduction

Only a few attempts have been made by ethnomusicologists to understand the nature of the Indian tribal music. In this regard special mention may be made of Bhattacharya (1968), Sinha (1970), Nag (1979) and Prasad (1985).

Bhattacharya (1968) has observed the melodies of the Abor, Badaga, Bhuiyan, Dhurwa, Parja, Gadaba, and others inhabiting different regions of the country. His main observation is that musical scale changes with the changes in the socio-cultural conditions. Taking into account the nature of change in tribal economic and spiritual life, material culture and language – as a result of contact with the 'outside' world – he has broadly classified the tribes of India into three groups: (i) primitive tribes, (ii) semi-tribes and (iii) semi-castes. According to him, music of the primitive tribes is predominantly diatonic, tritonic, or tetratonic, composed mostly of a single musical line and the rhythm predominantly asymmetrical, i.e. without any regular rhythm. In the music of the semi-tribes, the scales are predominantly tritonic or tetratonic, with occasional introduction of additional lines and asymmetrical and symmetrical rhythms. In the music of the third group, i.e. semi-castes, tetratonic and pentatonic tunes predominate. The symmetrical rhythm with the common time scales of three and four metres (units of time) are predominant and the music is often multilinear.

Sinha (1970) in her work on the folk music of various ethnic groups including that of the Bhumij, Kharia and Pahira tribes inhabiting the Pargana Barabhum of West Bengal has analysed the musical forms along the line of the folk-classical continuum. She has observed a continuity of music in the area through the primitive, folk and classical forms. In the process she has very explicitly shown the development of music from the three-note *sarhul* songs of the tribes to seven-note *kirtan*-type *nachni* songs sung by the non-tribal specialists of the area.

Nag (1981), who has studied the music of the Kinnara tribe of Kinnaura district from the *cis*-Himalayan region, finds that although their music apparently shows an overall similarity it basically differs with regard to the rhythmic and tonal organization in different territorial units. He also made a cross-cultural comparison of tribal musical forms including that of the Kinnara with the highly developed Indian classical music which he does not find relevant for determining the primitiveness of the former on account of two reasons. First, the pre-pentatonic, or pentatonic, musical scale of Indian tribes, thought to be an indicator of primitiveness, is also found to be used in Indian classical music. Second, the tribal music is basically rendered in group in contrast to the solo-singing of the Indian classical music. He observes that in group-singing it is difficult to have too many intricate patterns, or embellishments, as their synchronization by different members is difficult to achieve. Hence, the group-singing of tribes should be compared with group-singing, not with solo-singing of other cultures.

Prasad (1985) in his work on music of the Santal inhabiting Birbhum, a district of West Bengal, has analysed fifty-one melodies and found that majority of them (37 out of 51) rest on a particular melodic structure and that the changes brought into them are very much in conformity with the basic structure of their music. His other findings are that despite various changes in the melodies, the Santals have a tendency to perpetuate a core structural pattern of their music; that the relationship between the Santals and their musical instruments is organic; and that the techno-structural and social constraints limit the elaboration of the Santal music.

In brief, Bhattacharya has been concerned with the nature of primitivity in tribal music in terms of its musical scale; Sinha with continuity between the folk and the classical with tribal music at its base; Nag with the variation in music of a particular ethnic group living in different geographical settings; and Prasad with persistence in terms of structural organization of the tribal music.

Thus, in the studies cited above an overall attempt has been made to understand the nature of the tribal music of India within the frame of its major theme of discussion, viz. primitivity, folk-classical continuum, variation and persistence. This has been done only through the analyses of the musical structures of the various tribal groups. But the need for understanding the true context of the tribal music has not been realized. Music, especially tribal music, can hardly be studied in isolation from the social and ritual contexts of the people concerned. The present paper is devoted to this end.

The Social Context

Tribal music has a strong community basis. This fact can be understood in terms of musical-socialization, types of ownership, levels of participation, and the nature of role specialization.

Musical Socialization

Learning of music in a tribal society forms an integral part of the entire processes of association of its members. It is learnt along with the various customs and practices conforming to the standards deemed appropriate by society. But, as against an individual household of the non-tribal society, it is the tribal community as a whole that initiates its children in learning of music, viz. singing, drumming and dancing from an early age. The children in the Santal society, for example, are initially provided with the *katic murli* (flutes of smaller size) of five to six inches long with three to four emissaries to blow, and drums of smaller size to beat. They are also encouraged to learn music through participation in community singing organized on various festive occasions. This mode of musical socialization in the tribal society differs completely from the non-tribal one where its members undergo musical training at their individual initiatives. The Indian classical music, for example, is learnt by an individual member under a *guru* either of his own choice, or whom the guru finds suitable for learning music. Even the caste and regional music is learnt by a limited number of specialized professional singers and drummers, and also by those segments of society that are 'active bearers of its tradition'.

Types of Ownership

Music in a tribal society is not considered an exclusive property of its individual members, but of the community as a whole. Due to this reason, the tribal songs even if composed by individual composers remain anonymous. For example, none of the Santal songs are found to bear the names of individual Santal composers. Modernization of tribe has changed its character. Many of the Mundari songs composed by the literate Mundas bear the mark of individual composers. *Hisir*, a collection of Mundari songs composed by a number of literate Mundas and edited by Ramdayal Munda (1967), is an example. But the faculty of poetry composition is still not the exclusive monopoly of a few literate individuals in the Munda society. The Mundari songs are still composed by thousands of unknown illiterate Munda composers.

Further, among the Indian tribes, musical instruments are owned both by the community and by its individual members. Among the Didayies of Orissa, musical instruments are communally owned and looked after by a special functionary appointed by the community members (personal communication from Siddiqui). But this is not true for the Mundas and the Santals. Among the Santals, musical instruments, specially the *tumdak*, a cylindrical drum, are purchased and owned by an individual member who is economically sound; it is not a community property; its repairing cost is also borne by the individual concerned. From a list of the *jajmani* relationship provided by Kalipada Das, a Muchi of Sealah, it was observed that in some cases the *tumdak* is a joint property, i.e. of more than one individual member. But such cases are very few: out of eleven pairs of the *tumdak* in eleven villages of the Bolpur-Sriniketan Block only one pair has been jointly purchased by five Santals of Domdoma village whereas ten pairs have been purchased individually. However, irrespective of ownership, as observed in the field situation, be it individual or joint, every member of the community is allowed to play the drum. In fact the drum is purchased by an individual member keeping in mind all the villagers who would be using it. The purchaser also shares a sense of prestige of having the drum in his village. Thus the community basis is reflected not only in terms of ownership but also in terms of the usufructury right of the individually owned musical instruments.

Levels of Participation

Any musical performance in a tribal society involves all the members of its community. Boys and girls of different age-groups join the elderly men and women of the village. The children also watch them carefully and repeat their verbal and gestural expressions. The musical performance thus cuts across the boundaries of age and sex. Besides, everybody being a participant there is no defined category of audience or listeners. This, however, contrasts with the classical and the caste music where a clear-cut dichotomy between the performers and the listeners is observed. In brief, the tribal music is characterized by total participation.

As stated, in tribal society everybody is in musical performance, which is choral by nature with regard to singing. This group-singing is classified into: (a) 'the chorus of the primary type', where the joint singing starts from the beginning, and (b) 'the chorus of the secondary type', where the singing is started by a leader and followed by others (Bhattacharya, 1968:72). The chorus of the former type is the characteristic feature of the Santal, Munda, and Oraon (Prasad, *op. cit.*); Abor, Badaga, Juang, Kadar, Korku, and so on belong to the latter type (Bhattacharya, *op. cit.*). In this type of singing, the singers are not differentiated from one another. The chorus of the latter type is, however, the characteristic feature of the caste music marked by a differentiated role for the one who leads and for those who either follow, or answer.

Role Specialization

Apart from being a participant, everybody in tribal society is also a performer of music, i.e. everybody is a singer, dancer and drummer. As such there is no specialized role for singing, dancing, or drumming. However, differentiation of sex with regard to the use of musical instruments is accepted. Women are not allowed to handle the musical instruments of any type. For this, of course, there is no explanation.

Good Music

Tribal perception of music is positive. Music is always considered good, never bad. It is judged in terms of varying positive order. The Santal term of appreciation is *bhagiya rar*, (good melody) and *adi bhagiya rar*, (very good melody). Every music is good, and everybody is good musician. The notion of good music is reflected in a Mundari song as follows:

> *Soben sari bugin, jetae alope noe*
> *Hambal kutung, rabal kutung rulere rededede saria*

Tunturaba Oronglere pererere sari
Soben sari bugin, jetae alope noi
Hasa dumang mangmang, pital kartal cangcang
Mered nagera rulere redede saria
Soben sari bugin, jetae alope noe.

(All music is nice, do not say that any is bad. The *nagera* drum which weighs on the shoulder and the *daka* which is light, sound *rededede*, and when you blow through a *datura* flower, it sounds *pererere*. All music is nice, do not say the contrary. The earthen *dumang* drum sounds *mangmang* and cymbals sound *chang-chang*. The iron *nagera* sounds *rededede*. All music is nice, do not deny it.)

(Hoffmann, 1907)

The Ritual Context

During my acquaintance with the Santal music, I came to know that they bind or encircle the ground used for music and dance, or what is called *akhra bandhan;* that their drumming, dancing and singing cause rain; that their *bongas* (spirits or gods) dance with them in human form during *lagre*; and that singing and dancing at the *baha* and the *dasae* festivals make them obsessed with the spirits. All these led me to think of another dimension of tribal music. It was observed that, except *gam* (a narrative song), almost all forms of Santal music and dance have a ritual context. These are of different types, each marking a particular occasion. Such occasions are believed to be sacred-effective, viz. *baha* performance during March, *dasae* during September-October, *lagre* during April-May, and so on. It is not possible to deal with all of them within the limits of the space provided for this essay. I shall, therefore, restrict my discussion to only one of these, viz. the *dasae*.

The dasae form of music and dance

The Santals practise various types of *bakher* (charms) for warding off the evil spirits, believed to be the principal cause of sickness and disease. The charms are used also for curing the bites of poisonous insects and animals. A Santal boy interested in learning this art approaches the *dasae-guru* (preceptor).[1] The *guru* selects a place outside the village, called *akhra*, where every evening the *celas* (disciples) assemble to learn the spells. As they first enter the place, the *akhra* is opened up, so to say, and then while leaving it the guru 'binds' the place by muttering a certain *mantra*. Here the disciples, first of all, are taught the medicinal use of various kinds of herbs and roots. This continues for three months. The trainees are then initiated to various *dasae* songs and dances leading to 'spirit possession'. They also learn music and dance associated with *dasae daran*, (a ritual begging of corns) enacted after 'spirit-possession', and that forms the last part of the celebration.

When all these courses are over, the *guru*, in consultation with the villagers, fixes a day for the ritual performance known as *belboron*, which generally falls on the third day of the *Durga puja*. The *dasae guru* along with his *pat cela* (principal disciple) now venerates the *maran buru* praying to him to keep an eye on the events concerning the *belboron*. From this day onward the villagers are instructed not to play the cymbal and the drum until further instruction. If this is not followed strictly it may make the ritual ineffective, or may cause the wrath of the *bongas*.

A day before the *belboron*, the preceptor takes his disciples to a forest, or a field, in the vicinity of the village, for *ran sendra* (herb hunting), i.e. in search of medicinal plants. There the preceptor first identifies a plant, explains its application, and chants a *bakher* or *ran jagao*, or what is known as 'awakening the herb'. The charm uttered for awakening the plant runs as follows :

Jagao guru ho, jagao cela
Ran jagao guru ho, mantar jagao
Jagao cela ho, jagao mantar
Baro gonda mantar jharni
Jagao guru ho jagao cela ho.

(Awake O Preceptor!
Awake O Disciple!
Awake the Herb, O Preceptor!
Awake the Charm!
Awake O Disciple !
Awake the Charm!
Awake the 'Twelve Fours' of charms.)

The acts of identifying a plant, explaining its use, awaking it, digging it out and collecting it continue till the preceptor finds the available plants. Finally the collected roots and herbs are brought to his house.

Next morning, the disciples first smear with cowdung a portion of space in the courtyard of the preceptor's house and then go for a purificatory bath; and on return both the preceptor and the disciples worship the *dasae bonga*, the principal god of the festival known as *Kamru guru*. Ritual objects like water lily or lotus, unboiled rice, vermilion, incense, feathers of a peacock, smoke-pipe, hemp, blacksoot, *carcari* (a kind of grass), etc., are offered. Chickens are also sacrificed in the name of the spirit. When the worship is over the disciples, centering their preceptor, squat on the ground. The preceptor asks them one by one to identify each of the collected herbs and to explain their applications. This is followed by a session on 'spirit possession'. Singing, drumming and dancing begin as a gesture of invitation to the *baghut bonga* (the tiger-spirit). Shortly after this, a disciple or any other villager gets possessed and the rendering comes to a halt. A song rendered on the occasion goes like this :

Dau mar dau,
Mar mar dau
Dau mar dau,
Mar mar dau.
Taram rema cagam cugum,
Done rema sahai asahai.

(It is flaring,
It is flaring up.
It is flaring,
It is flaring up.
It follows stealthily,
It jumps over suddenly.)

The man in trance starts roaring and pouncing like a tiger and he goes on, like this with the beat of the drum. The tiger-spirit in him is then offered a chicken which he catches instantly and bites its head. By doing so the spirit is pleased and lets the person free from the trance. Thus ends the first session of the ritual.

In the evening, the disciples and their teacher gather again at the *guru raca* (the place of the guru) to enact the *dasae* play in the midst of the villagers, including women and children. The *dasae* songs begin with the drumming sound of the percussion instruments and the ringing sound of the *rankhi* (cymbal). The *buan*,[2] a musical instrument specially designed for the occasion, is handled to emit a reverberating sound. The first song, rendered in honour of the founding father of the *dasae* ritual, runs as follows :

Tokoe guru doe pir leda,
Tokoe cela doe akhra leda,
Desere gurma era,
Sunume sindur nudun,
Ainam Kajar nudun baherme.
Kamru guru doe pir leda,
Kamru cela doe akhra leda,
Desere guruma era,
Sunume sindur nudun,
Ainam kajar nudun baherme.

(Who was the guru who founded the hermitage?
Who was the disciple who established the *akhra*?
Wife of my teacher! Please give us oil and vermilion,
Please bring us a mirror and collyrium.
Kamruguru founded the hermitage.
Kamru's disciple established the *akhra*.
Wife of my teacher. Please give us oil and vermilion,
Please bring us a mirror and collyrium.)

Before the act of possession another song is rendered :

Guruma hakai ete,
Guruma dakai ete,
Kone guruma kasi avaere,
Guruma pinda baise,
Guruma machi baise,
Kone guruma pinda baise,
Kamru guruma pinde baise.

(Preceptor's wife is addressed,
Preceptor's wife is called,
The voice of which preceptor's wife is heard?

Preceptor's wife sits on the *pinda*.
Preceptor's wife sits on the cot.
Which preceptor's wife sits on the *pinda*?
Kamru's wife sits on the *pinda*.)

Now *kamru bonga*, also known as *jugi bonga* (the hermit-spirit) or *ganja bonga* (the hemp-spirit) in invoked:

Kasa tupri kasi avae
Kaun kaun deota aelo,
Avae se ho kamru guru
Khelaite aelo.

(Sound is produced by beating the cymbal,
Who are the gods who have come over here?
Kamru guru has come over here,
Through the person possessed.)

In the midst of singing and dancing, a member of the group falls down suddenly and begins to crawl around violently to the rhythm of the drum. Shortly after this the dance comes to a halt. As the person is under *rum*[3] (showing the signs of being possessed by a spirit), the preceptor approaches him and asks :

'O Respected Sir! What spirit you are? Why have you come? How can we serve you?'

The impersonated person answers :

'I am *jugi bonga*. I have come on your invitation. I will be pleased to smoke hemp on this auspicious occasion.'

The preceptor, then, offers him hemp in a smoke-pipe. The person possessed by the spirit smokes to his heart's content. Finally the preceptor sprinkles water on him, uttering '*saha gosain*', and pats his shoulder. Thereafter the *bonga* leaves the person. On the recovery of the person, the party begins singing and dancing with renewed enthusiasm in the name of the *carcari bonga*. The song runs as follows:

Lenga ka hate raja
Ya yelo deota.
Ghura ho ghura Sati
Barewae ghura.

(The spirit has come on the left arm.
Move, move around the boundary.
Move within the boundary.)

Now the *carcari bonga* enters into someone's body and the person starts jumping and dancing on the ground, waiving his arms violently. This particular kind of gesture indicates the arrival of the spirit. After a short while, the preceptor hits on both the arms of the man under *rum* with a scourge of *babui* grass. The obsessed one endures it without showing sign of being hurt. The *bonga* satisfied by him departs, leaving the person used as medium to return to his normal state.

Subsequently the *baghut bonga*, the *bagal bonga* (the cowherd boy spirit) and the *bachur bonga* (the calf spirit) are invited to appear one after another. The song rendered to call the tiger-spirit again who had appeared once before in the morning session runs as follows :

Haru harayre baghrae haru harayre,
Khelaylere baghae Khelayle
Baghe nacay baghe nacayre baghrae
Baghe khelayre,

(The fowl is let loose O Tiger!
O Tiger! you eat it up
You eat it dancing and enjoying O Tiger!
You eat it up O Tiger!)

With this song appears the *baghut* spirit roaring and jumping. Another song is rendered to invite the *bagal bonga* :

Bagal bagal bagal re,
Bagali tor kaha gaya,
Sugi gai bachure to baghe khelayre.

(O the Cowherd!
Where have you left your work?

The calf of the Sugi cow is being eaten up by the tiger.)

This causes the *bagal bonga* to appear. With his appearance the people surround the *baghut bonga* to avoid any confrontation with the *bagal bonga*. The *bagal bonga* then gives a call to the calf which causes the *bachur bonga* to appear and respond with a voice '*ombe*'.

As the spirit of the calf is lowing, the tiger-spirit makes an attempt to attack, but then is obstructed by the people sitting there. In some cases the *bagal bonga* protects its *bachur bonga* by a stick. This act continues for a while. Lastly, the tiger-spirit is offered a fowl to bite. The preceptor sprinkles water on all the three and requests them to depart. The persons in trance are now freed and they return to normal state.

Singing and dancing begin once more to invite *hanu bonga* (monkey-god). The song rendered for him is as follows :

Kal bhairon masan khan
Gangat gaurat sarimre
Hanuman Hanuman birjoi
Lankai digir ket.

(Glory to Kalbhairon.
Sitting on the Gangat gaurat roof,
Hanuman conquered Lanka.)

A disciple gets possessed by the monkey-god, starts jumping. The dancing group then dissolves and leaves the arena for the monkey-god. He climbs the trees and roofs of houses, starts plucking gourds and eating in imitation of a monkey. He also jumps from one roof to another and is then followed by the viewers to whatever places he goes to demonstrate frivolous and amusing behaviour. After a while he is brought back forcibly to the courtyard of the preceptor's house by a number of persons assembled at the dancing ground. There, he is prayed for his courage to enter into Lanka.

Let kutta Hanuman
Lonka gar jabi Hanuman.

(O insolent Monkey-god!
Would you go to Lanka?)

With the rhyming of this verse, the monkey-god goes on dancing until it is stopped. Lastly he is propitiated duly by the preceptor with the sprinkles of water and utterances of the words '*saha gosain*'. Then the monkey-god leaves the person, and this leads to resumption of singing and dancing.

A song is rendered to invite the *dhiri-bonga* (stone-spirit) :

Dor dorin dor dorin
Dahar dhuri ho otanokan,
Dor dorin hordahar likide likide,
Dor dorin dhiri gurgu calaome,
Dor dorin dhiri gurgu calao calaome,
Dor dorin dhiri gurgu calao Katinme.

(It rolls, it rolls
Causing the dust of the path to rise.
It rolls through quaking the narrow street.
Go rolling O Stone-spirit!
Cause to roll O Stone-spirit!)

This causes a disciple to be possessed by the stone-spirit. In that state he keeps his feet on a small cylindrical stone placed on a wooden sill, puts his palms on the ground to maintain the balance of his body and then goes on moving around. The preceptor allows him to go like this for some time and then sprinkles water with the utterance of '*saha gosain*'. This frees him from trance.

In the midst of singing and dancing the *bindi bonga* (spider-spirit) is invited :

Bindi gorh bindi gorh tilmin tiju,
Taram rema raimat lendon,
Taram rema legeme legeme.

(In spider's fort, In spider's fort,
There lies a larva.
It moves like a large centipede.
It moves smoothly.)

After a while, a person possessed by the *bindi bonga* comes with his hands up, moving his fingers in the way of a spider. The preceptor then requests the *bonga* to leave the person.

Thus several other spirits are invited to appear one after another until the preceptor declares the end of the ritual. Next morning, the disciples in a group visit every house of the preceptor's village to display the *dasae* dance. For this they receive some quantity of foodgrain. From that day onward to the 10th day of the moon, they go for *dasae daran* (*dasae* wandering) to the nearby villages where they display their dances and in return receive corns or cash from the villagers. This wandering is considered an essential part of the festival, as it provides them chances to exhibit their acquired knowledge of singing and dancing before the Santal of other villages. On this itinerancy if they confront any other group of the *dasae koras* (the *dasae* boys) they may indulge with them in a dialogue, singing *eset' seren*' (check song). It begins with the song rendered as follows :

Kulhi kulhite khelte aylam,
Duare duare bolte aylam,
Manjh kulhi rebon yapamen,
Deho guru ho cet' bon cekaya.

(We have come playing through streets,
We have come speaking from door to door,
We have met in the middle of the street,
O Guru! What shall we do now?)

This question would then be answered by another group in the following words :

Kulhi kulhite khelte aylam,
Duare duare bolte aylam,
Manjh Kulhi tala rebon yapamen,
Deho guru bon johar bihar.

(We have come playing through streets,
We have come speaking from door to door,
We have met in the middle of the street,
O Guru. We shall be saluting each other).

If the groups meeting each other do not want to prolong the dialogue they would be affixing vermilion mark on each other's peacock feather, or else they may continue asking one another in the song form. One such question-answer may, for example, be as follows:

Question : *Toka redo ho guru ho,*
Gaiko janam len guru ho,
Gaiko janam len.
Toka redo ho cela ho,
Bonga upal len cela ho,
Bonga upal len.
Cirti lagi ho guru ho,
Gaiko janam len guru ho,
Gaiko janam len.
Cirti lagi ho cela ho,
Bonga upal len cela ho,
Bonga upal len.

(O Preceptor! Where did the cows come from?
O Preceptor! Where did the cows come from?
O Disciple! Where did the spirit come from?
O Disciple! Where did the spirit come from?
O Preceptor! What for the cows were born?
O Preceptor! What for the cows were born?
O Disciple! What for the spirit was born?
O Disciple! What for the spirit was born?

Answer : *Dhiri rarure guru ho,*
Gaiko janam len guru ho,
Gaiko janam len.
Sinje buta re cela ho,
Bonga upal len cela ho,
Bonga upal len.
Des sawai lagi ho guru ho,
Gaiko janam len guru ho,
Gaiko janam len.
Disam sawai lagi ho cela ho,
Bonga upal len cela ho
Bonga upal len.

(O Preceptor! The cow has originated from the stony place,

O Preceptor! The cow has originated.
O Disciple! The spirit has originated from under the *bel* tree
O Disciple! The spirit has originated.
O Preceptor! The cow has originated for the progress of the country.
O Preceptor! The cow has originated.
O Disciple! The spirit has originated for the extension of the territory,
O Preceptor! The spirit has originated.

The *dasae* wanderers receive warm and hearty reception from the housewives. At the end of the performance they sing in their praise and of those who are standing to receive the compliments:

> The darkness being over, the morning star is up in the sky. We, your children, look at the star with hope and delight. Mother! It is you who is the morning-star. By your grace and blessing we have been able to visit every Santal village to meet every Santal mother and to strengthen the bond of brotherhood and relationship among the Santals. Mother! We are blessed to see your graceful face. May your love and affection for us flow like water from a hill spring. Accept our homage Mother! Accept our homage.
> The mother receives their homage with tears of joy which do not remain controlled at seeing so many sons together (Soren, 1982: 8).

Symbolic Interpretation

In this paper I have presented briefly the entire context of the *dasae* ceremony in three stages. The first is preparatory, when a group of adolescent Santal boys is initiated in medicine, music and medium for spirits – the three elements which together make the treatment of a disease effective. The second is the ritual session, when the training at the preparatory stage is put to test, specially of medicine, music and dance. Finally, the wandering session is meant for contact with the Santals across the village to maintain social cohesion by establishing harmony with the Nature in affirmation to an ancient tradition. However, it is only the ritual session, described here, which demonstrates as to how the Santals exercise symbolic control over the divine being through aesthetic performances of music, dance and drama – all in one.

The Santals believe that certain inexplicable eventualities are occurring in their society due to the intervention of the *bongas*. For self-protection they make supernaturalistic adjustments with them. There are prescribed ways. One such way structured for the occasion is the act of spirit-possession in which man is medium and music is what Saraswati (1982) calls 'ritual language'. Through this the guardian spirits are kept under control so that they may not endanger the Santals. The *baghut bonga* is invoked and venerated to protect people from tigers and leopards. The *carcari bonga* is venerated by beating with a whip both the arms of the person in a state of possession, symbolizing the act of 'protection' against the evil forces of the universe (Dupre, 1975: 98). So does the offering to the hemp-spirit.

The description of spirit possession prov. .es as to how the *dasae* form of music and dance becomes sacred-effective. Its sacred-effectiveness is, however, limited to the ritual context of performance, as commonly believed by the Santa. . It may be pointed out that the ritual context of performance marks the creation of the ritual time, that is, the sacred-time. As Clamagirand (1980: 149) has observed, performance of ritual acts like singing, drumming and dancing that become the effective cause of impersonations is intended to renew the sacred time of the beginning of the community so that steeped, again, in its source, the community can perpetuate itself. These ritual acts repeat the actions of the first ancestors – the founders of the community but they are now performed by actors totally removed from those mythical times. In the case of the Santals, the *Kamaruguru* is the founder of the rituals associated with music and medicine. Further, in the ritual context the *dasae* music and dance serve a mediating function between the Santals and their spirits or gods, leading the former to be obsessed by the latter for the purpose of interaction between the two. In other words, the *dasae* music and dance become essentially elements or what Saraswati (1982: 3) calls the code of ritual language, viz. *dhvani* (sound) and *mudra* (gesture), respectively. The sacred-effectiveness of the ritual code is proven beyond doubt as the spirits are brought into concrete observable context. Following Saraswati (1988), in the case of what is anthropologically known as spirit possession, man is transformed temporarily to serve as a medium and dies for the time being as a secular man, i.e. his secular personality is switched off. As he is elevated to the undifferentiated state he becomes a spirit or god. In that state of possession he personifies the spirit and is, therefore, treated as a reality. The fact of spirit-possession is made known by what the medium speaks. As one returns from the trance he regains his secular identity of a Santal.

Summary

The proper context of tribal music is both social and ritual. The social context is characterized by musical socialization, collective ownership of musical instruments and talents, non-differentiation of audience and performers, lack of role-specialization, and positive appreciation of music. The ritual context of music reaffirms the social concern and leads further on to man's highest perfection. The tribal aesthetic performances serve as a bridge between the secular and the sacred, between the visible world of man and the invisible world of god.

NOTES

1 *Dasae guru*, also known as *ojha guru*, is a charm doctor. He possesses knowledge in traditional medicine but is different from *raranic*, the medicine man. The ojha *guru*'s work always deals with the supposed supernatural causes of the disease.

2. To construct a *buan* instrument, a large hollow gourd is attached to the middle of the area of a bow with a string put through a hole at the bottom. When playing the open end the gourd is kept against the stomach of the player and struck with a little stick. An altering sound is produced, as the gourd is pressed tightly, or loosely, against the stomach.

3. It is a method by which spirits reveal their wishes, convey comfort, or discomfort, and assure the living of their fellowship (Culshaw 1949:78).

REFERENCES

Bhattacharya, S. 1968. *Ethnomusicology and India*. Indian Publications, Calcutta.

Clamagirand, B. 1980. The social organization of the Emа of Timor. *The flow of life: essays on eastern Indonesia*, (ed.) James J. Fox, Harvard University Press, Harvard.

Culshaw, W.J. 1949. *Tribal heritage: a study of the Santals*, Lutherworth Press, London.

Dupre, W. 1975. *Religion in primitive culture: a study of ethnophilosophy*. Mouton, The Hague.

Munda, R.D. (ed.) 1967. *Hisir* (The necklace). Sahkari Prakashan, Ranchi.

Nag, N.G. 1981. Some aspects of ethnomusicology of Kinnars with special references to issues relating to primitiveness. *Man in India*, 61: 305-326.

Prasad, D. 1979. *Hoffman on Mundari poetry*. Jyoti, Patna.

Prasad, O. 1985. *Santal music: a study in pattern and process of cultural persistence*. Inter-India Publications, New Delhi.

Saraswati, Baidyanath. 1982. Ritual language: a transanthropological perspective, *Man in India* 62(1).

Saraswati, Baidyanath. 1988. Transformation of man into god. *Lectures* at the Centre d'Etudes de l'Asie du Sud, Paris.

Sinha, Purnima. 1970. *An approach to the study of Indian music*. Indian Publications, Calcutta.

Soren, B. 1982. Tradition and history of the *Dasae* festival.

6

TRIBAL MEDICINE : A STUDY IN IRULAR SCIENCE AND SUPERSTITION

P. R. G. Mathur

Introduction

Ethnographic literature dealing with the ethnomedicine of the tribes of India is exceedingly limited. In 1987, I had organized a workshop on the anthropology of tribal health and medicine in forest environment. In his presidential address to the workshop Professor Surajit Sinha dwelt upon, on this occasion, the rationality and resistance approach to tribal health and medicine. This paper draws its inspiration chiefly from his thought.

While working on the tribes of Kerala for nearly three decades I was struck by the Irular categorization of illness and the method of treatment. Modern physicians are generally unfamiliar with such etiology of illness. It is useful to understand the culturally defined illness even for introducing modern system of medicine. Here I take the example of the Irular of Attappady.

The Background

Attappady is one of the important tribal areas of Kerala. It spreads over 730 sq. km in the eastern half of the Mannarghat taluk of Palghat district. The valley lies at a height of 750 m to 1,000 m from MSL. The Nilgiris and Coimbatore districts of Tamil Nadu form its northern and eastern boundaries, respectively. It is bordered by Palghat Taluk in the south and Mannarghat and Ernad Taluks of Malappuram district in the west. The valley is well-connected with the plains of Tamil Nadu and

Kerala. The Irular (14,908), Mudugar (1,691) and Kurumbar (988) are three important tribal communities inhabiting this area. They live in different geographical areas of Attappady. Among them, the Kurumbar have been identified as a primitive tribe subsisting on shifting cultivation and minor produce collection. The Mudugar also practise shifting cultivation, only a few of them have become agricultural labourers.

The Irular are small-scale settled cultivators who have been largely alienated from their land. The Attappady tribal population is distributed in 133 uniethnic tribal hamlets. Of these the Kurumbar is distributed in 16 hamlets, Mudugar in 22 and the Irular in the remaining hamlets. In addition to these traditional hamlets, there are half a dozen tribal colonies established by the government under different development schemes. Traditionally, each hamlet has a headman known as *oorumooppan* whose position is mostly hereditary in nature. They have the final say in the social and religious matters of the hamlet. They used to exercise great powers and influence among the fellowmen of the *ooru* and also act as the connecting link between the people and the erstwhile landlords. The *oorumooppan* of each hamlet acted as a mediator and arbitrator with power to inflict punishment for social and economic offences. The *oorumooppan* is assisted by two of his fellow tribesmen, namely, *kuruthalai* and *bhandari*, who were chosen by the hamlet people for discharging certain duties and functions. They also officiate as headmen during the absence of *oorumooppan* in recent years. In recent years, the institution of *oorumooppan* has lost much of its importance.

The *mannookaran* (soil expert) is another important social functionary. He should have good knowledge of the traditional agricultural practices, climatic conditions and fertility of soil, etc. It is he who fixes the date of the sowing of seeds and conducting rites and rituals associated with the cultivation. He also makes offerings to *karadaivam* (deity associated with health and agriculture) for a bountiful harvest and good health. His position is hereditary.

The Irular practise strict tribal endogamy and live mostly in the eastern half of the valley. This part of the valley is a rain shadow with an annual rainfall of only 30" to 40". Moreover this region is now left with denuded forests due to wanton tree felling. Till 1975 these areas were under the possession of *janmis* (landlords). The Kurumbar are confined to the reserve forest and vested forest areas which is in the north-west part of the valley. Most of the Kurumbar hamlets are surrounded by virgin forests. The annual rainfall of this area ranges from 150" to 200". Incidentally, this area lies adjacent to the Silent Valley National Park. The Mudugar lives in the south-west region, where the annual rainfall is 150" to 200". The Mudugar and Kurumbar intermarry. Each tribe has its own dialectical variation, but the predominance of Tamil is a well-known feature of the service centres including the PHC headquarters located in the Irular area, and practically no such facility is available in the Kurumbar area, due to inaccessibility.

These tribal communities who live in different ecological niches having different economic pursuits help us to study how the different environments and culture influence health, traditional curing techniques and herbal knowledge.

The researcher has been in constant touch with these tribal communities since 1975. In order to assess the health condition of these tribes interviews were conducted with the doctors of PHC sub-centres and traditional tribal medicine men. Records of outbreaks of epidemics during the last one decade have been examined.

An appraisal of drinking water supply and sanitary practices in relation to the environment has also been made. The health and medical behaviour of these communities in relation to the medical facilities made available to them also are observed. The differential preference of these tribal communities in selecting different systems in the context of the existence of medical pluralism have also been noted.

The data on the belief system associated with diseases were gathered by interviewing socio-religious functionaries such as headmen, aged men and women, and also tribal herbalists of these communities. The social and religious functions and lifecycle rites are also observed. The data regarding the tribal medical practices have been collected by interviewing all reputed tribal herbalists of Attappady (two herbalists of Kurumbar, one herbalist of Mudugar and five herbalists of Irular). After the interview, samples of medical herbs have been collected by visiting the neighbouring forests, for identification by a plant taxonomist and for the preparation of herbarium sheets. The diagnostic probing of the herbalist and his administration of the medicine were also observed.

Health Condition

The appraisal of drinking water facilities available at Attappady shows that majority of the tribal hamlets are still devoid of protected water. But in many of the tribal hamlets funds were spent for digging of wells without any benefit. Majority of them still depend upon rivers and springs for drinking water. These sources are not generally perennial and become dry in summer. In such situations they have to dig water-holes in the streambed itself. Almost all the Kurumbar take water from natural sources. Most of the programmes to provide drinking water have failed mainly due to improper implementation. The PHC with inpatient facility, two mobile medical units, two government dispensaries and also one ICDS medical unit are available for catering to the needs of the tribals of this area. But these service facilities are not being availed by the tribals due to the absenteeism among the health personnel and inadequate supply of medicines. It appears that these facilities are only on paper.

The doctors working in this tribal area opine that the main diseases prevalent among the tribal populations are skin diseases such as scabies, tropical ulcer, dysentery, respiratory trouble and STD of all kinds. In earlier days smallpox was a severe scourge that affected them periodically. Epidemics such as chickenpox, whooping cough, mumps are an annual phenomenon. Incidences of polio-myelitis are also reported. During 1981-82, an epidemic of dysentery occurred in the Kurumbar hamlets. This scourge has affected people of all age and sex. There occurred 33 deaths (among a population of 1,002 within a span of three months). Of these deaths children below 10 years constitute 65 per cent. Even though the same type of dysentery spread among the Mudugar and Irular, only the Kurumbar suffered to this extent. This shows not only the poor general health, hygiene and sanitation among the Kurumbar but also their vulnerability to communicable diseases and also the lack of health service facilities.

In general, among the tribes of Attappady apart from malnutrition, water and air-borne diseases and STD are still the major problems. Incidence of blindness, paralysis of various degrees, deaf mutism and epilepsy have also been observed. Alcoholism is also rampant among the tribal groups, particularly among those who are living near the growth centres. Illicit distillation of *arrack* and clandestine cultivation of *ganja* are also noted.

Among these tribal communities 95 per cent of the deliveries take place at home with the assistance of traditional tribal mid-wives or an aged-woman. This coupled with the poor nutrition of the mother, unhygienic surroundings and improper child care lead to high IMR.

They still seek the help of the traditional medicine men for a number of illnesses.

Theory of Illness

The tribes of Attappady worship a number of Hindu gods and goddesses such as Siva (Malleeswaran), Subramanyan, Peroorswami, Mariamma, etc. Their most important deity is Malleeswaran (Lord Parama Siva) whose abode is the Malleeswara Peak, the highest peak in the Attappady valley. They also propitiate Thondallur Mari or Thai (the Goddess of smallpox and chickenpox) by making fowl sacrifices. Blood-stained dysentery is also attributed to Mariamma. Each hamlet has a small shrine, or a sacred spot, beneath a tree, or an overhanging rock where idols of these gods and godlings (mostly stones) are installed.

Annual offerings are made to these deities. The propitiation is accompanied by merry-making and feasts depending upon the economic condition of these tribes. But the annual propitiation cannot be postponed and has to be performed even if it is only on a token level. Failure to do this, they believe causes illnesses and misfortune.

They also believe that the atmosphere is haunted by spirits, both benevolent and malevolent. According to them the malevolent spirits are constantly on a lookout for creating mischief. An individual moving alone on a desolate path, the forest area, is supposed to be highly vulnerable to such malevolent invasions. This kind of fright reactions is called *kannithattal.* The symptoms manifest in such cases are shivering at night, fainting at intervals and muttering of incoherent words. They think that it can also lead to madness. Malevolent spirits are moving in the form of whirlpools and hence are also called *kattuthattal* (*kattu* = wind). *Kattuthattal* is believed to be the cause of most of the children's diseases, and acute illness of the adults. The tribals of Attappady in general believe that there are certain individuals among them, who have command over such malevolent powers and can direct these powers as mercenaries to harm the rivals of those who seek their services. The two major magical beliefs associated with illness are called *odivekkal* and *mayyivekkal.* The *odivekkal* is effected with the help of mercenary spirits whereas *mayyivekkal* is effected by the administration of objects clandestinely after a magical spell over them into an individual. These objects include both herbal and animal poisonous matter like snake poison, or tiger fat mixed with poisonous herbs. They suspect *mayyivekkal*, if somebody falls sick all of a sudden, or somebody gets fatigued during a journey. Indeed, such magical attribution is quite predominant among the tribes of Attappady. It is also noted that patronizing tutelary deity, sexual rivalry, property disputes, etc., generally lead to such things.

Whenever an illness persists, irrespective of the usual therapies, their belief in such attributes gets strengthened. They try to identify the nature of supernatural causes by divination techniques such as: (a) *kuriyedukkal* (seed counting), (b) *varamyenginokkal* (trance dance), (c) *kodankinokkal* (scripture reading), etc. They ward off the identified manovolent invasions by (a) *pattuvekkal* (recitation of spells), (b) *bhootipidikkal* (ash smearing), (c) *ennayoothikodukkal* (application of charmed oil), (d) *smayyioothividal* (exorcizing), (e) *perissuvekkal* (votary offerings), (f) *thettukettal* (paying of fines), (g) *thakkidukettal* (talisman-tying), etc.

Therapeutic Recipes

The tribal herbalists occupy a higher social status. They generally administer the therapeutic recipes after divining the cause by magical means. Their curing recipes include potions, poultices, pills, fomentation, hot baths, ash smearing, etc. The tribal herbalists are called *vaidyakkaran*. The Kurumbar herbalists are known for their expertise as efficient healers even by non-tribals of the region. For the preparation of the recipes they use a variety of herbal and animal matter. Some of these healers are constantly on the move to treat illness among tribals and non-tribals, accepting remuneration for their services.

The following is a list of common illnesses and therapeutic recipes prescribed by the medicine men. The exact dosage and the quantity of ingredients required could not be given as the herbalists are not in a position to specify this aspect. The common illnesses are referred here in tribal terms *vis-a-vis* the plant and animal matter for the preparation of recipes.

Names of illnesses and therapeutic recipes

1. *Thalavettu (Headache)*
   a) Crush a piece of fresh stem or leaves of *Thalasithari (Clematis gouriana)* and squeeze the juice and pour it into the nose.

b) Juice collected from tender leaves of *Mookkuthikodi* and smeared over the forehead.
c) Keep a paste of tamarind for an hour on the head.
d) Collect the juice from the bark of *Bhoovina* and use it as salve over the forehead.
e) Boil the leaves of *Pada* for a while and allow to settle down. Keep the thick mass over the head and take bath after a while.

2. *Kachela Thalavettu (Fever and headache)*
a) Mash the roots and leaves of *Kurumthotti* and apply it over the head before bath.
b) Prepare a potion, using *Kolijeerakom*, *Cherukanthari* and seasoned tamarind; and drink.

3. *Perumandavettu (Headache occurring during sunrise)*
a) Mash a bulb of *Venkayam (Allivum sativum)* and smear it over forehead after diluting it in saliva.
b) Grind a mixture of roots of *Thottarvady (Mumosa hidica)* raw turmeric and roots of *Thakaram*, and smear this paste over the forehead.
c) A potion of mustard, pepper, coriander, nutmeg is drunk.
d) The leaves of *Vettumparaen Vittathulasi Ramathulasi, Vellaparalu, Seelasaranku* are squeezed, and the juice given to drink three times a day.
e) The juice collected from the roots of *Kevisimullu* is filtered through a cloth and poured into nose.

4. *Kacchel (Fever)*
a) Grind the tender leaves of *Kattivettu*, mix it with castor oil, and smear this over the head.
b) Mash the leaves of *Erumulakkatte* and smear it all over the body, and take bath after four hours in warm water.
c) Grind the roots of *Cheruchunda* and smear this over the body. This can also be given to drink.
d) Grind the roots of *Konte (Cassia fistula)* and smear it over the body.
e) A ground mixture of roots of *Konte, Ulakudi*, and leaves of *Sole* squeezed for juice; and this juice is given to drink.
f) Tender leavs of *Toomle* are ground and the paste smeared all over the face and head.

g) Mash the tuber of *Chikke* plant and apply this over the head in a thick layer for more than an hour.
h) *Kallukeera* leaves and the roots of *Thippali, Mannari and Pada* are mixed and the potion is drunk.
i) Prepare tablets from ground mixture of bark of *Athi, Kadampa, Karippatti* and take one tablet thrice a day.
j) The juice of bark of *Kadampa* and *Mullivenga* is ground with *Koramaavu Puttumannu* and this is smeared all over the body; and a sunbath is taken before the bath in warm water.

5. *Toothache with swelling*
a) Grind the leaves of *Komputhonda.* Place this smashed mass over the aching teeth for a while and spit out.
b) Collect stones found in bamboo internodes; this is used for the preparation of medicinal oil. Apply this oil in the aching tooth, cheek.
c) Boil *Karuvela* leaves in water and then plunge it into red hot white quartz. The steam emitting from it is directed to the aching tooth.
d) Boil the bark *Oankatta* (*Jooli*)/(*Genkonkbark*) and plunge into the red hot white quartz; and aching tooth is given a steam bath.
e) Juice of *Thumba* is collected and applied over the head.
f) Mash bark of *Karuvela* and keep this mash over the aching tooth.
g) Latex collected from *Babli* is smeared over the aching teeth.
h) Sap collected from *Alumanan (Ficus religiousa*) is used for mouth washing.

6. *Kathukuthel (earache)*

Grind the tuber of *Pinaki* plant along with common salt and mix this in warm water and filter through a cloth. This is used as an ear drop.

7. *Ear infection*
a) Collect juice from warmed tender leaves of mustard and use it as an ear drop.
b) Grind the *Kannaputti* and dilute it with cow milk and use as an ear drop.

8. *Eye pain*
   a) Juice from the stem of *Chullithandu* is used as an eye drop.
   b) Grind finely the tender leaves of *Assu cumin* seed and a pinch of salt and dilute it with water; and use as an eye drop.
   c) Mash the tender leaves of *Ponnavira and Chuvannulli* and dilute it with water; and apply as an eye drop.
   d) Powder the seeds of *Madhurichedi*; and this fine powder is applied in the eyes. It is also known as *Kannukollichedi.*
   e) Root of *Chutti* is kept over a red-hot iron and the juice emitting from it is used as an instant eye drop.
   f) Grind the leaves of *Ash* and onion, squeeze them through a cloth; and use the juice as an eye drop.

9. *Sores in eye*

   The tender leaves of *Arampuli* is ground along with *Venkayam*, and the solution is filtered through a cloth and used as an eye drop.

10. *Abscess*

    Grind the roots of *padissu* and smear this paste over the abscess.

11. *Waterbrash (Gandiyesalu)*

    The mashed leaves of *Ampukana* is mixed with lime and given to drink.

12. *Respiratory trouble*
    a) The tuber of *Passatti and Palpatta* ground together and mixed with water and is given to drink.
    b) Bark of the roots of *Kallring* along with *Beezhar* is ground and this paste is given to eat. For taste *Karipetti* can also be added.

13. *Backache*
    a) Grind the roots of *Kalle* and bark of *Kulamavu* and apply the paste over the backbone.
    b) Prepare a *beedi*, making use of the leaves of *Tuppai* and dry leaves *Kariumman*, and smoke.

14. *Bone setting*
    a) Collect the scrapings of bamboo stem, bark of *Mulluvenga puthumannu* (soil collected from anthill) bark of *Vellavega* and

seasoned tamarind and grind it together. This paste is applied over the broken limb. Diluted solution of *Napgi* flour is also applied over it. Give a bandage with fresh cloth with straight bamboo splints. Change the bandage and apply the above medicine on alternate days.

b) Grind the leaves of *Munka* (bamboo) along with white of *Rigg* and apply this after setting right the broken bone using bamboo splits; and give a cloth bandage to it. Change the bandage on alternate days for a month.
c) Pour the sap of *Kattalapala* over the bark of *Vellavela* and give a bandage. Repeat the medication and bandage every alternate day.

15. *Wound*

a) Grind the leaves of *Appasappu*, mix it with a mixture of lime, tobacco and arecanut and smear this over the wound.
b) Grind the leaves of *Vellakkara* and smear this paste over the wound.
c) Mash thoroughly the leaves of *Kathivettu, Nare, Railgoodu* and apply this to the wound.
d) Grind finely the scrapings of bamboo, arecanut, lime and tobacco and apply this. This is particularly good for wound over nails and limbs.
e) The bark of *Karinaram* is ground to a paste and applied.

16. *Dysentery*

a) Mash the root of *Pattokadi* and *Venkayam*; and take a bit of it. This can be given also for stomachache.
b) The mash bark of *Kattinaliga* and the juice of it is given to drink.
c) Prepare a curry of *Kuppakeera and Karimkeera* adding *Venkayam* and eat.
d) The sap of *Vazhapindi* and eat *Mathalanaranga* and tender leaves of *Pena*.
e) Prepare a potion from the barks of *Thanni, Karimanam poosa* and drink.
f) Grind roots of *Pulivarakkedi* and smear this paste over the breast for few days.
g) Grind also a mixture of crab (*Palukally nyandu*), *Thunalli athic* and *Kallithi* leaves and smear this over the breast.

17. *Cholera*
    a) The roots of *Kana* and *Velluva* are roasted fine and given to eat.
    b) Grind finely the barks of teak, *Eeti* (rosewood) *kodivetti* and give to drink in milk in small doses.

18. *Vomiting*
    a) Juice from the bark of *Nelli (Emblica officinalis)* is given to drink. This is also used for cough.
    b) Grind the roots of *Pookkila* and *Paralu* and mix it with half a glass of water and drink.
    c) Chew the root of *Ulakudy* and swallow the juice.
    d) Chew the root of *Idampiri valampiri* and swallow the juice.
    e) For vomiting associated with drunken condition make the patient chew tender *Pena* leaves.
    f) Vomiting blood: Grind the barks of *Vyanaman karivenga* and *Cholavenga* and give the solution for drinking.
    g) A potion is prepared from the bark of *Passunkanni*; drink it.

19. *Stomachache*
    a) Prepare a solution of the north bound root of *Ulakudi* plant and drink.
    b) The tuber of *Goomle* is ground and is given to drink.
    c) The juice from *Thottukurinchi* leaves is given to drink.
    d) The bark of *Meenvaiyye* is given to drink.
    e) Mash the bark of *Muringa and Karu* and drink the solution twice a day for 68 days.
    f) Chew the root of *Kattuthipali* and swallow the juice.
    g) Grind the bark of mango tree, *Nava* and *Naggary* and eat this paste.
    h) Grind together the barks of *Sale Veke, Nulluvenga, Ampukana* and *Ekepa*. Solution of it is given to drink.
    i) Root of *Kozholinchi* is eaten in raw condition.

20. *Stomachache with constipation*
    a) Grind a mixture of *Panavally kizhangu* and leaves of *Nelli (Embilica officinalis)*; and the juice is given to drink.
    b) Mash ginger, tomatto, seasoned tamarind and solution of it is given to drink.

d) Chew the root of *Katapukodi* and swallow the juice twice a day.
e) The root of *Neela avara* is crushed and kept in water and this solution is filtered and given to drink.

21. *Worm infestation*
a) The fruit of *Palitnee* is given to drink.
b) The root of *Pookkala* is ground and a solution is prepared in water and drunk.
c) Prepare a curry from *Pattathakara* and given to eat.

22. *Jaundice*
a) Grind barks of *Ellappala, Kolakkatta danchi* and mix it with the milk of black sheep. Smear this mixture over the head. This is also given for urinary trouble.
b) Eat the meat of the *Kenki* nuts.
c) Grind finely the leaves of *Kattukonka -chrukonka, Velippa* and add little *Kalkandam* and drink thrice a day for five days.
d) Grind to a fine paste *Keezharnelli* and add this to a black sheep's milk and drink.
e) Mash finely the *Kolakatta* roots and add this to black sheep's milk and drink.
f) Grind tuber of *Poomparuthi* and add this to the urine of white sheep and drink.
g) Squeeze the bark of *Vake, Karimanan ezhilampala*; the juice is given to drink in small doses.

23. *Piles*
a) Grind the *Vam, Kattuchera* along with *Chovannulli* and apply this around the piles.
b) Mash the *Ooncha* plant fully and prepare a solution and drink in small doses.
c) A potion is prepared from the *Masakotte, Kadampu* and *Konke* and given to drink.
d) Grind the roots of *Chuth* and smear it over the head and take bath at two hour intervals.
e) Grind the nuts of *Konkam* and eat a bit of it. This can be used for preparation of bread.

24. *Chest pain*
a) Grind the roots of *Kovikkoodara Mullu* and give a solution of it

in water to drink.

b) The tender leaves of *Rathire* are squeezed for juice and this is given to drink.

c) Grind the roots of *Uvvapullu, Valampullu, and Chandanapullu* and mix this in water and give to drink.

25. *Odema*

a) Squeeze out the juice of leaves of *Neerupidussi* plant and smear this juice all over the body and take bath after half an hour.

b) A potion of *Kalpasam, Kalvanali* mixed with cow milk is given to drink twice a day for five days.

c) The juice of *Oyneakodya* is mixed with raw turmeric. This is smeared over the crevices of the foot.

26. *Burns*

a) Collect the ash from the dry leaves of *Anasha* and mix with coconut oil, and smear it over the burns by a feather.

b) The sap of *Venke* stem is smeared over the burns.

c) Powder charcoal of coconut shell finely, mix with coconut, and smear this paste over the burns.

d) Keep the affected part covered with wet cloth for one hour and smear coconut oil over the burns.

e) Grind the bark of teak and charcoal of coconut shell to a fine paste and mix with coconut oil, and smear over the burns.

f) Fry few leaves of *Thuvara (Nednem)* powder and add it to coconut oil, and smear this Ever the burns.

g) Collect the ash of *Arssumana* leaves and coconut shell and add this to coconut oil, and smear over the burns.

27. *Body pain*

a) Grind the bark of *Adekampu kenka koli* leaves of *Kenki*, and *Kadukessi* given to drink in small doses.

b) Grind the root of *Aerigonte* and smear it all over the body including head.

c) The root of *Pennavinam* is chewed and the juice swallowed .

d) The root of *Tharani* plant and garlic smashed together and smearred all over the body, and bath taken only after two hours.

e) Warm the leaves of *Bakhnathodtu* and give with them a hot massage over the chest.

28. *Epilepsy*

Collect oil from *Anjlikkakuru* and apply over the head. This is good also for madness.

29. *Sores*

Grind the roots of *Pagan* and *Jooli* and smear this paste over the sores.

30. *Abscess*

a) Grind the bark of *Gooli* and apply over the abscess.
b) Grind the bark of *Lavanke* and apply this over the abscess.
c) Grind the tuber of *Vantukadikodi* and apply this on the abscess.
d) Grind the barks of *Rajapunna, Kollan, Munne and Kadamba* to a paste and apply this over the abscess.
e) Mash the roots of *Oottu*, tuber of *Vellakuva*, and smear it over the abscess and also give to drink a potion of dry chilly, cummin seed and seasoned tamarind.
f) Mash finely the leaves of *Chimkathal, Cheruvenkayam* and apply this mash over the abscess.
g) Root of *Erumanalanki* is mixed with salt and mashed; and this is smeared over the abscess.
h) Mash the barks of *Thanni, Cheenka, Manhe poosa*; keep this mash over the abscess.
i) Grind the tuber of *Nuduga* plant and apply over the abscess.

31. *Smallpox*

A potion of *Nunul* leaves, *Chuvannulli, Venkayam* is given to drink. *Poovapazham* is given to eat.

32. *Snake-bite*

a) The tuber of *Opnna* is crushed and smeared over the bitten spot.
b) Grind finely the tuber of *Kalavally* and smear over the bitten part.
c) The tuber of *Vattakadu korukki* is mashed and is applied over the bitten part.

33. *Foot corn*

Collect the oil of *Dhesirumrakoya* (*Cheru*) and apply this on the foot corn.

34. *Scabbies*
   a) Mash the leaves and stems of *Pulissi* and bark of *Neeka* and apply this over the scabs.
   b) Grind the roots of *Thumba* and apply this paste continuously over the scabs. This is particularly for the scabies over the head.
   c) Add a pinch of salt in goat urine, and smear it over the scabbies and take bath after two hours.
   d) Leaves of white *Ponncha* are mashed and urine of white sheep is added and the mash smeared over the affected part.
   e) Bark of *Ooma* is smashed and applied over the scabbies.
   f) Grind the *Poovarusukaya* and smear it over the spot.
   g) Grind together tamarind *Chuvannulli* and the root of *Konappullu*, and apply this over this spot.

35. *Whooping cough*
   a) Prepare a medicated oil by adding *Tharni* plant in *gingili* oil and apply over the head.
   b) An oil *Tudari* and *Koriyandel* seeds in a closed pot and allow it to cool down; repeat this for 41 days, and afterwards apply this solution once a day 41 days. During this period only meat and fish must be avoided.
   c) Juice of the *Amos* is applied over the head.

36. *Cataract*
   The leaves of *Veluparithi* are squeezed for juice and this is given to drink.

37. *Mouth sores*
   Chew few leave of *Narakodi* and keep this in mouth for three to five hours.

Science and Superstition

Thus, in the preparation of therapeutic recipes the Irular employ both herbal and animal matter for a variety of illnesses to which they are exposed. There are specialists of such illnesses as jaundice, snake-bite, etc. Deities believed to be associated with smallpox, chickenpox and blood dysentery are also propitiated. In Irular perception the atmosphere is filled with spirits, some benevolent, some malevolent; the latter often causing sickness of malignant type, that is, what cannot be easily comprehended. For this they perform curing rites. But, as evident from the above list of recipes, their knowledge of herbal medicine is vast and it would be wrong to generalize that they are a people wedded to superstition. What can be said is that for them the dichotomy between science and superstition just does not exist. They have constructed a holistic worldview where the body, mind and spirit are inseparable. As and when the harmony between them is disturbed sickness and misfortunes arise. To bring things to order one has to return to the primal source of existence, the Nature. Hence the Irular's taking to herbal medicine and performing curing rites for some illnesses is not in contradiction, as it may appear, to 'modern' man.

BIOLOGICAL, PSYCOLOGICAL INTERPRETATIONS

7

SMALL TRIBAL POPULATIONS : OBSERVED PATTERNS OF FERTILITY AND MORTALITY

Arabinda Basu

Introduction

In India demographic information of small isolated populations is still inadequate. It is, therefore, important to undertake an analysis of these data in order to develop additional insights and understanding of the demographic processes that determine the growth and structure of human population and the variety of factors which influence their expansion and occasional contraction.

The core of the present study is the analysis of fertility and mortality data obtained from small tribal population of India for which reasonably adequate comparable data are available. Direct and indirect factors responsible for fertility and mortality differentials have also been considered. Few small tribal populations could not be selected for the purpose of our present analysis because the type of data desired are not available for some societies and analyses of their data are not available in organized form.

Material and Method

The specific objectives of this study are to examine, in brief, the demographic features of eight small populations belonging to five ethnic groups, viz. the Purum (Chote) (includes two Purum isolates), Pahira (includes three Pahira sub-samples), Mallia, Chenchu and Kota to compare and discuss the levels of fertility and mortality and their implications for population structure. In addition to these eight small populations, the demographic situation of the Onge of Little Andaman, one of the most primitive population groups now living in the world, has also been discussed. Primitive populations are of considerable interest to the anthropologists because they provide good estimates of response to the conditions under which most of man's evolution has taken place. Moreover, small population size does provide certain advantages. Because, it is sometimes possible to enumerate and construct genealogies for the entire population and to make an analysis on the basis of all individuals rather than a sample.

In order to make a comparative study of the fertility and mortality levels of the selected populations, the following measures have been used :

1. Total maternity ratio
2. Maternity ratio
3. Survival ratio
4. Infant mortality
5. Childhood mortality

The working definitions of the measures that have been followed in the present study are :

Total maternity ratio : Mean number of live births per woman when all living ever-married women of age 40 to 45 years and above are considered.

Maternity ratio : Mean number of live births per woman when all living ever-married women of all ages are considered.

Survival ratio : Ratio of the number of living children to the number of live births.

Infant mortality : Death of live-born children prior to one year of age.

Mortality before 15 years : Death of live-born children prior to 15 years of age.

Population Studied

Purum (Chote) : The Purum is a small tribe, virtually isolated population of 1464 individuals (according to the census taken by the author in May 1975), also inhabits in nine villages in the southern part of the Manipur valley. On the basis of marriage rules and social norms though Purum may be described as a single population, yet on the genetical perspective and on the basis of the mating pattern, the entire Purum population may be divided into two partially isolated, territorially defined populations, Purum I and Purum II. An analysis of their mating pattern indicates that the integrity of the Purum as a breeding unit has been substantially maintained in all the eight villages referred to here as Purum I even with prolonged experience of culture contact with the neighbouring Naga, Kuki and Meitei populations (admixture rate in Purum I population is only 2.8%). On the contrary, considerable evidence of admixture (admixture rate = 35.4%) with the surrounding Naga populations was noted among the Purum II. Inspite of a high rate of admixture in Purum II population, it is evident from the genealogical charts that selection of a potential mate, other than from their own community members, was limited to a few Naga tribes from neighbouring villages within a radius of 8 to 10 km only, thus maintaining both physical and cultural isolation within a well-defined territory for a considerable length of time.

Pahira : The Pahira is a small, primitive, food-gathering population, inhabiting the hills and forests of Ajodhya and the Dalma hill ranges in eastern India. Their total population, according to an enumeration during 1963-64, was 1,353 (Basu, 1969). They are divided into three partially endogamous sub-populations – Northern Pahira, Southern Pahira I and Southern Pahira II. The Northern Pahira inhabit the foothills and slopes of the Ajodhya hills in the district of Purulia, West Bengal and the Southern Pahira I and II inhabit in the Dalma hills and the ranges further west across the river Subarnarekha, in the districts of Singhbhum and Ranchi, Bihar.

Mallia : The Mallia, an endogamous population of 1,162 individuals, according to a census taken in June 1974 (Sahu, 1983), are found only in Kapileswar village of Bhubaneswar, Orissa. The traditional occupation of these people was to serve the deity and to take care of the Kapileswar temple. At present they have been compelled to accept other occupations also.

Chenchu : The Chenchu are an Australoid tribe living in several districts of Andhra Pradesh in Southern India. The data analysed in this report are derived from the Chenchus of Achampet Taluq of Mahaboobnagar district, Andhra Pradesh (Sirajuddin and Basu, 1984). The Chenchus of Nallamalai forest hills in Achampet Taluq are an extant group that still subsists in hunting-gathering stage with incipient agriculture. The Chenchu population of Achampet Taluq is isolated from the other populations of adjoining districts of Kurnool, Nalgonda and Prakasam. According to the 1971 Census there were 3,439 Chenchu inhabitants in Achampet Taluq.

Kota : The Kota, a small tribe, represents a segment of south Indian population which has remained isolated for a long time in the Nilgiri hills (Basu, 1972). Their population, according to the census taken by the author, in 1961, was 1,112. The Kota is an agricultural community, inhabiting in seven villages in the Nilgiris.

General Reproductive Characteristics

Various measures of reproductive performance are presented in Tables 7.1 and 7.2. The mean number of live births (Table 7.1), when living married women of all ages are considered, ranged from slightly more than three births per woman for the Kota to less than five births for a Purum II woman. Thus, we see that small populations under comparison do not seem to differ much in mean live births when married women of all ages are taken into consideration.

TABLE 7.1: **Number of live births, number of living children and survival ratio in respect of married women of all ages**

Population	No. of married women	Mean No. of live births per woman or maternity ratio	Mean No. of living children per woman	Survival ratio
Purum (Chote) I	251	3.97	3.26	0.82
Purum (Chote) II	37	4.68	3.68	0.79
Northern Pahira	80	3.35	2.00	0.60
Southern Pahira I	128	3.32	2.18	0.66
Southern Pahira II	144	3.70	2.15	0.58
Mallia	-	-	-	-
Chenchu	504	3.67	2.66	0.72
Kota	326	3.11	1.63	0.53

Table 7.1 also provides mean number of children living at the time of the survey. Mean ranges from 1.63 among the Kota women to 3.68 among the Purum II women. Since there were significant differences between the samples in the mean number of living children (particularly between Kota and Purum women), a measure of child

survival, i.e. the survival ratio, has been calculated. The ratio of the number of living children to the number of live births was computed for each population.

TABLE 7.2: **Number of live births, number of living children and survival ratio in respect of married women 40 (or 45) years and above**

Population	No. of women	Age	Mean number of live births per woman or total maternity ratio	Mean number of living children per woman	Survival ratio
Purum (Chote) I	82	45 & above	5.04	3.78	0.75
Purum (Chote) II	14	-do-	4.57	2.79	0.61
Northern Pahira	9	-do-	6.44	3.44	0.53
Southern Pahira I	16	-do-	6.38	3.25	0.51
Southern Pahira II	11	-do-	6.18	4.18	0.68
Mallia			6.33	3.20	0.51
Chenchu	146	40 & above	5.70	3.81	0.67
Kota	120	-do-	4.11	1.78	0.43

Completed Fertility

Completed fertility is generally defined as the total reproductive performance of women who have completed the child-bearing period, women 45 years or more years of age. In the present analysis, women 40 to 44 years of age were also included.

The mean number of live births, of living children, and the mean survival ratio for women aged 40 or above for the eight populations are presented in Table 7.2. The mean number of live births ranged from slightly more than four for Kota women to slightly more than six for Northern Pahira women. Kota's overall mean number of offspring (4.11 per completed family) is considerably lower than most of the other small populations compared. The mean number of living children on the other hand ranged from slightly fewer than two children for Kota women to slightly more than four children for Southern Pahira II women, indicating significant differences in the number of living children between some of the population groups compared. It is further evident that the survival ratio – ratio of living children to total live births – is significantly lower for Kota, Mallia, Southern Pahira I and Northern Pahira in comparison to the ratio worked out for Purum,

Southern Pahira I and Chenchu populations as a result of relatively increased infant and child mortality.

Child Mortality

In Table 7.3 infant mortality and child mortality rates (mortality before 15 years) for each population group are presented. Infant mortality rates, reflecting deaths of live-born children prior to one year of age, are extremely high in Mallia and Kota populations in comparison to the rates estimated for Purum I, Purum II and Chenchu populations. Mortality before the age of reproduction (i.e. 15 years), an important measure of mortality, is also very high in Kota and three Pahira subsamples.

TABLE 7.3: **Infant mortality and mortality before 15 years of age**

	Total No. of live births	Mortality			
		Before 1 year		Before 15 years	
		No.	%	No.	%
Purum (Chote) I .	1000	55	5.50	164	16.40
Purum (Chote)II	173	19	10.98	32	18.49
Northern Pahira	365	-	-	164	44.93
Southern Pahira I	534	-	-	185	34.64
Southern Pahira II	662	-	-	216	32.63
Mallia	-	-	29.1	-	-
Chenchu	1852	216	11.66	484	26.13
Kota	1015	217	21.38	450	44.3

Levels of Fertility and Mortality

Fertility and mortality in each of the eight populations are presented in Table 7.4. The fertility levels of the population groups obtained from the value of total maternity ratio are presented in Table 7.5. Here the three-point scale of Nag (1962) has been slightly modified to four-point scale which I feel will be better suited for the range of particular fertility measure used here in the context of Indian populations. Mortality levels have been determined modifying slightly the conditions proposed by Nag (1962). The population groups that fulfil any of the following three conditions have been rated as high on a scale of child mortality: (1) 12 per cent or more of the children died before age 1 year; (2) 30 per cent or more of the children died before age 15 years; (3) 35 per cent or more of the children born to all living women were dead at the time of investigation. Populations that do not fulfil any of the above conditions have been rated as low in the scale.

TABLE 7.4: **Completed fertility levels and mortality levels in small populations derived from total maternity ratio and childhood mortality**

Scale of fertility level obtained from the value of total maternity ratio	Population groups according to levels of fertility	Scale of mortality levels obtained from mortality before 1 year & mortality before 15 years	Population groups according to levels of mortality
Very low (up to 2.50)		Low	Purum I, Purum II, Chenchu.
Low (2.51-3.50)	Kota	High	Northern Pahira, Southern Pahira I, Southern Pahira II, Mallia, Kota.
Moderately high (3.51-4.50)	Purum I, Purum II, Chenchu.		
High (4.51+)	Northern Pahira, Southern Pahira I, Southern Pahira II, Mallia.		

It is evident that fertility levels of small populations studied vary considerably. The extent of variability can be observed from the completed fertility levels of each population obtained from the values of total maternity ratio presented in Table 7.2. The lowest value of the total maternity ratio among the small populations is 4.11 (Kota) and the highest value is 6.44 (Northern Pahira). It can be observed from Table 7.4 that the fertility levels of four populations (Northern Pahira, Southern Pahira I, Southern Pahira II and Mallia) are high.

Table 7.4 also provides the levels of mortality of small populations on the basis of the scale of child mortality obtained from the values of infant and child mortality presented in Table 7.2. It can be observed from Table 7.4 that all the four population groups (i.e. N.P., S.P.I., S.P. II and Mallia) having high fertility levels are rated high in the scale of child mortality also, but all these populations do not show a decreasing trend. It may also be seen that populations (Purum I and Purum II and Chenchu) having moderately high fertility levels are rated low on the scale of child mortality. The remaining population group, Kota, reported to have a stable population, exhibit relatively low fertility and a very high rate of mortality.

Genetic Drift

Laskar and Kaplan (1964) formulated a measure of estimating the potential for drift to occur in a population. This measure, the co-efficient of breeding isolation, is calculated by multiplying effective population size (Ne) by the admixture rate and gives a good indication of the relative degree of reproductive isolation experienced by a breeding population. The smaller the coefficient the more the isolation, and greater the likelihood of random genetic drift within the population. According to Laskar and Kaplan the genetic drift is expected to have a considerable effect on the micro-differentiation of a population with a coefficient of five or less, but it would have only a slight effect in a population with a coefficient greater than 50. The coefficients of breeding isolation for the small populations of India are presented in Table 5. The coefficient of breeding isolation is 1.01 in Kota, 7.3 in Chenchu, 7.2 in Mallia, 7.6 in Northern Pahira and 10.2 in Purum I which indicates that genetic micro-differentiation due to random genetic drift is appreciable in these five isolates. Particularly in Kota the effect of drift is much more intense than in other populations compared. On the other hand, in two Pahira sub-samples (S.P. I and S.P. II) the coefficients of 49.92 and 45.97 indicate that genetic drift has a slight potential for differentiating the population.

Selection Intensity

The index of potential selection (Crow, 1958) incorporate fertility and mortality results in a single measure and this index is customarily used to indicate the potential effectiveness of selection. The values in small populations of India (Table 7.5) with the lone exception of Kota are distributed in a relatively narrow range between the extremes 0.31 (among Purum I) and 0.95 (among Mallia), and the values fall more towards the lower limits of the range 0.23 to 3.69 observed in 64 populations in different levels of culture by Sphuler (1976).

TABLE 7.5: **Breeding size, effective population size, coefficient of breeding isolation, variance due to drift and selection intensity**

	Year of study	Breeding size (N)	Effective population size (N_e)	Coefficient of breeding isolation (N_{em})	Variance due to drift (σdq^2) (when q=0.5)	Selection Intensity		
						I_m	I_f	I
Purum (Chote) I	1975	459	448	10.17	0.000279	0.198	0.095	0.312
Purum (Chote) II	1975	56	50	17.72	0.002515	0.227	0.122	0.377
Northern Pahira	1963-64	122	121	7.64	0.001033	0.815	0.175	1.133
Southern Pahira I	1963-64	204	192	49.92	0.000651	0.529	0.137	0.735
Southern Pahira II	1963-64	222	170	45.97	0.000735	0.484	0.137	0.687
Mallia	1974	-	430.7	7.2	-	0.687	0.159	0.951
Chenchu	1981	826	569	7.3	0.000220	0.501	0.204	0.808
Kota	1961	507	403	1.01	0.000360	0.79	0.83	2.25

Demographic Situation in Kota and Ongee Populations

Kota is one of the few populations in India that is experiencing numerical stabilization (Table 7.6). Since 1901 Kota population has remained virtually static or shows a slight downward trend. The fertility levels of the Kota do not appear to be unusually low compared to those other non-industrial or primitive societies like Ongee, Chenchu, etc., and are certainly high enough at least to sustain a moderately slow rate of population increase. The 4.1 live births in completed sibships indicate that fertility levels of the Kota accord well with many of the Indian tribal samples. On the contrary the average number of surviving off-spring in completed families is only 1.8 (Basu, 1972). Infertility appears to be much higher among the Kota than in the population of simple agriculturists, where it averages 3.5 per cent (Neel, 1958). The level of fertility of Kota women is thus partially offset or neutralized by the high incidence of infant and childhood mortality and partly to infertility in Kota women of 40 years and above.

TABLE 7.6: **Population figures of Kota and Ongee since 1901**

Year	Kota	Ongee
1901	1267	672
1911	1163	631
1921	1204	343
1931	1121	250
1941	952	150
1961	1112	129
1971	-	112

Of the small populations of the Andaman Islands mention may be made about the Jarawa, Sentinelese and Ongee. They are the remnants of the most primitive populations and are still living in a hunting and gathering stage of economy. The size of population of these communities is very small and some are beyond the stage of survivality. The Jarawas live in the western part of the south and middle Andamans. In a rough estimation the total Jarawa population has been recorded as 250 (Pandit, 1982). The Sentinelese live in the North Sentinel Island and their population, according to the 1971 Census, is around 100. Both the Jarawas and the Sentinelese have virtually no contact with the people living outside their territory.

In comparison to the Jarawas and Sentinelese the Onges of the Little Andaman are more exposed to longer society and their forest ecology has been disturbed to a great extent. In spite of this contact the Ongee still depends, to some extent, on hunting, fishing and collection of honey and wild produce from the forest.

The Ongee have experienced an uninterrupted decline in population since 1901 (Table 7.6). Over the years, since 1901, the population showed a fall of more than 83 per cent.

As the population of the Ongee has never been reliably or scientifically measured demographically, no systematic publications of the results are yet available on the actual demographic situation in order to ascertain the factors responsible for such a rapid rate of decline of the Ongee population since 1901 or even earlier. Some sporadic information concerning the demographic situation and composition of Ongee population as existed during 1955-56, 1963 and 1969 has been reported by Nigam (1962), Agrawal (1967) and De (1970), respectively.

Factors responsible for the decline in Ongee population have been discussed by some earlier authors. Cipriani (1966) and Agrawal have stated that decline in the Ongee population is due to high infant mortality while, according to Ganguly (1975), the decline is due primarily to extremely low fertility; Chaudhury (1967), on the other hand, stated that limited food supply and hazards of Ongee life are partly responsible for the retarded growth of Ongee population. But observations about the decline in the Ongee population so far repeated seem to me not based on precise and adequate data.

According to the 1977 estimation of the Anthropological Survey, the present strength of the Ongee population is a meagre 105. This clearly indicates that the population has come to a stage of total extinction. In fact diminution of number below a certain point destroys the demographic structure when resurgence becomes impossible. Livi (1949) also on the basis of his observation of the demographic situation on the number of small isolated populations found that those populations which are between 300 and 500 individuals may not be self-sustaining and have a high probability of dying out. In each population like the Onge, an analysis of potential mate pools would make it possible to evaluate the demographic and cultural determinants of the extinction process. Among the Ongee, the number of individuals in any age group may be so small and variable that the actual opportunities for availability of potential mates into that class may be limited. Besides opportunities afforded by the demographic structure of the population, the limits of availability of potential mates are also determined by cultural norms governing family relationship of mates.

Discussion

According to child replacement, or child survival hypothesis, of Notestein (1945: 30), increasing child mortality has often been associated with increased fertility. The extent to which this increased fertility compensates for child mortality, and the extent to which the effects are volitional is not distinctly clear. In the present analysis of small populations we have observed that at least in four populations (three Pahira sub-samples and the Mallia), out of eight populations examined, the high fertility can be associated with high mortality. On the other hand, in two Purum isolates and Chenchu populations the situation is somewhat different, where a moderately high level of fertility is not in response to high child mortality, rather levels of mortality in them may be rated as low. Kota of the Nilgiri hills, however, exhibit somewhat low fertility and very high level of infant and childhood mortality. It is thus seen that fertility and mortality levels of small populations of India are not similar.

The problem of the rapid state of depopulation of the Ongee is a matter of serious concern and needs immediate attention. We are aware that the growth and decline of a population depend not only on the fertility level but also on the mortality level and a balance of emigration and immigration. We have no record of any in-migration or out-migration so far as Ongee population is considered.

Plausible factors that may affect fertility levels and increase mortality rate can now be discussed. It has been stated that all human cultures exhibit a variety of biocultural mechanisms which regulate or limit reproduction. The low fertility levels in the population could be ascribed, in part, to the interaction of social factors that delay age at marriage and first pregnancy. The lower fertility may also be due to inadequate nutrition causing delayed menarche, longer than usual adolescent sterility period, irregularity or cessation of menstrual cycle, frequent occurrence of reproductive wastage and early menopause. Inadequate nutrition and poor health condition may retard intra-uterine growth and development and depress fertility by increasing ante-natal mortality.

Possible primary effects of blood groups, i.e. ABO(H) blood incompatibility as a cause of infertility, or affecting the number of pregnancies, among the fertile can be seen in the Ongee population.

It is apparent from the foregoing analysis that reliable basic data and relevant demographic information for proper measurements of the levels of fertility and mortality and factors responsible for rapid diminution of the Ongee population are still lacking. A proper evaluation of the state or nutrition and health of the Ongee population is, therefore, indispensable for health planning and supervision. We have also to examine contributing factors responsible for such a high rate of decline in the Ongee population.

The Kota are not an increasing population but are rated as a stable and constant population, and their demographic situation is not as severe as that of the Ongee. Diseases and factors associated with a high incidence of infant and child mortality and infertility in completed families among the Kota are to be properly examined and adequate measures initiated so that mortality decreases and the rate of population growth increases gradually.

REFERENCES

Agrawal, H.N. 1967. Reproductive life of Ongee women. *Vanyajati*, 15: 1239-149.

Basu, A. 1969. The Pahira: a population genetical study. *Am. J. Phys. Anthrop.*, 31:399-4516.

Basu, Arabinda 1972. A demographic study of the Kota of Nilgiri hills, *J. Indian Anthrop. Soc.*, 7: 29-45.

Basu Arabinda 1985. Contemporary demographic pattern of the Purum (Chote) with special reference to fertility and mortality. *Symposium on Purum (Chote) revisited.*

Chaudhury, N.C. 1967. Tribes of Andaman Islands. *India Museum Bulletin* 1: 51-58.

Cipriani, L. 1966. *The Andaman Islanders*. Weidenfeld and Nicholson, New York.

Crow, J.F. 1958. Some possibilities for measuring selection intensities in man. *Human Biol.* 30: 1-13.

De, D.C. 1970. A demographic study of the Ongee of Little Andaman. *Bull. Anthrop. Surv. of India*, 19: 1-16.

Ganguly, P. 1975. The Negritos of Little Andaman Island. *India Museum Bulletin* 10: 7-27.

Laskar, G.W. and B. Kaplan 1964. The coefficient of breeding isolation: population size, migration ratio, and the possibilities for ransom genetic drift in six human communities in northern Peru. *Human Biol.* 36: 327-328.

Livi, Livio 1949. Considerations theoriques et practiques sur le concept de minimum population. *Population Rev. Trim. de l'I.N.E.D.* 4: 754-756.

Nag, M. 1962. *Factors affecting human fertility in non-industrial societies : a cross-cultural study*. Yale University Publications in Anthropology, No.66.

Neel, J.V. 1958. The study of natural selection in primitive and civilized human populations, *Hum. Biol.*, 30: 43-72.

Nigam, R.C. 1962. The Ongee of Little Andaman - their settlements and populations. *Vanyajati* 10: 44-53.

Notestein, F.W. 1945. Population - the long view. *Food for the world.* T.W. Schultz (ed.). University of Chicago Press, Chicago, pp.36-57.

Pandit, T.N. 1982. Economy of the Onge. *Economic of the tribes and their transformation.* K.S. Singh (ed.) pp.183-193.

Sahu, P.N. 1983. Demographic and genetic constitution of a small population (the Mallia). *J. Indian Anthrop. Soc.*, 18: 55-60.

Sirajuddin, S.M. and Arabinda Basu 1984. Population structure, consanguinity and its effect on fertility and mortality among Chenchu of Andhra Pradesh. *Human Science* 33.

Spuhler, J. 1976. The maximum opportunity for natural selection in some human populations. *Demographic anthropology: Quantitative approaches.* E. Zubrow (ed.). University of New Mexico Press, Actuquerque, pp.185-226.

8

TRIBAL VALUE PATTERN : A CASE STUDY OF THE SANTALS

Lal Bahadur Singh and **Balanand Sinha**

Introduction

Tribes constitute about eight per cent of India's population. The Santals are one of the most important and numerically the largest homogeneous tribes of India. Concentrated mainly in the south-eastern plateau of Bihar, especially in the division of Santal Pargana, the Santals are not only remembered for their remarkable patriotic role in the war of Independence but are also admired for maintaining a distinct cultural personality. In recent years a good deal of interest has been evinced to understand tribal values (Manekar, 1972; Pandey & Singh, 1971). The present study was intended to explore the extent and composition of different values inherent in the life of the Santals.

The Santals have been characterized as follows: They are frank, open, honest and gentle, and have a natural love for calm, conscientious and happy life (Singh & Singh, 1982). They believe in social justice; any immoral and licentious act does not go unpunished (Singh & Singh, 1982). The Santals have a simple but highly respected social code of morality which helps them maintain their social solidarity, integrity and identity (Roy Choudhary, 1961).

A number of studies (Sachchidananda, 1965; Singh & Sinha, 1982; Surajit Sinha, 1957) have depicted the Santal's life as replete with high religious values. Consequently, their convictions and beliefs in religion work as an indispensable force in shaping their life from the cradle to the grave. Other studies (Das & Das, 1980; Majumdar, 1956; Triosi, 1979) show that change and modernization have not significantly altered their religious ideas and beliefs; their deep attachment to religion remains intact. They follow religious principles and dogmas quite meticulously.

Soren (1979), himself a Santal, has described Santals' love for their society: The Santals put the consideration of 'society' above the ambitions of 'individuals'. Their community life is well-organized and may be called a 'model of corporate living'. It rests on the concept and practice of equality, fraternity and social justice permeated through the idealism of socialism and democracy (D.P. Sinha, 1972). Kochar (1966) has described the Santals as having a very high level of social cohesion and social identity. The principle of togetherness and the spirit of brotherhood are greatly valued by them.

The Santals are very fond of music and dance (Bhattacharya, 1964). Art and painting have a special place in their life (Archer, 1975; Bhowmik, 1971). They prefer a life hemmed with natural beauty (Chattopadhya, 1972). All these attributes, adorning the life of the Santals, reflect the richness of their aesthetic values.

The Santals are now politically much more aware and conscious than they were ever before. Indistinctively there is a collective desire for self-governance. This desire has been expressed quite covertly, in the recent years, in the Jharkhand Movement. Their belief in traditional political system is deep rooted (Sachchidananda, 1972; Singh & Sinha, 1982). Traditional political dogmas continue to guide their political life to a great extent. They are, however, pacifists and have firm faith in democracy, socialism and civic liberty. Thus, so far as the political life is concerned, the Santals seem to be in a state of flux.

The tribals possess low economic value. Rath (1974) has pointed out that the tribals have a lower level of aspirations for income, education and occupation. Surajit Sinha (1957) holds a similar view. According to him, indifference towards a desire for high status and lower level of aspirations in terms of material gains are the characteristic features of the tribals. The same is true of the Santals.

Traditionality and orthodoxy governing the attitudes and behaviour pattern of Santals (Singh & Sinha, 1982; Soren, 1983) supposedly inhibit their potentiality for discovery and invention. Further, the tribals in general, and the Santals in particular, are often observed as being comparatively weak in their intellectual ability and lacking in scientific and numerical aptitudes (Singh & Sinha, 1983). Their way of thinking and behaving is simple and unsophisticated in the modern sense. A close observation of their temperament reveals that they are better fitted for manual exigencies; sophisticated sensory and motor activities do not match their temperament.

Thus, the analysis of the lifestyle and temperament of the Santals provides an *a priori* ground to characterize them as possessing a fair amount of religious, moral, social and aesthetic values and a low amount of economic and theoretical values. However, there is nothing conclusive as regards their political values.

Method

Subjects

One hundred and fifty Santals and 100 non-Santal uneducated youths, selected randomly from the villages of Godda district of Santal Pargana division of Bihar, served as subjects for the present investigation. Youths represent the larger bulk of the population of Santal Pargana They are in fact the dynamic force behind the making of a society and also symbolically the hope of a 'healthy' society. The specific reason for choosing Godda as the venue of the present investigation was that it is located in an interior and remote hilly tract which has not so far received much attention of the investigators. The respondents of this region are comparatively free from frequent and excessive experimental treatment and thus were expected to give their natural responses. Apparently, they were found to be more suitable for the present research than their counterparts from other regions of Santal Pargana. The two groups of subjects were comparable in terms of their age (18 to 24 years), sex (male) and economic condition (income ranging from Rs. 400 to Rs. 800 per month). The principle of randomization was not only followed in the selection of sample but also taken into consideration in the choice of villages from which subjects were chosen.

Test used

A value-ranking test developed by Dwivedi (1978) was used to assess value preferences of the subjects. The test measured preferences in seven value-areas such as theoretical, political, economic, social, aesthetic, religious and moral. There were eight items in each area. Thus, in all, the scale consisted of 56 items. The minimum and maximum scores one could obtain for each value area ranged between 8 and 56. A higher score was indicative of a high value-pattern in the concerned area and *vice versa*. Though the test had sufficient reliability, it was decided to compute it afresh by applying the test to a mixed group of 50 Santal and 50 non-Santal subjects. The computed alpha coefficient with r_{ij} of each dimension is presented in Table 8.1.

TABLE 8.1: **Showing alpha coefficient and r_{ij} of different value-patterns**

Value Pattern	Theoretical (8)	Political (8)	Economic (8)	Social (8)	Aesthetic (8)	Religious (8)	Moral (8)
Alpha	.59	.61	.71	.67	.66	.74	.62
r_{ij}	.15	.16	.23	.20	.20	.26	.17

Note: Number in parentheses below each value-pattern indicates the number of items related to each of the value-area.

The scale was converted into interview schedule before administering it. This was done keeping in mind the fact that the sample consisted of illiterate subjects.

Results and Discussion

In order to ascertain the interrelationship among the different value-patterns zero-order correlation was computed on the basis of pooled scores. Table 8.2 shows the findings.

The correlational analysis of data revealed that all the value-patterns were significantly interlinked with one another (r = .11 to .57) and bent upon to form a logical and meaningful cluster among them. Remarkably, social, religious and moral values were found to be highly interdependent (p = <.01), showing a highly positive relationship between social and religious attitudes (r = .59) but negative association between social and moral (r = .32) and religious and moral (p = <.01) attitudes. The present findings, however, lend support to the typical Indian mythological and philosophical proposition that high social values help in the development of religious feelings which, in turn, make an individual moralistic in his approach towards life. This assumption is also in tune with the observation of Saraswati (1977) who has suggested that religion emphasizes man's internal development and determines his way of life by ethical or moral values derived from faith.

Table 8.3 shows the summary of statistical comparison between the Santal and non-Santal students in terms of their value-patterns. A cursory look at the results reveals that while the Santals had significantly lower theoretical, political and economic values, they were well-endowed with social, aesthetic, religious and moral values. Interestingly, when the values among the Santals were arranged hierarchically, social value (Mean = 39.53) was found to be on the top and the theoretical value (Mean = 28.66) at the bottom of the hierarchy. Religious, moral, aesthetic, political and economic values received respective positions in the value hierarchy of the Santals. The reasons advanced to deal with the findings are give in the following headings.

TABLE 8.2: **Intercorrelations among different value-patterns**

Value-Pattern	1	2	3	4	5	6	7
1. Theoretical	x	17*	24*	15**	31*	13*	11
2. Political		x	28*	23*	12**	19*	14**
3. Economic			x	18*	16*	15**	12**
4. Social				x	21*	57*	39*
5. Aesthetic					x	27*	27*
6. Religious						x	43*
7. Moral							x

Note: Decimals are omitted; N = 250.
* $p<.01$; **$p<.05$

TABLE 8.3: **Showing comparison between Santals and non-Santals in terms of their different value-patterns**

Value Pattern	Santals (N=150)		Non Santals (N=100)		
	Mean	SD	Mean	SD	CR
Theoretical	28.66	5.11	37.54	5.88	12.33*
Political	32.37	4.77	35.81	6.21	4.71*
Economic	29.23	4.19	34.13	4.99	8.30*
Social	39.53	6.15	29.68	5.14	13.87*
Aesthetic	34.26	4.72	29.17	5.13	7.95*
Religious	37.46	6.01	31.97	4.80	8.07*
Moral	35.05	5.03	28.85	5.16	9.39*

Note: *$p<.01$; df = 248

Theoretical value

The Santals seem to be deficient in scientific zeal and aptitudes (P.R.

Sinha, 1982), the significant ingredients of theoretical value. They seem to be highly suited for manual jobs and not so for jobs requiring high skills. This explains why in comparison to the non-Santals they have significantly low theoretical values. Further, following a lead from the study by Majumdar (1961), it appears that the Santals are reality-evading, and their thinking and approach to life are often inadequate in the modern sense on account of their inherent traditionality, superstitions and orthodoxy. This also allegedly mars sufficient development of theoretical values among them.

Political value

Hymann (1959), the conceptual father of political socialization, has suggested that social institutions through their pattern of socialization, help in the development of culturally shared political values. In the case of the Santals social institutions and organizations like *khut* (family, lineage), *dhumkuria* (youth dormatory), *rajabasa* (*gram panchayat*), *kulhi durup* (a Santal form of *panchayat*), *jaherthan* (the sacred grove), *manjhi-than* (seat of the spirit of the founder headman of the village), *lobir* (hunt-council, the highest court of appeal), etc., contribute more to the socio-religious values than to political values and thus to an extent impede the development of political values among the Santals.

Kothari's (1970) concept of centre and periphery represents the two strands of political currents 'modernism' and 'traditionalism'. People concentrated in the 'centre' are considered to be more politically oriented and modern, while people lying on the 'periphery' of the society are less politically oriented and conscious and are more traditional in their political outlook.

As is obvious, the Santals are placed on the fringe of the Indian social structure. Despite the best efforts of national agencies they are still socially segregated and deprived people. The concept of 'centre' and 'periphery' fits well in the explanation of the low political values among the Santals.

In this connection it is also pertinent to mention here that the acquisition of political values by individuals largely depends upon their interaction with politically oriented people. Apparently, it shows the importance of social and political interaction in the internalization of political values. The Santals, on account of their shy, submissive, non-interfering temperament, and a strong in-group feeling, do not like to come forward for mixing, interacting and exchanging their ideas with their non-Santal counterparts who are politically more conscious and aware. Thus, the reason for the Santals exhibiting low political values can be attributed to their unique temperament, lack of sufficient opportunity and inadequate exposure to political stimulation.

Economic value

Orthodoxy and superstitions guiding the life of the Santals may be considered to be the contributory factors in the inculcation of low economic values among them. Weber (1958) in his *The Protestant ethic and spirit of capitalism* has contended that motivations and attitudes are the seeds of economic development. To him an individual causes his own poverty. McClelland (1961) has also underlined a similar notion. He subscribes to this view that orthodoxy and fatalistic outlook act as drags to the achieving tendency. The Santals are comparatively more traditional and orthodox in their attitudes and behaviour. Despite significant social, economic, cultural and technological exposure they still believe in the old practices and operation of traditional economic system – agriculture, the prime source of their subsistence (Donald, 1976; Verma, 1977). As Banerjee and Sarkar (1964) have observed, they are indifferent towards the use of modern technology. Thus the development of low economic values among the Santals is perhaps rooted in their traditionalistic viewpoint and the lack of will to change.

Social value

Segregated and isolated social groups in general have a high feeling of social insecurity. In order to get rid of such feelings they remain united. This in turn inculcates an intense feeling of togetherness in them. The Santals, because of their inherent traditionality and feeling of being in minority and social isolation, despite the considerable impact of social change and modernization, feel themselves to be socially insecure and consequently develop a strong in-group feeling and deep attachment to their society. For the Santals, service to society is an act of great virtue. The principle of equality, fraternity and social justice – the components of an 'ideal society' – is highly valued by the Santals (D.P. Sinha, 1972). 'Feeling of togetherness' is the characteristic feature of their life. The Santal villages are not merely clusters of families living in physical proximity but human habitations bound together by bonds of blood and commonness of interest. Thus, reasons for the Santals possessing high social values may be understood in the light of the structure and composition of their society and the feelings and emotions generated therein.

Aesthetic value

It can be commonly observed that the Santals generally reside amidst physical surroundings full of natural beauty and aesthetic richness considered to be stimulating and conducive for the development of high aesthetic values among them. Search for symmetry (beauty of form) is greatly valued by the Santals. Singh *et al.* (1987) have found that there is no dearth of aesthetic aptitude among the Santals. These observations may provide clues to the reasons behind the Santals scoring high on aesthetic values.

Religious value

Values are internalized during the process of socialization. Parents and other primary caretakers as well as other members of society play an important role in this process (Tandon, 1981). They serve as models of imitations for their children. The method of socialization adopted by them contributes towards the development of a certain value-pattern. The Santal parents are more religious and are very particular about the need of their children to learn religious ways, principles and values. The Santal children learn from religious folklore and stories which are important modes of value-transmission. The frequent viewing of and taking part in socio-religious customs, ritualistic observances and ceremonies and festive occasions like *karama, sohrae, sakrat, baha, magh sim, erok sim, mak more*, etc., help culturally shared value-modelling from the very beginning of a Santal life. Thus they imbibe high religious values.

Moral value

The Santals, in general, are frank, open and gentle and have a considerable faith in the principles of honesty, probity and dutifulness. They dislike unscrupulous deeds and are lovers of a calm, conscientious and happy life. They aspire to lead a just life. Violation of social justice is unpardonable for them. As Roy Choudhary (1961) has observed the Santals maintain a high standard of morality. They are conscientious and the rate of crimes of any sort in their society is negligible. Further, following Pandey (1985), conservatives are having high moral values. The Santals, on account of being relatively more conservative and orthodox (Jha, 1986), may, therefore, have high moral values.

Social deprivation encourages development of a socio-religious attitude and a sense of morality. The inherent social isolation, downtroddenness, tribalism and the traumatic feelings of minority provide enough ground for the Santals to consider themselves as one of the deprived sections of Indian society. Hence, this can also be taken as a reason for their being high on moral values.

REFERENCES

Archer, W.G. 1975. *The hill of flutes: life, love and poetry in tribal India*, New Delhi: S. Chand & Co.

Banerjee, H.N. and Sarkar, A.K. 1964. A study on the agricultural activities and ritualistic performances among the Santal of Belpahari. *Bulletin of the Cultural Research Institute*, Calcutta, 3, 52-61.

Bhattacharya, S.S. 1964. *Woodland verses, Bulletin of the Cultural Research Institute*, Calcutta, 3, 49-64.

Bhowmik, K.L. 1971. *Tribal India: a profile in Indian ethnology*, Calcutta: The World Press.

Chattopadhya, G. 1972. *The problem of tribal integration to urban industrial society: a theoretical approach*, K.S. Singh (ed.) *Tribal Situation in India*, Simla.

Das, K.K. and Das, T. 1980. Modernization of Santal communities of India, *Vanyajati*, 28, 3-19.

Dwivedi, K. 1978. *Value test*, Agra: Psychological Research Cell.

Donald, R.T. 1976. Santal religion, self-identification and socialization in Sohrae, harvest festival, *Man in India*, 56, 215-236.

Hymann, H. G. 1959. *Political socialization*, Glencoere: The Free Press.

Jha, S.K. 1986. *Family structure, parental behaviour and conservatism in tribal and non-tribal college students of Santal Parganas*, Unpublished Ph.D. Thesis, Bhagalpur University, Bhagalpur.

Kochar, V.K. 1966. Village organization among the Santals, *Bulletin of Cultural Research Institute*, Calcutta, 5, 11-19.

Kothari, R. 1970. *Politics in India*, New Delhi: Orient Longman.

Majumdar, D.N. 1956. *The Santal: a study in cultural change*, Manager of Publications, Govt. of India.

Majumdar, D.N. 1961. *Races and cultures of India*, Bombay: Asia Publishing House.

Mankekar, D.R. 1972. Understanding the tribals on the north-eastern border, K.S. Singh (ed.) *Tribal situation in India*, Simla.

McClelland, D.C. 1961. *The achieving society*, New Jersey: D. Van Nostrand.

Pandey, N.K. 1985. *Some psychological correlates of morality among college students*. Unpublished Ph.D. Thesis, L.N. Mithla University, Darbhanga.

Pandey, U.D. and Singh, R.P. 1971. The effect of sex and culture on achievement motivation, religious beliefs and religious practices, *Journal of Psychological Researches*, 5, 49-52.

Rath, R. 1974. From social isolation to stagnation: a study of Scheduled Caste groups, *Social Action*, 24, 101-116.

Roy Chaudhury, P.G. 1961. Bitlaha: a Santal ritual, *The Quarterly Journal of Mythic Society*, 52, 1-5.

Sachchidananda, 1972. The tribal situation in Bihar, K.S. Singh (ed.), *Tribal situation in India*, Indian Institute of Advanced Study, Simla.

Saraswati, Baidyanath 1977. Anthropological approach to the study of religion, Surajit Sinha (ed.) *Anthropology in India*, Vol.1., Calcutta: Anthropological Survey of India.

Singh, L.B. and Singh, I.K. 1982. Life of the Santals: from an elaborate angle, *Vanyajati*, 30, 25-31.

Singh, L.B., Singh, C.B.P. and Rani, A. 1987. Level of occupational aspiration and interest-pattern among Santal students, *Journal of Social and Economic Studies* (Under Communication).

Singh, L.B. and Sinha, B.N. 1982. Attitude of the Santal students: an empirical analysis, *Indian Journal of Social Work*, 43, 11-18.

Singh, L.B. and Sinha, B.N. 1983. The Santal Students: Their Intelligence and achievement motivation, *Indian Journal of Social Work*, 44, 167-173.

Sinha, D.P. 1972. *A study in traditional rural political institutions of tribals specially Santals in the district of Santal Parganas*; Unpublished Ph.D. Thesis, Deptt. of Pol.Science, Bhagalpur University, Bhagalpur.

Sinha, P.R. 1982. *A study of occupational aspiration values and vocational interest of Santal students of Bhagalpur University*, Unpublished Ph.D.Thesis Bhagalpur University.

Sinha, Surajit 1957. Tribal culture of Peninsular India, *Man in India*, 37, 62-71.

Soren, B. 1979. Santal Samaj O Samskriti Vivartan (Evolution of society and culture of the Santal), Surajit Sinha (ed.), *Rarh Anchaler Samaj O Samskriti: Gathan O Vivartan*, Proceedings of a Seminar held at Santiniketan.

Soren, B. 1983. Problems of education among the Santals and other Backward Communities, *Vanyajati*, 31, 12-16

Tandon, T. 1981. Process of transmission of values in the Indian child, D. Sinha (ed.) *Socialization of the Indian child*, New Delhi, Concept Publishing Company.

Troisi, J. 1979. *Tribal religion: religious beliefs and practices among the Santals*, New Delhi, Manohar Publications.

Verma, K.K. 1977. *Culture, ecology and population, New Delhi*, National Publishing House.

Weber, M. 1958. *The Protestant ethic and the spirit of capitalism*, Charls Scribners & Sons.

9

POLYETHNIC BEHAVIOUR : HINDU, MUSLIM AND TRIBAL

Kumkum Bhattacharya

Introduction

In a mostly rural setting, agriculture being the primary concern as well as an economically viable occupation, Hindu, Muslim and Santal occupationally follow the same path. These three communities are commonly found in the villages of Birbhum district, West Bengal. The principal crops raised are paddy, wheat, sugarcane, pulses and potatoes.

Muslim villages are hemmed in by Hindu villages and Santal villages occupy a unique position on the outskirts of both Hindu and Muslim villages, though mainly Hindu villages, often seeming to be a separate village altogether, and colloquially referred to as *majhi para*.

Numerical strength certainly belongs to the Hindu, by far the largest of the three communities and whose presence may be traced far back so as to make them indigenous without doubt. Next in numbers, but certainly not a close contestant, is the Muslim, partly composed of settlers through marital or consanguinous ties. Last in the running, if at all they can be considered to compete, is the Santal, known for their migratory habits and possessing an aura of being tribals or *adibasis*.

The Hindu have their great tradition which encompasses the whole country. The Muslim have their great tradition present in pockets of India, strong enough to be contended with. They also have affiliations outside the limits of the country which forms an important aspect of their life. They may be a minority in comparison to the Hindu but they have a large global brotherhood. The Santal have their little tradition known and contained within themselves, neither prolifically codified nor propagated. They are a scheduled tribe which gives them a unique position in comparison to both Hindu and Muslim.

A question may be asked about the basis of comparison between the three communities. The comparison, rather the attempt, is based on the fact that these three communities are occupying the same geographical, climatic and ecological environment and are more or less in close contact with each other, if for nothing else but their livelihood. The children attend the same school and they have recourse to the same health centres. Politically their constituency is the same as well as belonging to the same Anchal Panchayat. In fact, simply from the name of village it is not possible to identify the inhabitant community. Most of the villages on the Bolpur-Suri highway are more or less homogeneous in composition, thereby providing a unique opportunity to observe the village interactions as a whole in addition to the fact that these villages are physically close to each other to warrant frequent occasions for interaction (see Table & Notes). The discussion will also comprise comparisons between the three communities as it will then be possible to know the differences and similarities in the adjustments or adaptations each makes in this polyethnic situation. Situations where one community emulates the other will also be highlighted.

Facets of a Polyethnic Setting

a) *Territory*

'Man is a cooperative species, but he is also competitive, and his struggle for dominance has to be structured in some way if chaos is to be avoided. . . . Territorial rights limit dominance geographically' (Morris, 1982: 191). Certainly territory is an important facet for which one is 'prepared to be aggressive when there is threat of any encroachment' (*Ibid.*). To a casual observer the Hindu village Bergram and the Muslim village Khiruli would appear two hamlets of the same village connected by inside roads. However, soon this illusion is broken and one is faced with well-known and well-understood boundary demarcations. At present, there are two separate roads running parallel to each other from the Bolpur-Suri highway approaching the villages, when previously there was only one road approaching Khiruli. The Hindu of Bergram, when planning a road approachable in all seasons by extending the existing road and to make it rainproof, did not anticipate any objection on the part of the Khiruli Muslim. Rather they had thought that the Muslim would be grateful for this service as travelling to and from the village becomes practically impossible during the rains. Quite contrarily, the Muslim objected on the grounds that the road would then mean increased traffic and their women would be intimidated and feel encroached upon. As a result a totally separate road was built to Bergram. It should be pointed out that the women of Khiruli hardly bother about *purdah* nor do the men exhibit much concern about their privacy, so it may be concluded that the reasons were a kind of projection of territorial rights. The people of Khiruli repaired their road by packing it with shingle. However, apart from bullock-carts, cyclists, and the promise of easy accessibility during the rains, this road is hardly used by the people who prefer to cross the fields as the way is shorter to the bus stop. The Bergram road is widely used and it terminates right at the bus stop.

Through the interior of Bergram, next to the high school is a path that goes to Khiruli, and at a more or less mid-point there is a tiny culvert symbolizing the limits of either village. The children of Khiruli use this path to travel to and from school. Once while using this path I met a host of these children returning home and they asked me to accompany them. They pointed out the culvert, after crossing which, the first Muslim fields were pointed out. When we were approaching the houses I noticed that the girls and some of the boys washed their feet at the nearby tank. I asked them the reason for this and I was told that they had been told by their parents to come home with clean feet. When I pointed out that since their homes were still some distance away and that there were tanks nearer home and that they were making their feet even more dirty, they said that they would wash again. At first I was at a loss to understand the significance of this act but it is probable that this was a means of staking a claim upon their territory after having been in an alien territory (cf. *Ibid.*, 1982). I had earlier thought that this behaviour was in imitation of their Hindu counterparts who follow a ritual of purification after returning home. However, the use of the tank at the border of the two villages seemed to be an interesting aspect of territory.

In Khiruli there is a tiny Hindu low-caste settlement toward the western side of the village. This settlement is a little separated from the rest of the village. The mid-wife for Khiruli belongs to the Hadi caste, lives in this colony with family, being hierarchically superior to the Dom, the other major occupant. This Hadi family had a house within the Muslim territory which was exchanged for a plot of land in the Dom area on a mutual agreement basis by which both parties were satisfied. The Muslim did not feel encroached upon nor did the Hindu feel an intruder.

Santal territory is maintained in quite a different way. Wherever situated the boundaries are demarcated by the dominant non-Santal group. They are usually to be found at the edges of villages, quite distinct from the rest of the village, identified by a line of trees or bamboo groves. Usually the Santal homestead territory is completely hidden from view due to a thick line of trees. It is not intruded into, the reason being the low status ascribed to the Santal. However, often their agricultural land is seized in repayment of loans, or some other form of appropriation.

The Santal whose main livelihood comes from day labour in near or far agricultural fields and construction sites have to journey from one territory to another and on observation they appear to be indifferent to alien territory. Very rarely do they look here and there or stop to talk to people, but walk in a formation either singly or in pairs, talking softly among themselves. When I try to stop them in greeting, they quickly get the formalities over and walk on inviting me to visit their village. They seem to be aware that they are on alien territory and that I should meet them on their home ground. What is *majhi para* to the non-Santal is *hor ato* to the Santal. Sometimes they borrow the name of the nearest village or within which their village is situated as identification. This may be one way in which the Santal concede their territorial rights to the dominant community. Usually they maintain territorial relations with the dominant Hindu than with the Muslim, who, though numerically stronger, are still a minority.

b) *Physical structure of the village*

Studying the Hindu village, Bergram; the Muslim village, Khiruli; and the Santal village, Debagram *majhi para*; the physical structure and its variations immediately strike one. Bergram is wholly inhabited by Hindu caste groups which are Brahman, Kayastha, Sadgop, Sarnakar, Suri, Dom and Bayen. The village is divided into several *para* or colony-Brahaman or Bamun-para, Suri-para, Pal-para, Diyashi-para, Dom-para and Bayen-para which together is called *chotolok para*. (For caste-wise distribution see Table II, Notes). As one enters Bergram from the Bolpur-Suri highway, one will find the houses of the upper caste Hindu, i.e. the Brahmin and the Kayastha. Along the main thoroughfare, the Kayastha households are on the left and the Brahmin households on the right. Two Sadgop families share this *para*. One of the Sadgop is reputed to be the richest person in Bergram and owns a prominent house in this locality. The post office run by this Sadgop is situated near his house. The other Sadgop who shares this *para* is hierarchically superior to the other Sadgop of the village being a Kunwar Sadgop. As we move into the village off the main thoroughfare, we find on the left the Suri-para and the Diyashi-para which are prominent. The prominent *para* on the right are the Pal-para and the school-para or the area of the High School, library, hostel, playgrounds and teachers' quarters. Almost hidden from view and tucked away in one corner, on the left, is the Dom and Bayen-para. There are two temple-like structures where local deities Dharmaraj and Beraichandi are housed. Most of the houses have their own deities which they tend themselves. One Suri family has a separate temple of their own for which they have employed a Brahmin to do *puja*. The *chotolok* or low caste have their own Kali temple situated at the base of a tree which they themselves maintain and worship. There is an open raised platform behind the Bamun-para and opposite Dharmaraj's temple which is earmarked for the annual *Durga puja*.

The various *para* appear neat, with tanks behind houses, in which few people have different shares. Cows, bullocks, lambs, goats, geese are to be found in plenty. The *chotolok para* appears desolate and depressing, houses are small with little land. The houses have no courtyard which is almost a customary part of the houses in *bhadralok* or upper caste *para*.

Coming to Khiruli, the village plan is simply a maze. Approaching through the main thoroughfare, one will first spot the *masjid* and the *idgah* situated on the banks of a large tank called Sutroe. Behind the *masjid*, overlooking the tank is the *majhi para*, east of which and contiguous to it lies the *pub para*, on the east, and on the other side of the *masjid* lies the *paschim para*, on the west. The Upper Primary School is situated on the bank opposite the *majhi para*. Along the main thoroughfare, near the entrance of the village are two tanks on the left and the graveyard. The water of these tanks is used for drinking and cooking. The Sutroe is used for bathing, bathing of animals, washing utensils and clothes and for fishing – the fish are supposed to be big and tasty. Contiguous to the *paschim para* is the Dom para, through which it is connected to Bergram. I have tried many times to view Khiruli in these simple geographical terms but even repeated visits over a long period have not enabled me to untangle this maze. Houses are almost piled upon each other duc to frequent break-ups by death or quarrels among family members over inheritance or polygyny. There are tiny alleys leading to independent houses, sometimes having common roofs, walls and sometimes even sharing an entrance. The *majhi para* is the most crowded of all; there the living quarters, animals' quarters and granaries may be in three different places. Going toward the two ends of the village the houses are less crowded but having little privacy. Pattern of settlement is clearly according to lines of kinship rather than along economic or social status.

The houses have more or less the same structure as Bergram houses, with a central courtyard, where most of the household activities are performed, a verandah along which the rooms lie; the verandah in most houses is used for sleeping. Most of the houses in Khiruli, unlike Bergram, are made of mud with thatched roofs. There is only one two-storeyed brick-and-mortar house near the *masjid* which is also made of brick and mortar. Activities of the village centre around the *masjid*; slaughtering of cows either for religious or commercial purposes is often done under a tree opposite the *imasjid*. Cultural functions of a religious nature like *milad*, etc., are organized at the *masjid*, sometimes in houses too. Apart from its daily use where men congregate to read the *namaz*, it is the scene for meetings of the village elders to settle disputes as well as being the place where children come to learn Arabic and recitation of the *Koran*.

Apparently, Khiruli has a simpler structure when compared to Bergram with its many *para* but there are clear-cut boundaries between each *para*, whereas in Khiruli it is difficult to identify between the three *para* or the houses. Even the *Dom-para* merges with the *Paschim para*. Houses in Khiruli are devoid of appropriate artefacts to indicate personal boundaries, which can only be identified when pointed out. Within houses again there are divisions among the various units of a joint family. The kitchen is the best indicator of the individual territory as there are as many ovens as there are sisters-in-law.

Moving on to Debagram *majhi para*, one finds that the houses are organized around a main road. The Santali term for road is *kulhi* which plays an important role in Santal life. The road or *kulhi* in Debagram traverses between a huge tank and a row of houses. The houses of those holding offices of headman, *majhi-haram*, the assistant headman, *jog-majhi*, the village messenger, *godet*, and the witch-doctor, *janguru*, are on this road. In front of the *majhi-haram's* house is the *majhi-than* or sacred place which is a raised mud platform under the shade of a tree. The *majhi-than* is very important to Santal belief and religion. The houses do not crowd into each other, ensuring privacy. The houses have an open courtyard into which visitors enter and are offered hospitality. A very narrow, low-ceilinged verandah is sometimes to be found, beyond which are the rooms, very low and dark. These rooms are not generally used, except when there are guests and liquor is served. The animals' quarters are in one corner of the courtyard. The kitchen too is in one corner of the courtyard. One common feature in all the Santal homes is one big tub into which starch and waste water is poured for the animals to drink. Each house is the personal property of the inhabitants. Each house has distinct artefacts indicating the territorial limits. The common animals to be found are pigs, goats, ducks and hens. Cows and bullocks are not seen in abundance.

Debagram *majhi para* is not divided into para, rather it maintains the contiguous nature of the village road. The houses are neat and orderly, made of mud with thatched roofs. Some of the houses have the traditional red/black border on its walls. There has been an increase in the number of households during the recent past and yet there is no apparent crowding of houses (see Table II, Notes). There is a creche about three years old which is open from ten in the morning to five in the evening, mothers leave their children on their way to work. The children are provided with free mid-day meal and are looked after by Santals. The portion of the highway on which Debagram is situated is crowded with shops, a bank and the irrigation office. Express buses also stop here. The Santal village is almost screened by the row of shops.

Arena of Interaction

Apart from the institutionalized arena of interaction, like schools, agriculture, local political bodies and such like fields, it is the social-cultural interaction of the three communities that presents an interesting picture. Inclusive in such a description is the intra-village interactions, i.e. between the members of the village.

a) *The village*

To start with the latter form of interactions, i.e. intra-village, the distinctive features that emanate may be described as follows: Bergram is apparently a homogeneous Hindu village, constructed along hierarchical lines of caste. The social distance between the caste groups is remarkable and certainly it influences interaction. Even when we think in terms of bhadralok-chotolok dichotomy (Table II, Notes; Sinha and Bhattacharya, 1969), interaction is found to proceed along certain lines. The latter form of stratification is based on considerations of economic status, wherein the Suri is considered bhadralok, though in terms of caste hierarchy they are closer (socially) to the Dom than to the Sadgop. Then there is the residential pattern of the various castes as mentioned earlier.

Talking to a cross-section of people, especially women, of any one *para*, one repeatedly faces a decided opinion about freedom of movement. Very rarely do the women and children move out of their *para*, though the men enjoy more freedom. In reality, there is very little visiting of homes by women who confine themselves to their homestead; they only visit other homes during marriages and deaths and other such ceremonies, but that too along the lines prescribed by caste. They leave their homes to visit their natal villages. Children too play in their own *para*, i.e. with children belonging to the same caste group. There is strict prohibition against visiting the *chotolok para*. In fact, the *chotolok para* is so hidden, both physically and socially, that even visitors like social workers, government personnel, etc., rarely go into this *para*, confining themselves to the more affluent homes and the school.

Among the Brahmin families, there is restricted movement largely determined by economic status and a certain amount of rivalry. One of the Brahmin families is very poor and they receive no help from other Brahmin families. Instead they obtain some help, both in terms of friendship and material aid, from a Kayastha family across the road. The well-to-do Brahmin family is not held in high esteem as it is too involved in agriculture and does not live up to the expectations. The Sadgop are the numerically strongest group settled in the Pal and Diyashi-para. Though hierarchically equal, there is absence of affinal ties. Marriages very rarely take place between the members of the same village within caste groups. The social behaviour of these people is governed by norms and conventions of both caste and class.

However, there are some changes that may be observed, especially with respect to the behaviour accorded to the *chotolok*. One major change, according to some *bhadralok* women, is the greater freedom that the maids, who are usually Dom by caste, are allowed in household work. The Dom, a service class, owning practically no land, are entirely dependent upon the *bhadralok* for employment both in the field and homes. In recent times the Dom are allowed to do these kinds of work which were earlier prohibited to them. In many houses one can see that the distance between the clean and 'unclean' castes is on the decrease. I was often told that values have changed over the years and the luxury of a maid doing more to help outweighs other social considerations. I was also told that these days the Dom are no longer satisfied with work or employment in homes or fields under the previous conditions of part payment in kind and part in cash, but prefer working as daily labour as the wages have been sufficiently increased. It is not unlikely to come across *mahendars* (domestic servants) from other villages working in the *bhadralok* homes. Once I had a chance to observe a unique interactional scence. The dramatis personnae were: Renupada Ghosh (Kayastha), Adhir Ghosh, Nabanidhar Pal (Sadgop), and Hatu (Dom). The *bhadralok* men were clustered together and the *chotolok* were seated on a bullock-cart at some distance. They were discussing the possible outcome of the recently held general elections. Adhir Ghosh informed me that he had taken a bet with Hatu that the CPI(M) would win most of the seats in Birbhum – at stake was a meal. Hatu has definite leaning toward the CPI(M), being an active member. However, the interesting point was that there was a bantering note in Adhir Ghosh's tone implying the opposite, that Hatu's party would be trounced and with it Hatu.

Men are more free to move about the village, but they seem to be bound to some implicit social mores. They do not go to the *chotolok para* unless they have to, even then not everybody goes as it is not a highly approved behaviour. There is often some talk of illicit relationship between *bhadralok* men and *chotolok* women. Generally such things are not mentioned to strangers, but I was fortunate to stumble on to this kind of information while talking to a college-going girl who remarked that on the surface there is no truck between the *bhadralok* and *chotolok* but underneath a lot of these respectable men maintain peculiar relationships with low-caste women.

There is a certain amount of factionalism between the various caste groups as well as within the same caste which influences the interactions of men. The existing rivalry or factionalism between groups is rarely mentioned or highlighted. Even when someone starts discussing it on frequent probings on my part, the topic is changed or dismissed as of being no concern to me. Often I have been thwarted in my efforts to distinguish rival groups or discover the causes of rivalry, instead I have been placated with platitudes that the village is more integrated these days and that the social relations are cordial.

Coming to Khiruli, the pattern of interaction is seen to follow simpler lines, though apparently the various ties of kinship seem to create confusion. Khiruli is a truly homogeneous village except for its tiny Dom settlement. The Muslims are all Sheikhs, most of whom are related to each other through marriage or familial ties. Marriages take place within the village frequently, and even when they take place across villages, the new kinfolk or the groom may decide to move into his bride's natal village. The groom is sometimes brought in as *ghar jamai*.

As mentioned earlier, there are three *para* in Khiruli, but no strict lines are drawn. The women, supposed to observe *purdah*, move about freely in the village, in fact they literally roam around. There is no time which is inconvenient to go to someone's house – either to borrow or return something, or to exchange a piece of news or generally air one's grievances – the explanation offered is that they are relatives. Children are forever outside their homes, freely going to the Dom-para, though they claim that they do not go. At least the girls do not go usually to the Dom para but they had no qualms in following me on my first day out of curiosity. The children of the Dom-para freely play with the Muslim children. The Dom youths have very good relationship with the Muslim youths, to the extent of exchanging clothes, eating out of the same dish, except beef. This information was freely given to me by many of my Muslim informants but there was some hesitation among their Hindu counterparts. On my pointing out specific instances of Hindu-Muslim friendship the Dom boys told me that since they were part of the same village such close associations were bound to happen, as if implying that their intimacy was incidental rather than by choice. I once saw a Muslim woman quietly slipping into a Dom house to exchange gossip. I was told that since she lives close by she comes often to chat and pass the time of day. Excepting her, I have not seen any other-woman entering the Dom-para.

Women of Khiruli claim that they do not go to any other *para* other than their own, which may be due to limited time, distance from their homes and the ties of kinship. However, this disappears when I am in the village, as then it makes little difference which *para* they follow me to. Children of course follow me into the house I enter and it presents an interesting sight as usually I am given tea and puffed rice which I have to consume under of the gaze of 30-35 pairs of eyes on an average. The number of women is not so large but five or six of them are around.

Another predominant kind of behaviour common among Khiruli women is their habit of answering my questions to their neighbours which nobody seems to resent except me who is forced to listen to second-hand information. There can be no topic upon which decided opinions are not offered, especially the greatness of Islam, comparison with Hindu notions of cleanliness, etc. There are certain areas left alone as being the concern of the men like whether their children will continue their education. I have already mentioned that Khiruli offers little privacy and the houses are piled on to each other. The people too are constantly in touch, meeting and gossipping. Their quarrels too are not private, in fact it provides an arena for further interaction. I have also observed a crowd collecting in no time to witness a quarrel in a family or hotly discuss a recent quarrel. I have also observed women rushing off from their discussions with me on hearing that a death has occurred. They literally clutch their sarees and run. I once had an opportunity to observe the operations of cutting a new tank in the place of an old one and then too I had seen women and children running with all kinds of fishing equipment to catch fish if there be any.

The large number of children is one thing that strikes one in Khiruli. I was proudly told by one of the older women that no Hindu village could boast of so many children. Certainly Khiruli is teeming with children which is not so apparent in Bergram as there the children maintain territorial restrictions in their movements.

There is some amount of economic disparity among the people of Khiruli but it is not blatantly observable. The Dom of Khiruli also own land which they put to agricultural use and none of them have to work in others' fields. Moreover, according to the Dom informants there are quite a few rich Muslims, certainly richer than them. There are some very poor Muslims who barely make both ends meet. The stratification in Khiruli follows *baralok-garib* pattern, i.e. based on economic status of the people (*Ibid.*). Islam has provision for charity and care for the poor and the infirm and this helps in maintaining the semblance of egalitarianism. It is not uncommon to hear both men and women reiterating the point that everybody is like themselves – poor – poorer than the Hindu of Bergram. There is also some rivalry which may be known from their comments regarding their kin or neighbours. Many young girls have reported that the people of Khiruli are jealous and intolerant of others' success – it may be noted that these statements were made by girls belonging to the richer families. However, I have noticed young children hiding their catch of fish for fear of arousing someone's jealousy or 'black eye'. Talking to the men, on the other hand, I did not find any deliberate attempt to run down anybody, they have often reported to me that their village is united and that there is no factionalism. When questioned about the frequent quarrels due to which joint families break up, the answer is that quarrels are usually over land, authority, antipathy between sisters-in-law and poverty. Talking to the women one may know that during quarrels within a joint family the villagers take sides.

As most of the people are related to each other, kinship imposes responsibilities, generates hopes of gaining by inheritance which creates jealousy and bias. The people of Khiruli have all this in full measure though they are not so vocal about the latter exigencies of kinship.

The relationship between Muslim, Dom and Hadi is found to be free of constraints. The Hadi women serve as mid-wives for the Muslim women, as there are no mid-wives as a separate caste in the Muslim community. This relationship is based on money, each pays according to one's means in cash or kind. Sometimes extra payment is also made if a son is born or a child has been born after long years of marriage. The Hadi women told me that the Muslims are very polite, pay generously and respect her, which she does not get in Hindu households. About the Dom relationship with the Muslim I have already mentioned.

Observing the Santal in Debagram *majhi para*, the picture that emerges is as follows. The village is quiet and sleepy, during the day-time, houses wear a deserted look as both men and women leave for work, either in their own fields or in others'. The children are either quietly playing or are in the creche or in school. Unlike the Muslim of Khiruli, the Santal do not crowd into each other, rather their interactions are on a restrained key. There is no segmentation of the village indicative of either social status or hierarchy, rather each house forms a segment or unit of the village (for details see Sommers, 1977 : 80, 85). Bergram has its *para*, Khiruli has its kinship and in Debagram the house/home is one of the most important aspects of their life. Thus, a contrast is provided when compared with Bergram or Khiruli. In fact household territory is given due respect and not intruded upon. People visiting their homes are *para hor* or relatives and an elaborate ritual of greeting is often observed depending on kin-status. Usually, formal visiting of homes is a part of festivals and ceremonies. The ritual follows a sequence – as first water is given to the guest to drink or wash, after which greetings are exchanged and then *handi* or rice beer with puffed rice is served. No sign of excitement is witnessed, the whole house does not rush out to see the visitor. Each one slowly trickles in maintaining a distance. Conversation is in muted tones and the range of topics large.

I had the opportunity to observe the Santal in their festive spirit which provided an insight into the Santal way of life. Sohrae, their most important festival, which lasts for five days in the month of *Pous*, i.e. December-January is a rejuvenating one. During these days the village has a different look, no longer sleepy, the people look happy and cheerful. *Handi* flows like water and every house, be rich or poor stocks up well for these five days. During three days people visit each other, daughters come from their husbands' homes. The people who hold important posts like *majhi-haram*, the headman, and *jog-majhi*, the assistant headman, play an important role.

In Debagram, the festivity centred around the *jog-majhi's* courtyard, the dancing started from near the *majhi-than*, moving to the edge of the village. All other activities came to an end and there was only merry-making; singing and dancing went on for long periods of time and all kinds of musical instruments were brought out. I saw little girls being helped to wear *sarees* to deck themselves out prettily and being taught to dance in a line along with the older girls, little boys were being encouraged to play their flutes and indulge in *sogoi* which is a kind of teasing of the dancing girls making use of whistles and gestures. I did not observe young girls and children drinking *handi*; they seemed more interested in dancing, singing and dressing up. The *jog-majhi* and the present *majhi-haram's* mother did the honours in receiving the guests at the *jog-majhi's* house with mustard oil and vermilion. The young and old participated in the fun together, in fact the camaraderie between the young and the old was remarkable. The old are the fountainhead of many songs and jokes and the young are eager learners and listeners. I saw many old women being persuaded to join the dance or sing a particular song by young boys and girls. During these five days I went to four Santal villages close by and found the same joyous spirit prevailing.

b) *Behavioural poses adopted by the three communities*

In this polyethnic situation, the three communities are bound to come in contact with each other and as already mentioned there are institutionalized arenas of interaction. Moreover, there is an under-current of social-cultural conditions or forces which strongly influence the interaction between the three communities. The communities necessarily fall into a dominant minority category involving both overt and covert competitiveness. The traditions of each in close proximity undergo changes in the stance/pose adopted by each of the three communities. The Muslim of Khiruli, both men and women, are unequivocal in their praise of Islam – how many times I have been told of the difficult path of Islam, the total dedication that it demands and involves repeated punishment of the body by frequent fastings, and the young age from which practice of Islam is begun to create true believers, and the provision in their religion against all kinds of evil, and for charity, honesty, etc. The women, almost involuntarily, start comparing the Hindu customs with theirs and dismiss them as being far inferior to theirs. Almost without prompting they bring in Hinduism and its 'peculiar' customs – one not allowing the widow to eat fish, meat, eggs and certain other things about which one women jokingly remarked that why should the widow starve herself to death; another is the Hindu way of performing ablutions – many women remarked with derision that the Hindu women, otherwise so conscious of cleanliness, do not use water after urination. They also told me that their rites of death are more elaborate and complicated than the Hindu customs of burning the dead. Hindu religion to them is rather 'soft' whereas Islam demands strenuous participation which the hard-boiled, resilient Muslims can fulfil. The Muslims are braver, stronger, more violent, never take an insult lying down and all this is due to the magic of their religion and diet which is high-protein in nature. Their food enables them to be more fertile which helps in adding to their growing numbers by which they move into big power category. Their identity as Muslim is an important factor in their lives and even children of three years, if asked, will say that he is a Muslim.

However, their passion for Islam is not often carried into their daily lives, rarely have I found a woman saying her *namaz* five times a day though they claim otherwise. If I pointed out to the women that they were ignoring the calls for *namaz*, they answered :

1) they are so busy that it is not possible to say *namaz* regularly;
2) they are not well and they should not say *namaz* when they are ill, but they will make up later;

3) they have to be in *pak saf* or ritual cleansing, and with little children it becomes difficult. When I asked some men why they did not say *namaz* regularly, I was told that those days (harvest time), they had no time for anything other than agriculture; also at present, the habit of saying *namaz* is on the decline.

The mosque at Khiruli has a loudspeaker fitted on to the towers so that the call for *namaz* is heard by all, even those in distant fields. However, some of the older Muslims deplored the fact that congregations for *namaz* had declined since their days, when they did not need a loudspeaker.

The Muslim when comparing themselves with the Hindu face some difficulty in deciding on the caste group to which they can relate. Usually, they appear to look down upon the lower castes like Dom, Bayen, etc., while, in reality, other than restricting comensal relations, they maintain cordial relationship with the Dom and Hadi in their own village. Santals, they do not consider to be any force at all. Their whole point of contention lies with the Hindu *bhadralok*. In spite of being an egalitarian society, they have easily been able to assimilate the hierarchial pattern of behaviour of the Hindu caste groups in maintaining social distance with the lower castes and the Santal. Even among themselves they follow a stratification system based on economic status which is not as rigid as the Hindu caste system. However, it must be pointed out that the Muslim of Khiruli are egalitarian in principle where the rich and the poor are mutually dependent upon each other and there are not many pollution taboos.

The Hindu of Bergram, unless drawn into a discussion regarding their Muslim neighbours, will never voluntarily talk of them. To them their neighbours do not pose any problem, rather they are depended upon for odd jobs. There is no social intercourse between the Hindu and the Muslim. I have found only two instances of formal friendship between a Hindu and a Muslim, of which one I know in some detail. Achinta Ghosh (Kayastha) and Rawson Mulla of Khiruli were friends from a young age and they formalized their association when they grew up. Achinta Ghosh has died but his sons try to maintain the relationship by calling Rawson Mulla 'uncle'. Rawson Mulla in talking of Achinta Ghosh expressed with some gratification the respect he is still shown by his friend's family but obviously the frequency of his visits has decreased over the years. It is rare to find close friendships between the people of these two contiguous villages. The Khiruli

Muslim have many Hindu associates in the towns due to business purposes. Some college students have Hindu friends. One of my informants, Ali, who is in the fishing business has extensive dealings with Hindu merchants and he took pains to tell me how well he is received in Hindu households, even by the women. Another of my informant, a student of Bolpur College, Ghulam Murtuja, told me that he preferred his Hindu friends because he felt he could be free of Muslim fanaticism. He claimed that his friends or their families did not make any discrimination regarding him which was a source of gratification to him. He further told me that he was not fond of beef as it made people hot-blooded and violent as well as aroused base desires in men. Many of the men of Khiruli told me that the people of Bergram often call them for catching fish, helping during harvesting, catching thieves, repairing houses and other jobs. The Muslim seemed to expect to serve (in return for payment) the Hindu *bhadralok* and did not see any anomally in the image they projected and what the Hindu actually thought of them. Obviously there is an attitude prevalent among the *bhadralok* Hindu that the Muslim are a part of the serving class and it is not unlikely that the Muslims are not cognizant of this. By virtue of being a minority, the Muslim are subjected to a putting-down pressure from the dominant Hindu, generating a feeling of insecurity and anxiety. This is expressed overtly in their desire to do better, project their superiority in terms of their religion and global brotherhood, constant comparisons with Hindu customs as well as their firm belief in their physical strength and prowess. Covertly their anxiety and insecurity is expressed in their ever increasing families, their sense of gratification to be on cordial terms with the Hindu; it is also expressed in their maintenance of social distance from certain groups both within and without which goes strongly against the tenets of Islam.

On the part of the Hindu, there is a tolerance, may be superficial, toward the Muslim, but if one probes a little, one will find an undercurrent of antipathy. When talking of their Muslim neighbours the women of Bergram refer to them as unclean, having no sense of family planning, violent and short tempered. Muslims are called '*bhai-saheb*' which is a kind of mockery as well as indicative of their peculiar distinctness from themselves. The Muslim children studying in Bergram High School often complain of partisanship on the part of the teachers who are all Hindu. Some of them have told me about the treatment meted out to them in Hindu households where if they have tea they are expected to wash their cup and dish as well as wipe the place where they sat. The Muslim children are aware from a very early age as to how to behave in a Hindu house though inwardly they seem to resent it. One Hindu Brahmin girl related an incident of her visit to a Muslim house in Sattore, a village beyond Khiruli.They had prepared many delicacies for her but her status prevented her from eating anything. They were very disappointed and asked her to at least make herself a cup of tea which she complied with, and they were happy. She mentioned that her Muslim friend had visited her often and she was forced to return the visit as a courtsey.

To the Muslim of Khiruli, the Hindu of Bergram are richer, better educated and have more chances of success. They can employ more servants in the home, farmers in the field and thus the burden on their children is reduced so that they can concentrate on their education. Also, they can afford to employ tutors for private coaching. Many of the educated boys of Khiruli earn a living out of coaching Hindu children. They are sometimes criticized for ignoring their poor Muslim brothers and sisters for money. Zakaria, a college student of Khiruli, is considered an example of a model youth as he coaches many girls of Khiruli so that they do better and not always for money.

Toward the Santal, Hindu and Muslim adopt different stances. The Santal form a small minority who generally work as day labourers either on fields or construction sites. They inhabit fringes of villages and their presence too is analogous to their position. They are not in any position to enter into direct competition with either the Muslim or the Hindu. Their special status as 'scheduled tribe' also makes them separate from the larger Hindu society of which they could be considered as 'part society'. However, their way of life is such that they are contained within themselves – there is little overt expression regarding their feeling about the Hindu or the Muslim. The Hindu is more or less indulgent toward them but is also wary about them as they are unable to predict Santal behaviour due to ignorance of their customs and an exaggerated opinion about their drunkenness. The Muslim, on the other hand, ignores them as much as possible, but tries to make fun of them. The Khiruli Muslim do not have any interaction with the Santal of Rahamatpur *majhi para*, the nearest village and very few Santal work for them. According to the Rahamatpur Santal, they prefer working with the Hindu as they receive better treatment as well as help in times of need. The Santal also avoid the Muslim, sending their children to the Rahamatpur Upper Primary School which is farther than the one in Khiruli. I have often observed Muslim children mimicking Santali if they ever stopped to talk to them which the Santals took quite good-naturedly.

The Santal have evolved a novel way of dealing with their minority status. They are otherwise one of the most polite and most respectful people when in their own milieu especially with older people and yet when they talk to non-Santal or *diku*, they employ a disrespectful form of 'you' quite unceremoniously ('*tui*' in Bengali). It is generally always overlooked as their language is so different from ours and we are unaware of their linguistic embellishments and such like reasons. There is a kind of compunction when talking of them – the Santal is so poor, uneducated, etc. Then there is the myth about their drunkenness which reaches alarming proportions as their festivals come closer, during which time they are left strictly alone. The Santal too make full use of this myth, behaving as they want after consuming liquor. I was warned against visiting Santal villages during Sohrae. In Debagram, a non-Santal who had come to drink *handi* during Sohrae was unceremoniously shoved off after my arrival. The person was forced to leave which under normal circumstances he would never have had to do. Once on my way to Debagram during Sohrae, our bus was stopped on the road by a group of Santal men and women who were singing and dancing.

They had stopped the bus to demand money. They were all obviously under the influence of liquor, climbing all over the bus and the women were being deliberately provoking. The driver did not have to be cajoled too long – he paid a part of their demand, promising the rest on his return journey. They had asked for only Rs.5. The driver told me that this was a recent phenomenon and everybody including the government turns a blind eye to them during these five days. Their way of demanding money brings to mind the similar way the Hindu youth collect donations for the Puja, the difference being the force they use, there is no cajoling element in their behaviour.

The Santal are not completely untouched by living in this polyethnic situation. Their participation, aided by government policies as well as their own need to succeed, has increased from what it was earlier – at least the extent of their participation has certainly increased. The creche in Debagram *majhi para* is one such service widely used by the Santal. Debagram has become crowded with all kinds of shops that have become established on its main road. There is a bank at the bus-stop, the irrigation office has long stood there. As a result of this increased business, many Santal have come from far to settle down here in search of employment. The number of households has increased from 26 to 40 in a matter of a few years. Some of the Debagram Santal have started their own shops. I was told by the Janguru's son who runs a cycle repair shop that he would keep his shop closed only for the last two days of Sohrae as he does not want to lose business. He also told us that his sister's husband could not come because he had to harvest the potatoes before they become rotten and that he must remain to prevent theft. Certainly this is a change that may be attributed to polyethnic situational forces.

Conclusions

In this paper I have tried to explore the nature of polyethnicity and the concomitant interactional behaviour of three ethnic groups under the pressure of a polyethnic situation.

To examine two definitions of a plural (polyethnic) society: (a) a society integrated economically under the control of a state system dominated by one of the groups but leaving large areas of cultural diversity in the religious and domestic sectors of activity (Barth 1969:16); and (b) '. . . the highest common factor of their wants, i.e. the various sections of the plural society is the economic factor' (Farnivall, 1967: 449); we find that economy is the most important factor, in fact the factor that makes for polyethnicity. There are various extra-local 'demographic, economic, political factors such as population pressure on land, the pattern of land distribution, . . . government policies on induced change' that influence polyethnic situations (Bhattacharya, 1970: 73).

However, as I have already mentioned, there is a strong undercurrent of social-cultural factors that affect and influence the intensity of participation of the various sections of the plural society in the economy. From the point of view of my special interest (psycho-anthropology) and my attempt to highlight yet another facet of a polyethnic setting, it is these social-cultural forces that have directed the course of my fieldwork.

Traditional norms, values, rules, customs and the ways of life create an underpinning of notions about themselves as well as others which are being tested in the arena of interaction. For any meaningful interaction to occur these preconceived notions become necessary to enable one to predict behaviour.

Talking of a plural society, one will have to take into account the relative power vested in each of the segments – in this instance Hindu, Muslim and Santal. The extent of power vested in or exercised by each group may be known from the extent of exploitation of the opportunity structure. Among the Hindu, there is, apart from caste hierarchy, a class distinction of *bhadralok-chotolok*. The *bhadralok* is equipped to take advantage of the opportunity structure by exercising control over the *chotolok's* access to the said structure. Among the Muslim, though apparently egalitarian, there is a kind of social stratification based on economic status – *baralok-garib* – and it may be seen that the *baralok* can equip themselves to pitch in competition with the Hindu bhadralok. *baralok* exercises control over *garib* in more or less the same way as his Hindu counterpart, *bhadralok*, does over *chotolok*; one major difference being the fact that it is not sanctioned in Islamic tradition and because of close kin ties due to which the control is not quite complete.

The Muslim, when comparing their status in the backdrop of Hindu society, cannot fit themselves into the hierarchy to their best advantage, and the Hindu, when assigning status to the Muslim, assigns to them a low status, though with some reservations. The Santal in this setting is in part encapsulated by the greater Hindu society by occupying for long a fringe position both physically and socially. The Muslim accord no such recognition to the Santal, rather they maintain social distance with them. However, the Santal by virtue of special recognition as a scheduled tribe by the state system, as well as due to changes in their own aspirations are becoming more eager to participate in the resources of the plural society and better their position.

Against the background of this prevailing power structure, the interactions of the three ethnic groups have been found to follow a pattern based on this power structure. Polyethnicity leads to patterns of interactions based on socio-cultural factors which undergo a series of changes and adaptations leading to increased participation. Hsu (1972: 466) has described the interaction of culture and personality as a 'two-way traffic in spiral progression' and not merely cyclical. A similar kind of analogy may be appropriate here for an understanding of a polyethnic situation and its interactional pattern. Interaction of the various sections and the socio-cultural matrix of the plural society may be thought of as a spirally progressing phenomenon mutually reinforcing one another.

In this paper through the physical and social facets of a polyethnic situation I have also tried to trace the patterns of interaction between the three sections of this particular plural society, as well as compare one community with the other two.

I have also attempted to describe the interactional pattern prevalent within the three communities in order to understand the social-cultural factors that make for the norms and values of a particular community to provide a basis for prediction of behaviour.

NOTES

TABLE I: A brief overview of the villages and their composition beyond Bolpur town within a distance of 15 km on the Bolpur-Suri highway. The villages are on the right-hand side of the highway except Debagram *majhi-para* which is on the left.*

Village		Composition
Ballabhpur	-	Hindu
Kendradangal	-	Muslim
Sattore	-	Hindu, Muslim
Rahamatpur *majhi-para*	-	Santal
Khiruli	-	Muslim
Bergram	-	Hindu
Bergram *majhi-para*	-	Santal
Debagram *majhi-para*	-	Santal
Gonoria	-	Hindu
Parui	-	Hindu, Muslim

* This is to show the contiguous element inherent in these villages.

TABLE II

a) Bergram

Caste	No. of households	
Brahmin	5	
Kayastha	3	
Sadgop	16	*bhadralok*
Samakar	1	
Suri	6	
Dom	14	*chotolok*
Bayen	10	
	56	

b) Khiruli

Caste	No. of households
Sheikh Muslim	80
Hadi	1
Dom	8
	89

c) Debagram *majhi-para*

Group	No. of households
Santal	40

1. *Majhi-para*	:	Santal hamlets are colloquially referred as *majhi-para* implying a colony.
2. *Hor ato*	:	Santal refer to their village as *hor ato*, meaning village of men. The impersonal and limited *majhi-para* is transformed into personal and free territory.
3. *Para*	:	Literally means a colony but there is no word in English expressing the actual meaning, therefore, I have used *para* in the Paper.

REFERENCES

Barth, Fredrik (ed.) 1969, *Ethnic groups and boundaries, the social organization of cultural difference*. George Allen and Unwin, London.

Bhattacharya, Ranjit K. 1970. Social and cultural constraints in agriculture in three villages of West Bengal, *Science, technology and culture,* edited by Surajit Sinha, New Delhi.

Farnivall, J.S. 1967. *Netherland India, a study of plural economy*. Library of Congress Catalogue Card No.39 - 20815.

Hsu, F.L.K. (ed.) 1972. *Psychological Anthropology*. Schenkman Publishing Co., Inc., Massachussetts, U.S.

Morris, Desmond 1982. *The pocket guide to man watching*, Triad, Granada, Britain.

Sinha, Surajit and Bhattacharya, Ranjit 1969. *bhadralok* and *chotolok* in a rural area of West Bengal. *Sociological Bulletin* 18, (1).

Sommers, George E. 1977. *The dynamics of Santal traditions in a peasant society*. Abhinav Publications, New Delhi.

THE CHANGING, THE UNCHANGING TRIBES

10

HINDUIZATION OF TRIBES : CRITIQUE AND PERSPECTIVE

H. K. Bhat

Introduction

Defining Hinduism

Hindu is a controversial term and yet widely used in social and intellectual contexts. Different authors attribute different meanings to this term. A terminological clarification may, therefore, be attempted first.

The western scholars have seen Hinduism as a 'composite of faiths with essential characteristics like reverence for the cow, belief in the transmigration of soul (*atman*), acceptance of Brahman's leadership and belief in the divinity of Brahma, Vishnu and Shiva (Creator, Preserver and Destroyer of life, respectively)' (Swain, 1970: 208). According to *Webster's Dictionary*, 'Hinduism is a complex body of social, cultural and religious beliefs and practices evolved in and largely confined to the Indian sub-continent and marked by a caste system, an outlook tending to view all forms and theories as aspects of one eternal being and truth, a belief in *ahimsa, karma, dharma, samsara*, and *moksha* and the practice of the way of works, the way of knowledge, or the way of devotion as the means of release from the round of rebirths.' *The Encyclopaedia of Religion and Ethics* defines Hinduism in special terms: 'Hinduism is the title applied to that form of religion which prevails among the vast majority of the present population of the Indian Empire' (Hastings, 1974: 686).

Of the Indian scholars, Sen (1961) takes a wider view: 'The term Hindu is derived from the river Sindhu (Indus), for the Persians referred to India as a land beyond the Sindhu. Hinduism would thus appear to be a generic term meaning the religions of the people of India (p.17). 'Hinduism is a *dharma,* rather than a religion. It has more to do with the nature and behaviour of man rather than with conduct (p.38). Hinduism also points out that difference in metaphysical doctrine need not prevent the development of an accepted basic code of conduct. The important thing about a man is his *dharma,* not necessarily his religion' (p.40).

Among the Indian anthropologists, Baidyanath Saraswati's definition is the lone attempt to define Hinduism. He considers it 'as a religion of religions' and gives a precise explanatory definition: 'Hinduism is an evergrowing religion federating those faiths of inalienable worth whose origin it is possible to trace in the continual process of evolution and accretion in the collective ideas of the Vedic *rishis,* well-marked into the threefold phase of *karma, jnana* and *bhakti,* whose adherents are permitted to enter into a sacred shrine commonly known as Hindu temple; and whose propounders are intrinsically connected with one another through *guru-shishya parampara* of direct or indirect order, but none are granted absolute authority of guiding the unknowable whole truth' (1970: 24-25). In a later deliberation (1986), he came out with a theoretical interpretation of Hinduism, or what he labels as 'Sanatan Hinduism'. Pointing out to the inappropriateness of the term Hindu, he says: 'Hindu does not emerge as a category either in ritualistic tradition, or in a secular traditional identification in such critical contexts as marriage, inheritance, food and occupation. It is, indeed, an official (Census) category persisting as a legacy of the foreign rule in India. In the past, we have been referring ourselves as "Sanatani", the followers of Sanatan Dharma, the Eternal Tradition (Religion) whose source is not in space and time. Even today this term is commonly used by the *pandits* in their traditional scholastic debates. Alternatively the term "Varnashrama Dharma" is also used to signify those people of the past who follow the primal system of *varna* and *ashrama.* Perhaps, Sanatan Hinduism will be a compromise term. For, no other term lesser than it would convey the persisting features of our faith, its both primal and contemporary characters' (1986). Saraswati holds that Sanatan Hinduism is like a proverbial elephant and one can touch upon only some of its primal characteristics. Five of these, he has pointed out considering that by no means that is all, viz. (1) *Nirbandha* (without ties), (2) *Nilakantha* (assimilation of an element without causing loss to its identity), (3) *Nityasuddha* (eternally pure), (4) *Nityamangala* (eternally auspicious), and (5) *Nityananda* (bliss eternal) (*Ibid*).

One problem with Saraswati's approach to the study of religion is that he does not approve of the traditional anthropological method. He proposes a new approach which he calls 'transanthropological' (Saraswati,1984), the method which is not yet spelt out by him. He has also not clarified as to whether the so-called tribals come within the fold of Sanatan Hinduism. Let us, therefore, turn to the more widely followed trends in the anthropological interpretation of Hinduism in tribal context.

Hinduism in Tribal Context

Tribals in India have lived in forest, hills and isolated regions for thousands of years. The Hindu scriptures – the *Vedas*, the *Puranas*, the *Ramayana* and the *Mahabharata* – contain good accounts of the tribal people of ancient India. According to Suniti Kumar Chatterji, four main races and cultures welded together into one people, the Hindu people. These are (1) Austro-Asiatics represented by the Mundas, the Khasis and the Nicobarese; (2) Mongoloid people speaking dialects of the Sino-Tibetan family who are represented by the Nagas, the Bodos and the Kukis; (3) Dravidians represented by the Malers, the Oraons and the Gonds whose tongue belongs to the Dravidian family; and (4) Aryans who are the migrants to this land (*cf.* Vidyarthi and Rai, 1977). J.H. Hutton has also expressed a similar view. He considered Hinduism as an amalgam between the pre-Aryan Indian beliefs and the Rigvedic religion. Since they have a common substratum, he argued, the distinction between Hinduism and tribal religion is useless (*cf.* Ghurye, 1963).

The bulk of tribal population is said to be isolated in ecology, demography, economy and traditional political system from the other ethnic groups of India. During the British rule the tribal people were not brought into the mainstream of Indian population, obviously as a consequence of the British policy of divide-and-rule. The post-Independence situation has somewhat changed. To protect the interest of the tribal people many of them have been scheduled, for the purpose of special treatment. It may, however, be pointed out that 'tribe' and 'scheduled tribe' need not be the same population. For centuries tribal communities have lived as a part of the Indian peasant system. In the process of peasantization many of them identify themselves with one of the world religions, viz. Hinduism, Islam,

Christianity and Buddhism. In the 1961 Census, 89.39 per cent of India's tribal population was returned as Hindu, 5.53 per cent as Christian, 0.34 per cent as Buddhist, 0.21 per cent as Muslim and 4.53 per cent as followers of other religions.

The Hinduized Tribes

Census interpretation

In the 14th and 15th centuries many Westerners came in contact with people following diverse religious practices. The religions of the people called primitive or tribal were included under the blanket term 'animism'. The colonial scholars used this term for the entire indigenous population of India, ignoring the fact that many of these communities have lived civilized life for millinnia and have contributed to the formation of the world's most ancient civilization. In India the question of the status of tribal religion came up at the time of decennial census. Let us first discuss the views of the various Commissioners and Superintendents of Census of British India.

Majority of the early Census Commissioners felt that it is futile to distinguish between animism and Hinduism. Later some of them classified a certain section of the Indian population under 'tribal religion'. J.T. Marten, Commissioner of the 1921 Census, was the first to do so. J.H. Hutton, Commissioner of the 1931 Census used 'tribal' in contradistinction to Hindu, Muslim, Christian, etc. He was of the view that tribal religions provided the raw material to build Hinduism. He had conceived of the process by which a tribal became a Hindu. According to him, the tribal groups are those which 'have not reached the stage of accepting Brahmans as priests, or of attaching any sanctity to the cow, or of worshipping in Hindu temples of their own villages . . . the line is hard to draw between Hinduism and tribal religions. The inclusion of the latter within the Hindu fold is easy, and wherever hill or forest tribes live in permanent daily contact with Hindus, their religion rapidly assimilates itself to that of their neighbours though the old method of thinking is unchanged' (*cf.* Ghurye, 1963: 4). W.G. Lacey, Superintendent of the 1931 Census for Bihar and Orissa, has also described the process of Hinduization of aboriginals.

Indian anthropological interpretation

Most Indian anthropologists followed the colonial view of tribal population. Ghurye was an exception to this general trend. Reviewing the various Census Reports of British India, he observed that 'almost all the so-called aboriginal tribes of the (central) region have a Hinduized section, small or large, that they have been in fairly intimate contact with the Hindus for a long time, and that they have common interest with the Hindus in matters of religion and gainful occupation. They have shown a tendency to look upon themselves as Hindus or as people closely connected with the Hindus. They seek to improve their social position by asserting themselves to be Hindus and then establishing a claim for a status higher than that of the lowest or even lower castes. They are imperfectly integrated classes of Hindu society. They are in reality Backward Hindus' (Ghurye, 1963:18-19).

Considering the extent of Hinduization, some anthropologists have classified tribal population under various categories. D.N. Majumdar's classification (1957) leaves hardly any tribal community outside Hindu contact. The three stages listed by him are: (a) Tribals outside Hindu influence; (b) Minor castes, who have adopted Hindu customs, beliefs and practices; and (c) Hinduized tribals but keeping some social distance from upper castes. B.K. Roy Burman's classification (1971) takes account of orientation towards Hindu social order. He has identified four categories of tribal communities: (a) Incorporated in the Hindu social order, such as Bhils, Bhumijs, etc.; (b) Positively oriented towards the Hindu social order, such as Santal, Oraon, Munda, Gond, etc.; (c) Negatively oriented towards the Hindu social order, such as Mizo, Naga, etc.; and (d) Indifferent towards Hindu social order, such as Arunachal tribes.

The process of Hinduization

N.K. Bose was perhaps the first to delve deep into the aspect of Hinduization process. In his famous paper, 'The Hindu method of tribal absorption' (1941), he described meticulously the decisive factor of articulation of the backward tribal economy with the more advanced plough-based economy of the Hindu peasantry. He takes up the case of the shifting cultivator Juang of Orissa to explain the Hindu method of absorption: As the plough-cultivator Hindus penetrated into the original Juang territory and cleared up the jungles, the latter were forced to withdraw into more restricted valleys and higher hills. But they were more numerous than the hills and the jungles could support through their accustomed primitive method of production. Under the circumstances a section of the Juangs were forced to adopt wet cultivation in the valleys between the hills and also to specialize in basket-making. Thus they have been tagged on to the larger body of Hindu society which is sustained by the more advanced production technology of plough cultivation.

While Bose considered socio-economic factors (such as Hindu productive organization ensuring minimum economic security, assurance of ethnic monopoly of a craft occupation, preservation of group identity as a *jati* and a degree of cultural autonomy to pursue distinct ethnic customs), Surajit Sinha drew attention to a much larger process of assimilation. Drawing upon his major fieldwork on the Bhumij, he has summed up his views on what he called the Indian civilization mode of tribal absorption in the following words: 'In a paper "State formation and Rajput myth in tribal central India", I have dealt in detail mainly with reference to the Bhumij tribe of Barahabhum, how state formation and the associated creation of a myth of Rajput ancestry provided a structural base for integration of tribes with the social organization of Indian civilization (S. Sinha, 1962). In the case of chieftancy of Barahabhum there is structural evidence that the traditional segmentary clan-territory units of the tribal Bhumij were reorganized into a hierarchic feudal state with a Raja of Pargana claiming Rajput-Kshatriya status at the top having control over the lower order of chiefs, namely, Taraf Sardars, Sadiyas and Ghatwals. Roughly corresponding to the feudal hierarchy there was a socio-ritual hierarchy of endogamous grades, namely, Rajput-Kshatriyas of Namahal grade, Rajput-Kshatriya of Dasmahal grade, Ataichey Bhumij, Nagadi (Ordinary) Bhumij. It was pointed out that state formation was facilitated, in the case of the Bhumij, by the adoption of plough technology which was reinforced by extensive practice of tank irrigation. Extensive land-grants to the Brahmans indicate the role of the immigrant Brahmans in providing the tribal chieftains with prestigious myths and ritual symbols in support of their Rajput status' (1982).

The picture of Hinduization drawn by Bose, Sinha and other anthropologists, including the Western scholars like Martin Orans (1965), emerges mainly from the viewpoint of Brahmanic social organization. But there could be other dimensions too. A more universal process of Hinduization can be looked into.

New Perspective

In this section, I wish to present my own ideas of the process of Hinduization, an alternative approach to study Hinduism.

First, a more comprehensive definition of Hinduism may be formulated as follows: 'Hinduism is that vision of reality, beliefs, rituals, practices and values as found in, or in accordance with, the *Srutis, Smritis, Itihasas, Puranas, Kavyas*, etc., either in its pristine form, or in adaptive transformation from within, expressed orally, or in textual form, in Sanskrit, or in any other regional languages of Indian subcontinent. Irrespective of one's knowing or not knowing, calling or not calling oneself a Hindu, if one falls within the range of the above characteristics he can be called a Hindu'. Empirically it can always be established that there has been a movement within from the periphery to the core, or *vice versa*. In the situation Hinduization cannot be considered as a phenomenon parallel to proselytization of the kind adopted by Semantic religions.

Anthropology of Hinduism has so far adopted three basic approaches which using Sanskrit terms I would describe as follows:

1) *Deshatmaka* (spatial-distributional). This approach is influenced by diffusionism. M.N. Srinivas and N.K. Bose are the leading scholars of this school of interpretation. In his famous book *Religion and society among the Coorgs of South India* (1952), Srinivas analyses the Great Tradition of Sanskritic Hinduism. He talks of regional spread, peninsular spread and all-India spread of Brahmanic practices and beliefs. He also describes the process of Sanskritization, combining both the distributional and processual aspects of Hinduism. Sanskritization refers essentially to the phenomenon of cultural mobility that brings tribal groups into the fold of the Hindu caste system, or Hinduism. Bose also combines the distributional and processual aspects in his study of the Juang tribe of Orissa. Unlike Srinivas, he did not emphasize the sacerdotal elements. In his view the Juang tribe was Hinduized mainly through techno-economic transformation.
2) *Kalatmaka* (temporal-processual). This approach has developed from the insights of Robert Redfield, Milton Singer and A.L.

Kroeber. It has been widely applied to the study of both contemporary and historical processes of transformation of Indian society. Surajit Sinha is the leading figure. Following Redfield, he has applied the tribe-caste and tribe-peasant continua as a conceptual framework for the study of tribal transformation in central India.

3) *Deshakalateeta-mulyatmaka* (trans-spatio-temporal and value-based). This approach has been advocated by Baidyanath Saraswati who considers religion as a transcendental phenomenon, and hence calls for a transanthropological perspective. But as of now, this is in a formative stage.

Looking into the contemporary scene we find that religion and nationality are fused into one criterion of identification. Thus emotionality, or sentimentality, gets doubly strengthened within the space-time framework. This I would call *Deshakala-bhavatmaka* (spatio-temporal-sentimental) approach to study Hinduism.

REFERENCES

Bose, N.K. 1941. Hindu method of tribal absorption. *Science and Culture*, 7, pp.188-94.

Ghurye, G.S. 1963. (1943). *The scheduled tribes*. Popular Prakashan, Bombay.

Saraswati, Baidyanath 1970. *Contributions to the understanding of Indian civilization*. Karnataka University, Dharwad.

Saraswati, Baidyanath 1984. *The spectrum of the sacred: essays on the religious traditions of India*. Concept Publishing Co., New Delhi.

Saraswati, Baidyanath 1986. Five characteristics of Hinduism. Paper presented at the National Seminar on *Hinduism*, Nehru Memorial Museum and Library, New Delhi.

Sen, K. 1961. *Hinduism*. Penguin Books.

Sinha, Surajit 1982. *Tribes and Indian civilization*. N.K. Bose Memorial Foundation, Varanasi.

Swain, J.E. 1970. *A history of world civilization*.

11

PRIVATE PROPERTY FORMATION AMONG HIGHLAND TRIBAL COMMUNITIES OF NORTH-EAST INDIA

S. N. Mishra

Introduction

In this paper we propose to study the phenomenon of the rise and growth of private property in the means of production among the highland tribal communities of North-East India. A study of this nature, apart from being purely of historical interest, is equally important for its contemporary relevance, insofar as private property formation in these communities has acquired such speed and coverage today as it never had through their known history. Furthermore, since the property relations provide, as if, the ground or constitute the base over which stand the production, distribution and exchange relations of an economy, an understanding of the changes in the nature and scope of the former is bound to enrich our understanding of the latter. And this is of crucial importance specially for those who are engaged in the design of development strategy in and for the region. For the purpose of this essay we shall simply take private property to be a bundle of rights over a particular means of production an individual or family exercises or enjoys to the exclusion of all others, which may be individuals, families, clans, village, tribe or the state. In the most developed form of private property it is well-known that such a bundle comprises rights to permanently possess, to bequeath, transfer (alienate), lease, mortgage, hypotheticate and sale without restrictions. To reach this stage is itself the result of a historical process. Our goal is precisely to go along and lay bare this process.

In our focus of study are those tribes which inhabit the mountainous tracts of Arunachal Pradesh, Nagaland, Manipur, Mizoram and Meghalaya. The tribal communities settled in the plains, like those of Brahmaputra, Barak (Surma) and Imphal rivers and also those of Tripura plains are excluded from our purview. The period covered is from late the 18th century to the present times. For the period prior to this there is precious little information available on the social and economic life of the mountain tribes. There are of course scanty references to their political and economic relations with the neighbouring kingdoms in the plains in the chronicles of the latter. Although useful by way of supplementary information, from these references alone one cannot hope to reconstruct the property relations within the tribes existing before the 18th century. It is with the British and through their pen that for the first time worthwhile written records begin to appear. The British contact with the hill tribes inevitably followed the grant of Diwani of Bengal in 1765 and was completed with the Treaty of Yandabo in 1826 and annexation of Assam. And then began their penetration into the hills – first into North Cachayr, Jayantia, Khasi, Garo Hills, then Naga Hills and finally Lushai Hills – a process that eventually culminated into a semi-administration of these hills by the end of the last century. Penetration into the Arunachal hills had been slow and halting so much so that it had remained incomplete when the British left the country in 1947. It is during this period of over a century and a half of contact, penetration and eventual administration that records relating to hill tribes were compiled. First in the general reports like those of Pemberton (1835), Robinson (1841), Dalton (1872) and Mackenzie (1884) and then in the form of ethnographic accounts of specific tribes, of which those by Hutton (1921), Mills (1926, 1937), Hodson (1908), Shakespear (1912), Parry (1932) and Gurdon (1914) form the high watermark.[1] In the post-Independence period more such accounts were added. It is from this material that we hope to reconstruct the property relations prevalent in the hill tribes before the British appeared on the scene and then to take note of the new elements introduced by them including the modifications their actions brought about in those relations. We shall then examine the mechanism by which development plans and the market together, in the post-Independence period, have given a boost to private property formation that goes on apace currently. Finally, we shall have occasion to reflect upon the predictable consequences of this process on the traditionally equitable economic life of the tribes.

Traditional Property Relations Prior to the British

From the early British reports what stands out to be the single most important common feature of all the tribes in the mountainous tracts of the region is their living by shifting agriculture supplemented by animal husbandry, gathering of forest produce, hunting, fishing and basic handicrafts geared to fashioning of own-use simple tools and making of household utilities including cloth, goods of personal ornamentation and residential decoration. The means and methods of these activities were remarkably similar from tribe to tribe. Shifting agriculture in particular did not involve animal-drawn plough and was solely based on human energy.

Through this mode of living the tribes largely satisfied their basic needs but contrary to general belief they were not self-sufficient, and some of them not even in respect of food. For this reason they traded among themselves and exchanged goods with the traders from the plains at the foot of the hills and also with neighbouring regions of Burma and Tibet. At the doorways of the passes from the hills to the Assam and East Bengal (Bangladesh) plains called *duars*, there were numerous trading posts where seasonal exchanges took place. This is not the place to go into the details of the trade relations but for purposes of illustrating inter-tribal trade[2] we may mention Nishi (Dafla) exchanging *mithun* (*bos frontalis*) for rice and cloth and Miris exchanging salt for the same purpose with the Apa Tanis; Mishmis exchanging their cane helmets, bags and coats with Adis (Abors) and Noctes for rice and cattle; Lhota Nagas selling salt to Rengma who in turn selling it to Sema, and Aos selling cloth for Konyak *dao*. In the trade with the plains metal and metal goods specially iron and iron-tools, salt, grain, cattle and cloth were the major items which the tribes acquired in exchange for their forest produce such as musk, tusk, hide, wax, munji, mismi-teeta, etc. And to these were added some cultivated items, chiefly cotton, ginger, black pepper, mustard, opium and red chillies. Khasis distinguished themselves by exporting, apart from cotton, oranges and iron (smelted out of scrapped ore found over their plateau) to Sylhet plains.

Almost all trade transactions, inter-tribal and with the plains were carried out in barter form exchanging goods for goods. Only some Naga groups are reported to have used a form of currency[3] as a medium of exchange between them. Money as a medium of exchange was virtually absent. This had two clear consequences. Firstly, there would not arise trade balances for the tribes. Secondly, exchangeable surpluses (net of imports), if any, would fail to be commuted into money and then accumulated as money-capital. Between and within tribes, animals, specially *mithun*, to some extent played the role of a medium of exchange and a measure of value. But being perishable, subject to devaluation through aging and at the top of it a consumption item greatly in demand for ritual feasts and ceremonies, could not be a dependable means of surplus accumulation for anybody for long. Yet those who had relatively large numbers of *mithun* over a stretch of time were recognized as the wealthy of the tribe.

Besides trade with the plains described above, lack of self-sufficiency induced them further to carry out frequent predatory raids on the plain's settled population near their foot-hills. This was done mainly for looting of grain, cattle, utensils and such necessities. Victims will occasionally be carried off to the hills in the hope of receiving ransom afterwards. Head-hunting for ritual purposes notably by Nagas and Garos has been noted as another motive behind the raids. Raiding, however, could not be a pastime as it involved risk of band members losing life and involving punitive reprisals well into the hills. In the declining days of the Ahom Kingdom, weak kings, in order to prevent raids, permitted the neighbouring tribes of Arunachal to collect annual dues called *posha* from their subjects at the border of the kingdom in the form of grain, cattle, salt, cloth, etc. So did the successor English government until *posha*, having been commuted into money and paid through treasury, was finally abolished towards the end of the 19th century.[4]

This then was the highland tribal economy of the North-East Region based on shifting agriculture, hunting, gathering, trade and predation, to the exception of Apa Tanis and Angami Nagas who had adopted settled agriculture. It is in this background that we have to discuss the traditional forms of property. Each village had its well-recognised territory which, when need arose, was defended with force, failing which recognition was sought through ceremonial or matrimonial alliances or by seeking protection and becoming a tributary to a strong village as among the Nagas. In this way was maintained the territorial rights of the village community. By virtue of being members all individuals and families had rights to practise agriculture, hunting, fishing and gathering within the village territory. If a member left the village all his rights ceased to exist but could be reobtained provided the chief, the elders' council or the village head, *gaonbura*, consented. In some tribes village territory could be divided between clans and further between lineages of a clan retaining a part as the common village land, as among the Khasis, Garos and some Naga groups. Each clan owned its land permanently with rights of the clan members to use it exclusively. There could also, however, be rule prescribing reversion of a part of the clan land at the time of its every subsequent subdivision as among the western Rengma Nagas.[5]

Shifting agriculture by virtue of the fact that the cultivated block shifts annually or at intervals of two years to different locations within the village territory or within the clan territory it does not permit private right of permanent ownership or possession of individual pieces of land by the members. Invariably every year a new block of forest land is cleared collectively and then distributed among the members of the village or clans for private cultivation. The distribution is done by the elders or the chief in consultation with the elders, normally on the basis of number of months to feed in a family. After a year or two of cultivation the whole block is left fallow untill it is opened up again and the process is repeated after several years corresponding to the shifting or *jhuming* cycle as it is called in the region. At the subsequent reopening it is only by chance that a family may get back the same piece of land in the block which it had cultivated at the previous opening. Indeed, the family's requirement of land for cultivation may turnout to be more or less now depending upon how its size and composition changed during the intervening period, which normally stretched over 15 to 20 years.

There are exceptionally few writers who did not confirm common ownership of land among the hill tribes of the North-East region, Hutton (1921) is one among them who claimed that among the Sema Nagas, 'All land is now privately owned'. In fact he goes further to claim it for most Naga tribes, 'for almost all the land in the Naga Hill District is now privately owned, and has long been subject to sales, gifts, marriage settlements, and even mortgages of sorts'. Yet at the same place he contradicts his position by saying that 'much land is of necessity owned jointly by brothers and even cousins, the eldest allotting the land for yearly cultivation' and admitting that 'land held in common by the whole community . . . probably still exists in one or two of the most eastern Gema villages. . .'.[6] Apparently Hutton confuses clan and sub-clan (lineage) common ownership right over parts of village territory with private ownership of land. A similar mistake had been made by Gurdon (1914) when the common clan lands among the Khasis – the *ri kynti* lands – were characterized by him as lands under private ownership. Had it not been the case, how and what for the common village lands, following Mills (1937) quoted earlier, among the Rengma Nagas would increase at every successive division of the clans. If Hutton was right one wonders what prevented the British to impose and collect land revenue from private land owners instead of house tax which yielded a lower amount. In brief, Hutton had assumed too much for himself and seems to have been a partisan of private property theory *vis-a-vis* the English debate on forms of property in land in India.[7]

While dealing with property in land it is important to bring the rights of the chiefs in the picture. Not all tribes in the highlands of the region had chiefs. And even among Naga groups known for their powerful chiefs, the Aos did not have them and their village affairs were managed by a council of elders who vacated office at fixed interval to their immediate lower age-group members.[8] Others like Mishmi, Konyak and Sema Nagas, Kuki-Lushai groups, Khasis and Garos had chiefs. Generally each village would have its chief who functioned independently of other village chiefs. But in the interest of peace some chiefs would enter into ceremonial or marriage alliances with others. Among Konyak, Sema Nagas and Lakher-Lushai groups the chiefs were drawn from particular clans, the so-called 'Royal clans', chosen with meticulous care in favour of the pure-blood line. By this arrangement while such clans acquired the flavour of a superior caste, the village chiefs became 'brother chiefs', helping each other in maintaining peace and warding off enemy attacks.[9] Another way of maintaining peace was by engaging in tributory relations. The chief of a weak village would seek protection from the chief of a powerful village or be forced into it by the latter on condition of paying tribute and obeisance. Tributory relation would also arise when one village with plentiful land would permit people of another village with land shortage to cultivate some land in its territory on payment of tribute.

A village chief had several privileges. But here we shall focus briefly on *labour-service* and *grain* (or a sheef of crop harvest) dues only which have a bearing on property rights in land. Among the chiefly Naga tribes it was *labour service* for the chief's *jhum* fields, and among the Lushai-Kuki groups in some, for instance, Lakhers it was *grain dues* and in others both. The rate of both the dues varied from village to village. Hutton (1921) says in some Sema villages right to free labour was not there; in others it varied from 4 to 16 days labour a year from each household, 'for one-half of which in some villages, the chief must give a nominal payment of a little salt or a small piece of meat to each worker'.[10] For the Lakher, Parry (1932) mentions two forms of grain dues: *sabai*, a fixed number of baskets of paddy from every household, and *rapaw*, number of baskets in proportion to householder's volume of crop harvest. In most Lakher villages *sabai* was the only due payable 'in recognition of his chiefship'. However, in Chapi and Savang groups of Lakher the village chiefs collocated *rapaw* as well 'for the privilege of cutting *jhums* in his land'. When this is read with Parry's contention that a Lakher chief is 'the owner of the village lands',[11] it becomes immediately transparent that *rapaw* was land rent. Now the question before us is why *rapaw* was confined to the above two groups while *sabai* was the general rule in all Lakher villages. There is no doubt that *rapaw* was a later development, most probably following the grant of *pattas* to the chiefs by the British, a point to which we shall return later, whereby Chapi and Savang chiefs claimed ownership right in land and succeeded in imposing land rent on the villagers.

Thus, the traditional *grain dues* were payable to the Lushai-Kuki chiefs–*sabai* in the case of Lakher — by right of their being chief and not by their right of land ownership. Land commonly belonged to the village and/or the clans. Similar was the position among the Khasis where chiefs were elected and had no right to land rent or land-revenue.[12] For the Naga groups no English writer in any case has claimed that Chiefs were the owners of village land. The free *labour service* rendered to them was by virtue of their being chiefs. In this context it is also worth bearing in mind that a great part of the grain thus collected or the additional produce made possible through free labour service customarily went back to the people through feasts and festivals. In summary, in the tribes with chiefs or without chiefs, land was the common property of the village and/or the clans.

In contrast to land, the next important means of production, namely, animals, in particular *mithun* were privately owned. So were the few and simple tools and implements used in shifting agriculture, hunting, gathering, fishing and crafts. Ceremonial goods and ornaments were of course privately owned, but these, being no means of production, are out of our purview.

British Measures Favouring Rise of Private Property

One of the most innovative measures introduced by the British favouring the rise of private property among the highland tribes of the North-East was the introduction of money. Money was introduced in several ways. Initially it was through *trade levies* and *trade monopolies*. After the grant of Diwani of Bengal when the officers of the East India Company began controlling the foot-hill *hauts* in Shylhet and Goalpara they soon enforced customs duties to be paid in money by the Garo and Khasi hillmen. The latter were thus obliged to sell at least part of their goods for money. Then followed monopoly control of trade with these tribes specially in cotton and salt. Garo cotton came in for increasing demand for Manchester's booming textile industry. The English purchased cotton and sold salt for money. The Garos, whose main item of export was cotton, had no alternative but to accept money as the medium of exchange for their trade at the foot-hill *hauts*.[13] Occupation of Khasi hills in 1833 gave the next opportunity for monopoly mining and trade in lime, coal, metals and minerals. The Khasi chiefs, one after the other, were made to enter into agreements which in due course were given the shape of *Sanads* whereby they were made to cede to the company Government the mining and trade rights in the above items in their respective territories and were to receive half of the profits, in money of course, arising out of sale, lease or any other disposal of these items.[14] A remarkable feature of these agreements was that the Khasi chiefs received money for an ownership right which they had never had in the past.

In the north, the *posha* dues given to Arunachal tribes, a point noted in the last section, were commuted to money towards the last quarter of the 19th century until *posha* was altogether abolished.

The third and very effective method of introducing money was the imposition of a general house tax on the population in all the administered hills of the region. It was realized in money through the chiefs and village *gaonburas*, not without hardship to the hillmen at the beginning.[15] As the administered area increased so increased the revenue from house tax.[16] The highlanders met their house tax dues partly by exchanging their goods for money, partly by coolie labour on government works for which they were paid in money and partly by coming down to work in the tea gardens. Since working as wage labourers was something unthinkable for the tribesmen and administration of the area required construction of paths, roads and public buildings at administrative headquarters, the chiefs and village heads were made responsible through signed agreements for providing the required labour for porterage for which the latter were paid money wages. To add to this, but one-shot affair was to recruit a contingent of 8,000 tribesmen to serve in Europe during the First World War. A considerable amount of money was brought this way which resulted in soaring prices inside the hills. Sema recruits could pay back their grain debt and Wanching and Wakching ornament-makers made fortunes. [17] A similar thing happened due to money gained in war work during the Second World War. It was reported that some Nagas were 'rolling in money' and had taken even to buying condensed milk at a rate of one rupee per tin. And finally money 'poured' through the Baptist Missions who paid regular salaries to pastors and teachers and made gifts to converts.[18]

It is not surprising therefore that by the first quarter of the present century, as Hutton and Mills claim, money has generally been accepted as a medium of exchange, a means of payment for grain debts and marriage price in the administered areas. Above all it became a store of value and a means of accumulating private wealth, arising out of profits earned through trade and sale of surpluses by the producers. Thus while the foundations had been laid, sporadic money wealth had still to wait for the post-Independence period for becoming a source of private capital and capital accumulation.

The second most important innovation the British made was to confer private property rights in land on the chiefs of the Lushai-Kuki and Khasi-Garo clans, by issuing *pattas* and *sanads*, a right they never had before as we have seen in the last section. Having had the experience of innumerable military expeditions in the hills the British had realized that they could not put their administration on a secure footing without the support of the chiefs. Hence this concession at the expense of common property in land. The result was imposition of land rent and privatization of village commons by the chiefs whenever and wherever opportunity arose. We have noted this in the case of Lushai hills in the last section. Among the Garos the *nokmas*, as a result of this conferment, emerged as a 'landed aristocracy' and undertook large-scale cotton farming by enlisting the services of the growing body of landless peasants and imported labour. Cotton-growing was purely for commercial purposes of earning money and wealth.[19] The Land Reforms Commission for Khasi Hills (1974) while reviewing the rights in land said that it was necessary to explain to the people that 'land revenue (rather land rent) is an introduction of the British, copied later by some *ri kynti* owners and certain chiefs'. This had thus set the precedent for some dans to sub-divide their common lands and claim their share as private property. Both these processes of private property formation circumscribed and abridged the right of permanent entitlement to land for subsistence enjoyed by all the members of the village and the clan. In these hills efforts were also made by the British to introduce here and there permanent, wet rice culture which automatically required permanent possession of the land pieces thus cultivated.

Post-Independence Development

The processes just described which came to take root during the British rule received tremendous boost when the five-year development plans opened unprecedented opportunities and public expenditure rose by leaps and bounds in the post-Independence period. Just to give an indication, the per capita plan outlay in Arunachal rose from Rs. 224 in the Third Plan to Rs. 4,500 in the Sixth and was slated to double during the Seventh Plan. Similar was the position of Nagaland and Mizoram, being far above the country's average.[20] The effects of the development plans on the economic life of the highland tribes I have discussed in some detail elsewhere.[21] Here I shall briefly focus on ways of money-earning, money-capital accumulation in private hands and growth of private property in land.

Out of the plan and non-plan public expenditure money flows in private hands in three major ways : (1) as profits from contract works on public construction activities; (2) as salaries from state and central services, and (3) as outright transfers in the form of subsidy and grant associated with private beneficiary-oriented projects in agriculture, horticulture, animal husbandry, small-scale industries and craft, transport services and so on. A second source of money income is the sale of surpluses by well-off cultivators, specially from the produce of cash crops and plantations.

According to one study in some parts of Meghalaya as much as 45 per cent of the area under cultivation was found to be under cash crops and plantation.[22] Logging from privately owned forests by chiefs and private individuals provides the third source of money income earnings.[23]

Savings from money income increasingly find an outlet to turn into money capital. Certainly this is a small class of elite that has reached this position. This class has taken shape out of the erstwhile chiefs, *gaonburas*, clan leaders and their descendants. The outlets for money capital investment lie in the sphere of contractor business, trade, transport, merchandise, orchard and plantation development, permanent agriculture and dairy. The balance of liquid savings are either kept in hoard, lent on interest or deposited in Banks where these are available. In 1984 all the highland States and Union Territories in the region had very high deposit-to-credit ratio,[24] with Meghalaya 4 : 1, Nagaland 3 : 1, Arunachal Pradesh 4 : 1 and Mizoram 4 : 1. In this context it is advisable to bear in mind that the rate of urbanization in the region during the post-Independence period has been fastest in the country.

Besides the emergence and growth of private capital let us have a look at the process of private property growth in land. A major goal of the development plans has been to convert the shifting cultivation area in the hills into permanent agriculture, orchard or plantations depending upon the elevation, gradient and suitability of the lands. Considerable incentives are offered to the people for this purpose. And no sooner such conversion takes place the land comes under permanent possession of the families concerned. For all practical purposes it is treated as private property subject to sale, lease and inheritance. It is here again that the elite class referred to earlier has seized the opportunity of privatizing the village and clan common lands. This process is on and will continue until a cadestral survey is done to map out the ownership rights. But this is not in the interest of the elite at the moment as it will take away the opportunity of privatization. Be that as it may, there has developed a general urge among the highlanders to take to permanent agriculture and thereby acquire private property in land. According to NSS (1976-77) in the region an overwhelming majority of the tribal families had taken to permanent agriculture wherever it was introduced by the governments in the region. And between 40 and 70 per cent of shifting cultivators had come to have some land under permanent cultivation, in other words, private property in land.[25] The whole process of agrarian change has given impetus to the rise and development of markets for land, labour and lease cultivation. This is reflected in the declining proportion of cultivators and rising proportion of agricultural labourers in the occupational distribution of main workers in the highland States and Union Territories of the region.[26]

Concluding Observations

To sum-up, prior to the British rule land for shifting cultivation was the chief means of production and was held as common property of the village and/or the clan among the highland tribal communities of the North-East India. All members of the village or the clan had permanent entitlement to land for cultivation. Everybody had equal right to hunt, gather, collect firewood and housing material in the common lands. In the tribes with chiefs, the chiefs enjoyed certain privileges. But village lands were not their private property. Animal stocks and simple tools and implements used in various activities were, however, held privately as family or individual property. Goods were exchanged for goods within and between the tribes and also with the traders at the foot-hill *hauts*.

As the British began to penetrate and eventually administer the hills beginning from the last quarter of the 18th century they introduced money. In fact in the transactions with the government they made the use of money obligatory. By the early decades of the present century in the administered areas money had become a medium of exchange, a means of payment and above all a store of value for those who made profits in trade or had surpluses to sell. Secondly, although the general British policy was not to interfere in the internal life of the people, in the interest of seeking support for their administration, they conferred upon the chiefs private property rights in land of their respective villages in the Khasi-Garo hills and the Lushai-Kuki areas. This was the origin of private property in land.

The real opportunity for money accumulation in private hands and its turning into private capital was opened up by the development plans in the post-Independence period. All-out efforts to convert shifting cultivation into permanent agriculture, orchard and plantation created a general urge among the hillmen for private property in land. The elite class drawn from erstwhile chiefs, *gaonburas* and clan leaders seized this opportunity to privatize the common lands. This elite which controls the political processes and governs the highland States and Union Territories of the region has on one pretext or the other postponed a cadestral survey until now, as this will inhibit the process of privatization. In the meanwhile markets for land, labour and lease cultivation have taken root and are expanding. Since the potentials for private capital accumulation and land acquisition are far from exhausting, the processes of private property formation and growth are bound to continue in the foreseeable future at the expense of the common property rights of the people.

NOTES

1. For a selection of the early writings see Verrier Elwin, *India's North-East Frontier in the 19th century*, Oxford University Press, 1959.
2. For details see Pemberton R.B., *Report on Bhutan* (1839) William Robinson, *A descriptive account of Assam* (1841) Alexender Mackanzie, *A history of relations of the government with the hill tribes of north-east Bengal* (1884).
3. These were (called Lays) in the form of large disks cast out of brass or an alloy of brass and tin originally obtained from Shans in upper Burma and later manufactured in Assam. There were also currency in the form of large spear heads. See Hutton J.H., *The Sema Naga* (1921) and Mills, J.P., *The Ao Nagas* (1926) and *The Rengma Nagas* (1937).
4. On *posha* See Pemberton, *op. cit.* and Mackenzie, *op. cit.* and Barpujari, H.K., *Problems of hill tribes: the north-east frontier*, 3 vols. Lawers Block stall, Gauhati. I have touched it in some detail in my paper, Arunachal's tribal economic formations and their dissolution, *Economic & Political Weekly*, 18 (43), October 22, 1983.
5. This had the effect of gradual increase of the area under village common since such transferred pieces of land, says J.P. Mills. "Would remain common land for ever". See his, *The Rengma Nagas* (*op. cit*).
6. Hutton, J.H. (1921), *op. cit.* pp. 155-156; Gurdon, R.T., *The Khasis* (1914).
7. See Henery Summer Maine (1871) *The village communities in the East and West*; Baden Powell (1896) *The Indian village community*; Louis Dumont, The village community from Munro to Maine and also Daniel Thorner, Marx on India and the Asiatic mode of production, in *Contributions to Indian Sociology*, IX 1966.
8. Mills, J.P. *The Ao Nagas* (1926), *op. cit.*
9. Furer Haimendorf, *The naked Nagas* (1939); Hutton, J.H. (1921), *op. cit.*; Mills, J.P., *The Rengma Nagas* (1937), *op. cit*; Shakespear, J., *The Lushai Kuki clans* (1912); Parry, N.E., *The Lakher* (1932).
10. Hutton, J.H. (1921), *op. cit.*, p. 147.
11. Parry, N.E. (1932), *op. cit.* p. 252.
12. *Report of the land reforms commission for Khasi Hills* (1974), Government of Meghalaya. Details of the Khasi land tenure is to found in Chowdhury, J.N., *The Khasi canvas*, (1978) and Mathew, T. (ed.), *Tribal economy of the north-east region* (1980).
13. Bhattacharjee, J.B. (1977), *The Garo and the English*, Radiant Publishers, New Delhi.
14. Barpujari, H.K. (1970), *op. cit.*, vol. I & II. See also Chowdhury, J.N. (1978), *op. cit.*
15. Many in the Lushai Hills were unable to pay the house-tax in money for which reason for a time it was collected in grain but was shortly replaced by money again. See Barpujari, H.K. (1970), *op. cit.*
16. Allen, B.C., Gait, E.A. and others, *Gazetteer of Bengal and north-east India* (Reprint 1979), Mittal Publications, Delhi.
17. Barpujari, H.K. *op. cit.*, volume III.
18. Furer Haimendorf, *The naked Nagas* (1937, revised 1946), *op. cit.*
19. Bhattacharjee, J.B. (1977), *op. cit.*

20. Figures available with the Planning Commission.
21. Mishra, S.N., (1985), *Tribal economic transformation: the north-east Indian pattern*, V.R.F. Series No. 117, Institute of Developing Economies, Tokyo.
22. Sukumaran Nair, M.K. (1983) *Agrarian relations and shares in Meghalaya*, Ph.D. Thesis, NEHU, Shillong.
23. In Nagaland, Meghalaya, Manipur and Arunachal Pradesh forest area is predominantly under the ownership and control of district councils, village communities, chiefs and individuals. See *Basic statistics of north-eastern region* (1980) North-Eastern Council, Shillong.
24. Statistics obtained form Reserve Bank of India Office, Delhi.
25. National Sample Survey, Some results of the survey on *jhum* cultivation in the north-eastern States (31st Round, July 1976 – June 1977), *Survekshana*, April 1979.
26. For details see Mishra, S.N. (1985), *op. cit.*

12

INDUSTRIALIZATION AND THE NATURE OF TRIBAL TRANSFORMATION

Pranab Kumar Das Gupta

Introduction

The mid-19th century was a crucial period so far as the industrialization in India is concerned. During this period, the first successful jute and cotton mills were established, coalfields were connected by rail to the port of Calcutta and rapid expansion of railway lines throughout the country began. For about half a century following this period, industrial growth in India was limited to these four sectors. In the first decade of the 20th century, the establishment of Tata Iron and Steel Company at Jamshedpur was a fillip to the industrial progress. After Independence, the Second Five Year Plan was another booster to the industrial development and several heavy and basic industries were established in different parts of the country, including rural tribal belts.

India is a country with an appreciably surplus labour force and there has never been a shortage of unskilled labourers for urban-industrial sectors. The workers are rather *pushed* to the labour market on account of non-sustaining capacity of land, scarcity, and lack of economic opportunities in their village environment. It has been observed that while largely self-sufficient agricultural communities, sparse population, maldistribution of population, and absence of need for money income made the recruitment of unskilled and semi-skilled labourers difficult in Africa in the initial phase (Berg, 1965), in India and other parts of overpopulated Asia, supply and recruitment of labourers were made easy by a generalized rural misery (Myers, 1959).

The Gonds joined the Parasia Coal Mines in Chindwara mainly on account of an inadequate income from their unhealthy land-holdings (Kurup 1959: 79). Orans (1959: 222) observed that a majority of the Santal industrial labourers in Jamshedpur were pushed out of their villages by dire need. Under such circumstances various tribes in different parts of the country have taken up industrial-urban jobs.

Displacement of Tribal Population

Intrusion of industries into the tribal areas has both adverse and congenial effects on the economic life of the tribal people. The large-scale displacement of the tribal population on account of acquirement of their villages for the establishment of industry and the ancillary township is one of the principal adverse effects. The major power and irrigation projects and the establishment of heavy and basic industries in the First and Second Five Year Plans such as the Mython, Konar and Panchet in Bihar; Mandira, Machkund and Hirakud in Orissa; steel projects of Rourkela, Durgapur and Bhilai in Orissa, West Bengal and Madhya Pradesh, respectively, are among the many undertakings that have resulted in a substantial displacement of tribal people. The cash compensation which was given to them was rapidly used up and in course of time they found themselves without money as well as land. They joined the ranks of landless labourers without training, equipment or aptitude for any skilled or semi-skilled jobs. Statistics show that in Bihar, West Bengal and Orissa out of 14,561 tribal families displaced from 62,494 acres, only 3,479 have been allotted alternative land (Elwin, 1963: 104-5).

In Rourkela alone 1,231 tribal families were uprooted. In addition to the monetary compensation an equal quantity of land was allotted to the oustees. Sixteen reclamation camps were set up. In such camps subsidy was given for reclamation of the land and also for cultivation. The people, mainly young men did not like to leave the industrial site and were interested to have jobs in the industries. To meet the requirements of such persons three rehabilitation colonies were established near Rourkela (Roy Burman, 1965: 26). For establishment of Chittaranjan Locomotive Works (CLW) altogether 330 Santal families were displaced owing to acquirement of six villages. Out of these, 81 families (24.5%) settled on the land which was acquired by the government for resettlement. Each family was allotted a small portion of land for construction of a hut only. Neither agricultural land was provided nor were any avenues for suitable occupation created. Consequently, the rest on their own initiative moved and settled in the neighbouring areas of Chittaranjan. Very few of the displaced Santal got employment in the CLW. Most of them worked as daily labourers under contractors in various construction works of the CLW (Dasgupta, 1964: 92). A large number of tribal people were also uprooted for the establishment of the industrial complex at Hatia, Bihar. These villagers have by and large become unskilled industrial labourers (Vidyarthi, 1970).

Another type of displacement caused by the non-sustaining capacity of land is large-scale seasonal migration to the industrial-urban sectors in search of temporary jobs. Such migration used to take place also to the tea gardens of North Bengal and Assam in the early days of plantation.

Drifting into New Occupations

When industries intruded into the tribal areas, most beneficial aspect of this was that the tribals got the opportunity to have an alternative occupation in the industries to refurbish their sagging agricultural economy while still living in the village and maintaining agriculture. They had to evolve a number of socio-economic strategies maintain this dual role. Since they belonged to the unskilled categories they did not have to bear much strain in adjusting to the nature of occupation in the industries. Morris (1960: 187-89) has observed that the major proportion of labour required for modern factory/industry in India is of unskilled sort and their nature of work in the factory is undistinguishable from that done in the rural areas.

The author has studied a number of tribes in West Bengal and Bihar in the industrial context and a summary of his work is furnished below to illustrate the nature of adaptation of the tribes involved in industrial urban jobs.

In the CLW though the number of Santals of neighbouring villages employed permanently in the factory is negligible yet a good number of them work as unskilled casual labourers in different construction and maintenance works in the factory and the township. A sample of 440 casual labourer reveals that 79 per cent of them are residents of villages within a radius of seven miles from the factory and 59 per cent live within five miles from the factory. The Santals near the CLW are primarily agriculturists. Most of them own a little land along with which they cultivate land owned by others as agricultural labourers or as share-croppers (*bhag chasi*) for which they receive half or one-third share of the product. It is observed that the casual labourers from the neighbouring villages live in their village home and keep contact with agriculture. This is a sort of compromise between agriculture and industry and this dual role gives a psychological relief and economic advantage to the people concerned as they are not totally shifted from their traditional occupation. Even the Santals who are permanently employed in the factory are attached to the field. It is common to find land being cultivated outside the factory walls. Those who have shift duties utilize their spare time in agricultural operation and during sowing and harvesting seasons avail themselves of their leave due. Regarding socio-cultural consequences it may be concluded that the change which may justly be called a structural, or institutional, change has not affected the Santal culture. The political power and structure remained unaltered, observance of religious rites and festivals unhampered, and adherence to traditional values unchallenged. Some superficial changes may obviously be observed but this change has not yet gone deep into the core of culture (Dasgupta, 1964).

During March-April 1967, a preliminary survey of some of the iron ore mines in Naomundi, Barajamda and Gua of Singhbhum, Bihar, was undertaken by the author. Operation in these small mines may be divided into seven major stages – earth-cutting, drilling and blasting, ore-collecting, ore-dressing, stacking, transport and railway wagon loading. Tribes, primarily Ho, of the neighbouring areas form the bulk of the labour force in these small mines. Two persons, usually husband and wife, or brother and sister, form a work unit. The men are usually engaged in earth-cutting, ore-dressing, loading and unloading trucks filling baskets, etc., while the women do the job of carrying baskets. The *pairing* of a male and a female in the formation of a work unit is a common phenomenon in those mines.

To get an idea of the occupational structure in the villages around the iron ore mines, a snap survey of two main hamlets of Barajamda and Khasjamda villages was undertaken. It was observed that a few families had agriculture as the only, or primary, source of livelihood. It is basically a mixed economy of agriculture and mine labour, and both men and women in almost equal number work in the mines (Choudhury and Das Gupta, 1970).

The author studied the Ho in the industrial context of Chaibasa Cement Works (CCW) in Jhinkpani in Singhbhum district of Bihar during 1969-70. The CCW employs roughly 2,000 workers and the Ho constitute about 44 per cent of the total workforce. They happen to be the most numerous ethnic group in the factory complex. Majority of them are unskilled and live in the neighbouring villages. Around Jhinkpani an unpredictable agricultural economy based on the vagaries of rainfall failed to sustain the growing tribal population and pushed a section of them out of the realm of village economy in search of other economic opportunities. The industrial complex of Jhinkpani provided them with such an economic source. However, majority of the industrial workers also continue to do agriculture. Land is still considered as the ultimate, or the long-term, source of security, whereas factory job is viewed as a temporary or short-term security or gain. The Ho industrial workers were found to utilize the factory income in expanding their agriculture. During the peak agricultural seasons like sowing and harvesting, the industrial workers avail themselves of their due leave, or engage agricultural labourers on payment. Some of the Ho workers who hail from distant villages live in the factory township. High rate of polygony among the workers living in the industrial town appears to be a social response to the requirements of maintaining the agro-industrial economic pursuit. One of the two wives from polygonous marriage of a town-based industrial worker lives in the village and looks after the agricultural work while her counterpart stays in the town and maintains the household there. Jhinkpani offers a model of adaptation to the industrial system by a tribal agrarian people through the maintenance of a dual role in the village as well as in the industry. Operation of such a binary role involves processes like combination, compartmentalization, attenuation and compromise in the respective areas of operation. One of the major consequences of such a bi-cultural existence of the Ho has been the low degree of commitment in the industrial job (Das Gupta, 1978). A more or less similar situation prevails in Bailadila, Bastar, where the Bison Horn Maria have been involved in the urban-industrial occupation (Naskar and Das Gupta, 1984).

About three-fourths of the eight lakh tea garden labourers in India work in tea estates of Assam and North Bengal and about 90 per cent of them are tribal labourers from Chota Nagpur and Madhya Pradesh. They work as pluckers mainly and the women constitute more than 50 per cent of the labour force. Much of the traditional customs and rituals of these tribes have been attenuated or have gone out of vogue, yet each group maintains its ethnic boundary through rules of commensality, dialect, etc., in a polyethnic situation (Das Gupta and Khan, 1983).

The Nature of Transformation

From the above account it appears that the nature of adaptation of the tribes in the industrial context of India is marked by the following features :

1. The tribal labourers are rather pushed to the industrial-urban job market owing to the non-sustaining capacity of land;
2. Most of the tribal labourers belong to the unskilled or semi-skilled categories and they are marginally placed in an industrial organization owing to lack of education and skill;
3. Adherence to traditional culture and agriculture involves bi-cultural way of existence with the consequence of split-commitment;
4. The tribals do not seem to lack in motivation, but they do not possess the resources and social arrangement for acquiring the requisites for smooth transition to industrial culture.

Retrospect

The present paper answers partly some of the basic questions raised by the Government of India under check-points for examination of Integrated Tribal Development Projects (ITDP) in the context of heavy industries (pamphlet published by the Ministry of Home Affairs on *Tentative outline and check-points for examination of Integrated Tribal Development Projects*, page 67).

The Government of India has taken a decision that the development of zones of influence of the industrial complexes should be prepared as a part of the project and approved before the project is clear. The Working Group on Tribal Development During Medium Term Plan, 1978-83, therefore, recommended: (a) comprehensive planning of zones of influence of industrial and mining complexes, both existing and new ones, should be taken up on a priority basis immediately; and (b) the development of the zones of influence of industrial and mining complexes should be a joint responsibility of the project and the local government both of them assuming a positive role in these common endeavour (*Report*, Ministry of Home Affairs, 1978: 79-81). The

Working Group also observed that the representation of the tribals in the skilled workforce in the new industries is insignificant and therefore recommended that 'an aggressive programme for inducting tribals at higher skilled levels should be taken up in areas having industrial enterprises'. They proposed that a scheme may be prepared in which part of the cost of employment of tribes at skilled level may be met by the Government.

The author did not make any evaluative study of any ITDP in the industrial context. However, overall findings of his various studies which have been mentioned before may be helpful in policy and planning of the ITDP.

REFERENCES

Berg, Elliot J. 1965. The development of a labour force in sub-Saharan Africa, *Economic Development and Culture Change*, 13: 394-412.

Choudhury, N.C. & Das Gupta, P.K. 1970. Impact of industrialization on the tribals: a preliminary statement. S.C. Sinha (ed.), *Research programmes in Cultural Anthropology and allied disciplines*, Anthropological Survey of India, 190-211.

Das Gupta, P.K. 1964. Impact of industrialization on tribal life, *Bulletin of the Anthropological Survey of India*, 13, (1-2), 85-106.

Das Gupta, P.K. & Iar Ali Khan 1983. *Impact of tea plantation industry on the life of tribal labourers*, Anthropological Survey of India, Calcutta.

Elwin, V. 1963. *A new deal for tribal India*, Ministry of Home Affairs, New Delhi.

Kurup, A.M. 1959. Changing phase of tribal economy: a study of tribal coal miners, *Bulletin of the Tribal Research Institute*, Chindwara, Vol. 2(3-4), 77-91.

Ministry of Home Affairs 1978. *Report of the working group on tribal development during medium term plan 1978-83*, New Delhi.

Morris, David M. 1960. The labour market in India, Wilbert E. Moore and Arnold S. Fildman (ed.) *Labour commitment and social change in developing areas*, New York, 173-200.

Myers, Charles A. 1959. 'India', in Walter Galenson (ed.), *Labour and economic development*, New York, 19-74.

Naskar, S.K. & Das Gupta, P.K. 1984. An economic profile of the Bison Horn Maria in the industrial context of Bailadila Bastar, *Human Science*, 33, (2), pp.91-101.

Orans, M. 1959. A tribal people in an industrial setting, Milton Singer (ed.), *Traditional India : structure and change*. Philadelphia, 216-235.

Roy Burman, B.K. 1965. Cultural factors in economic development and technical change in tribal India, *Journal of Social Research*, 8, (1), 21-32.

Vidyarthi, L.P. 1970. *Socio-cultural implication of industrialisation in India: a case study of tribal Bihar*, New Delhi.

13

KINJOLI: A TRIBAL VILLAGE FLOATING BEYOND THE NEW WIND

Raghunath Singh Negi

Introduction

The long-awaited inauguration of the Zonal Anthropological Museum at Jagdalpur on 7-8 April 1978, gave me an opportunity to visit Bastar once again after a long span of time, nine days short of 15 years to be exact. I was there for fieldwork during January-April 1963. I made a traverse through the Abujmarh, which had remained uncovered during the previous field trips. Earlier, in February, between 13th and 21st, I had to perform the pleasant, but arduous, task of introducing Bastar and its fascinating people to the then Director of the Anthropological Survey of India, the late Prof. N.K. Bose. This quick survey of the Bastar tribal situation in the company of Prof. Bose, a great anthropologist, and the exciting journey through the Abujmarh stirred my emotions. On 16 April 1963, I had left Bastar for the last time and now I was again on the road to Jagdalpur on 6 April 1978. Prior to this I have worked in Bastar during 1958 to 1961 spending four to six months each year, gaining a first-hand experience of the fascinating Bastar tribal life and culture. This was the time when I came to know Dr. Surajit Sinha both as a man and as an anthropologist. My field mate during those journeys into the nooks and corners of Bastar was my esteemed friend, Shri Syed Hasin Ahmed, who is again back in Nagpur from where those field studies were launched by us. Together we lived in many villages, in some places more than in others. Kinjoli, the village where we lived the longest and returned time and again, has fascinated our hearts.

The Village Studied

Kinjoli, situated about 20 km in the northwest of Jagdalpur, is predominantly a Bhatra village. It is the village where Late J.S. Tandon, a close friend and a colleague, worked from 1957-61. Each year he lived there for four to six months, and his total stay was a little over one year. Tandon had quantified the multi-ethnic character of the village.[1]

The village was divided into six hamlets, two of which were quite far away – they were rather closer to other villages and as such their socio-economic interaction with the parent village was minimal. The rest of the hamlets were compactly situated within the village boundary but were distinctly set apart to be recognisable as units. The principal reason for such setting was the segregation of the socially higher and lower groups. For example, the Mahara, the so-called untouchable caste and the lowest group even in a tribal set-up, are clustered in a separate *para*.

The village was set along a linear pattern but not clearly one-dimensional. A main thoroughfare divided the village into two halves. From the main thoroughfare flowed small lanes in each direction to various *paras*. The central place in the village was prominently distinguishable, as the village *thanagudi*, the school house, the *panchyat ghar* and a small village tea shop were located around it.

The main thoroughfare connected the village to Bastar-Jaitgiri Road, which branched off from the main highway to Jagdalpur at Bastar village and ran through the Bhatra tract right up to the Orissa border, connecting Bakawand, the Block headquarters. On the other end it passed through the agricultural field to Umergaon and ultimately to join the Jagdalpur highway near Asna. This was the shortest route to Jagdalpur but during these days it was only a cart track. At best one could cycle down, as myself and Ahmed often did. This was how the village looked between December 1959 and April 1960, when we were working among the Bhatra, the Mahara and the Muria of Bastar, and made our frequent trips apart from a month-long stay.

The Village Revisited

And it looked exactly the same when I visited the village in February 1963, with Prof. Bose. The unaffected welcome pleasantly surprised Bose, and he was fully convinced that his junior band of workers was really at home with the people. There was even a slightly embarrassing situation. We were standing in the central square when the word went round that I was back in the village. The young boys and girls came and encircled me, some hugging passionately. They persistently wanted to know where I was all these days and insisted that I should stay in the village, at least, for one day. I expressed my inability saying that I was with my officer who is pre-occupied and has come there just to have a glimpse of the village. On this one young girl exclaimed 'Oh that bald old man' in Bhatri, a dialect akin to Oriya which was intelligible to Bose. But he turned away as if he did not hear. Later he briefly remarked, 'It appears you are well-known in the village.' I embarrassedly replied, 'Sir, not so well as Tandon', conscious that my answer was not at all coherent.

In April 1978, when I arrived in the village, with some of my colleagues, I felt as if I had really not been away for all those 15 years. Almost nothing had changed. The main thoroughfare, through which we drove up to the central place, in front of the school house was just in the same condition. The general look of the young people, and their curiosity at the approaching vehicle, was the same, only now there was another generation of the youngsters looking, an almost one generation time had passed in between. As soon as I alighted from the vehicle I noticed a person stealing glances at the vehicle and just on the point of disappearing. At once, I called out his name, and Sindhu, one of our friends of old days, turned around, looked and took some hesitating steps before he finally strode to meet me half-way, since I had also started walking towards the village tea shop owned by his brother where he was standing when we arrived. I asked him whether he recognized me. He did. His was the next question, 'Where is Hasin?' With this, the time gap was completely bridged, between us. We started making inquiries about each other and many other things, oblivious of the curious onlookers, including my colleagues who had accompanied me. Sindhu explained his stolen glances and his hesitant steps. He first thought that we were revenue officials and had come to realize the *taccavi* loan and so he wanted to flee before he could be caught. We had a big laugh at this. I could see Sindhu still possessed the same agility and quickness which he did 20 years ago.

When we started from Jagdalpur for Kinjoli earlier in the morning I was having the same old route via Bastar village, in mind. But recently a road from Asna has been constructed linking Bakawand, the Block headquarters. Thus, the distance to Bakawand is reduced by nearly

16 km. The road is in good condition and must be serving the entire Bhatra tract in the north-east of Jagdalpur, much more effectively than the old road. Following the new road we reached Kinjoli via Rajnagar and Bakawand. At Rajnagar we met the old postman of the area and he vividly remembered Tandon, since he used to deliver his post. It was at Rajnagar we realized that Tandon was still very much remembered not only in Kinjoli, but in other villages of the area also.

It was a holiday for the school and we made ourselves comfortable at the school house. Soon the village *kotwar*, the *athpaharia*, the *raut* and the *patel* reached the place as is customary for these village officials to receive the visitors. The Secretary of the village *panchayat* was also there. (He is a poet of sorts and did not want to miss an opportunity to regale the visitors with his compositions.) I found that Sindhu had spread word that we had come; and since anybody from the organization to which Tandon belonged was most welcome in the village; the villagers had assembled in good numbers to make us feel at home.

In Bastar certain age-old institutions from the days of the Kakatiya rulers are still persisting. The *thanagudi* and attending *athpaharia* is one such institution. In every village there is a sort of rest house which is termed as *thanagudi* and by turn the villagers are put on duty for 24 hours, called *athpaharia*. Whenever any visitor, specially an official, comes to the village, he is straightaway directed to the *thanagudi* where the *athpaharia* makes him comfortable and fetches the *patel* (the village police official), *kotwar* (the village watchman) and the *raut* (a person belonging to a clean caste, who can fetch drinking water and cook food for the visiting official). In Kinjoli, *thanagudi* was not in a very good conditions even in the late 50s and early 60s. At that time we had camped at the *panchayatghar*, a brick structure constructed in the year 1955. It was quite a big structure with a big central hall and two side rooms. Perhaps with the construction of the *panchayatghar* the *thanagudi* went out of use and so was not so carefully maintained, as is the case in other villages. The villagers chit – chatted with us and wanted to know when Tandon had died and how. They also inquired about Mrs Tandon, who had lived in the village with her husband. It was really gratifying to see how well Tandon was still remembered in that village. I gathered that whenever these villagers face any problem, they wish that Tandon Sahib were there, so that they could go to him to seek his advice, and solve their problems. This is, of course, the greatest tribute that a field researcher can ever expect from the people amongst whom he has worked.

While my colleagues stayed in the school, I went around the village with Sindhu, to see if there had been any substantial change in the settlement pattern, the material condition and the general outlook of the village people. I found that the *paras* were as they were before and there was no change in their setting. The houses were almost the same, except some new thatches here and there. I visited the house of Jatgirin, an 89-year old lady (unusually she remembers her exact age). She could hardly see, but she remembered me very well. Hearing my voice she recognized and inquired about my family and where I stayed all these years. She told me everything about her family and her problems. Her daughter Ara, living in the same house with her husband Jhitru who is Raut by caste, and cooks food for the visiting officials, was also very much pleased to see that I was back in the village. She also excitedly informed me of her son's marriage in about eight days, and invited me to attend the wedding.

The Bhatra are divided into several sub-groups, such as Bade Bhatra, Manjhola Bhatra and San Bhatra. The Bade Bhatra are further sub-divided. In Kinjoli, most of the Bhatra belong to this sub-group and a few are San Bhatra. As implied by the term *bade* and *san*, the former are the highest in social hierarchy and the *san* (small) are the lowest. It appears that in north Bastar there is a well-defined process of social mobility, by which the lowly placed Muria become San Bhatra, and ultimately, with the economic and social upliftment, may even obtain the higher sub-group status of the Bhatra.

Marriages are restricted within the sub-groups with clan-exogamy. Among the Bade Bhatra and Raut it was found that more often a number of villages form some sort of a circuit, for selection of mates. The frequency of marriages between the villages within the circuit is much more than outside. It may thus be found that in a village a number of wives may be originating from a particular village, and also may be related to one another (patrikin). In this manner some sort of close breeding is being followed which will have the effect of increasing the homozygosity of the genotypes. This phenomenon has sometimes been explained in terms of lack of proper communication. But in the recent years even with the vast improvement in the communication network, there is practically no change in the marriage structure, a challenge to the notion that communication influences marriage distances. It is thus apparent that mating structure is independent of communication.

In the Bhatra tract, specially in Orissa, the *Satya Mahima Dharam* movement, popularly known as the Bhagat movement, started in 1837. It is a reformist movement having some followers in the area. But I was surprised that this movement had not made much progress, at least in Kinjoli. The two Bhagats whom I could meet this time were the old *sarpanch* (his father was among the first lot to become a Bhagat) and his son. Perhaps not more than two families follow the *Satya Mahima Dharma*, this includes the family of the village *kotwar*. It seems that since the Bhagat movement did not help the Bhatra to attain a 'very high' status in social hierarchy the attraction towards it was lost. The Bhatra are one of the most status-conscious people in the whole of the Bastar region.

Materially also, I did not find much change in the village. To start from the village tea shop, it had the same old equipments which used to be there 20 years ago. In the few houses which I visited, I found that the material gains were not very many and the household utensils were almost the same as 20 years ago. The modern communication system and the Block development programme had apparently brought about little change in the material life of the villagers. One thing which struck me most was that while the old traditional institutions and land-marks in the village were well maintained, the new features introduced by the State development agencies were ill-maintained. The school house was in a very dilapidated condition. Actually, one of the roofs of the back room was just hanging and could fall apart any moment. So also the *panchayatghar*. It had been partitioned into 3-4 rooms, where, I was told, the school teachers were residing permanently. As such the building had become non-functional in the sense that it did not serve the purpose for which it was built. One additional feature which I found in the village was a small well-kept house of a *seth* (wealthy Baniya) who had come permanently to reside in the village. This house has come up next to the *panchyatghar*. Perhaps the presence of the *seth* has saved the village folk from the trouble of taking their marketable goods to Jagdalpur or Muli marketplace, as they used to do in the olden days. At the same time, it is clear that the exploitative agency has made inroads right into the village, with predictable results.

While driving from Raipur one could notice the well-maintained National Highway to Jagdalpur. This was not the dream of the people walking down to Jagdalpur 20 years ago for the whole day. Now one can reach there within a few hours by a luxury bus or taxi. However, from Keskal to Jagdalpur the general landscape has remained unchanged. The pedestrian traffic on the road can tell you even now exactly whether you are passing through the Muria or San Bhatra or Bhatra tract. No change is perceptible in the dress pattern or the distinctive hair-style of various populations. The body built and the features have also generally remained unchanged. What is changed is the small hutment shops on the roadside, having grown phenomenally, especially in Pharasgaon and Kondagaon. The business houses have prospered, but the hutments of the larger population of Bastar remain the same.

An unfortunate incident had marred our visit. The old *athpaharia* was bitten by a mad dog just a year ago and till this day he showed the acute sign of hydrophobia. Since morning the village prist and witch-doctor were singing to overpower him by magical spells. At long last he was roped. I do not know what eventually happened to him. Since the modern system of medicine has not yet reached the village, obviously he was left to the wisdom of his people.

My revisits confirm the 20 years of unchanged Kinjoli. The eternal tribal life flows there beyond the new wind blowing in other parts of the world.

NOTE

1. The ethnic composition of Kinjoli, as recorded by Tandon :

Ethnic Group	*Occupation*	*No. of Families*
Bhatra	Agriculturist	194
Mahara	Weavers & Cattle-herdsman	38
Raut	Cattle-herdsman	12
Panka	Weavers	11
Keota	Parched rice & gram-seller	8
Sundi	Wine distiller	7
Mongia	Rope-maker	2
Lohar	Blacksmith	2
Panara	Flowerseller	2
Kumhar	Potter	1
Halba	Teacher	1
	Total:	278

J.S. Tandon 1959. The Bhatra of Bastar, *Bull. of the Deptt. of Anthropology*, 8, (2), pp.33-54.

INDEX OF TRIBES

ABOR,
melody 131, 135; Adi 77; exchange 227

AHOM,
state 44, 227

APA TANI,
cosmogonic myth 65, 66, 67, 81; exchange 227; settled agriculture 228; worldview 118

ARGONAUT,
of the Western Pacific 101

BADAGA,
melody 131, 135

BHATRA,
unchanging village 247-253

BHIL,
Hinduism and 221

BHUIYAN,
30, 111; melody 131

BHUMIJ,
28, 29, 32, 40, 41, 51, 53, 54, 56, 120; Hindu social order 45, 221; Kshatriya status 30, 222; melody 131; non-tribe relations 38-39, 42; state-formation 43; Vaishnava impact 46

BIRHOR,
119; worldview 17, 108, 110-113, 115, 117

BODO,
219

BORI,
cosmogonic myth 65, 81

BUGUN KHOWA,
cosmogonic myth 66, 89

CHENCHU,
demography 169-182

CHIMBU,
in the New Guinea 102

DAFLA,
118; cosmogonic myth 72; Nishi exchange 226

DHAMMAI MIJI,
cosmogonic myth 68

DHURWA,
melody 131

DIDAYIE,
musical instrument 134

GADABA,
melody 131

GALLONG,
77; cosmogonic myth 65, 82

GARO,
35; chief 230, 233; head-hunting 228; hillmen 232; Hills 226, 236; land-man ratio 39; tribal lore 124-127; village land 229

GOND,
30, 219; Hinduism and 221; industrialization 240

HALBA,
253

HO,
27, 30; industrialization 242-43

HOPI INDIANS,
53

HRUSSO AKA,
cosmogonic myth 65, 69, 74, 82

IRULAR,
curing practices 151-166; science and superstition 21

JAINTIA,
44; Hills 226; Jarawa 19, 179; population 178
JENU KURUBA,
natural right denied 50
JUANG
28; Hinduism and 221, 223; melody 135

KADAR,
melody 135
KHAMPTI,
cosmogonic myth 68
KHARIA,
131; Hill Kharia 120; melody 131, worldview 113-14
KHASI,
44, 79, 219, 237; belief 67, 70, 75, 76, 79; chief 229, 230, 232, 233; cosmological conflict 18, 19; export 227; Hills 226, 233, 236; hillsmen 232; village land 228, 230
KINNARA,
melody 132
KORKU,
melody 135
KOTA,
119; demography 169-182; worldview 118
KOYA,
120; worldview 118
KUKI,
171, 219, 237; chief 230, 231, 233; village 236
KURUMBAR, 152; hamlet 154; herbalist 156; intermarriage with Mudugar 153

MALER,
219
MALLIA,
demography 169-182
MARIA,
Bishon Horn 243, 245
MEITEI,
171; creation ritual 72-74; priest and priestess 75; state model 44
MINYONG,
cosmogonic myth 66, 69, 74, 82
MIRI,
cosmogonic myth of Hill 65, 68, 69, 81; exchange 227
MISHMI,
77; chief 230; cosmogonic myth of Idu 70, 226; of Kaman 66, 70, 82; of Taraon 66, 68-69, 83; exchange 227
MIZO,
44; Hinduism and 221; Lakher 236, subgroups 230; Lushai 230, 236; chief 231, 233; Hills 226; village 235
MOKLUM,
cosmogonic myth 68
MUDUGAR,
152, 153, 154
MUNDA,
10, 111, 219; Hinduism and 221; melody 135; musical instrument 134; song composition 134
MURAI,
248, 253

NAGA,
171, 219, 237; head-hunting 228; Hills 226, 229; Hinduism and 207; use of currency 227; Angami settled agriculture 228; Ao 237; exchange 227; Konyak chief 230; exchange 227; Lohta exchange 227; Rengma 229, 230, 237; exchange 227; Sema 233, 237; chief 230; exchange 227; private land 229
NEGRO,
American society and 46
NICOBARESE,
219
NOCTE,
77; cosmogonic myth 69, 70; exchange 227

OIKOUMENE,
Kroeber on ancient 40
ONGEE,
19, 29; cosmology 17, 85-103; demography 170, 178-182
ORAON,
219; Hinduism and 221; melody 135

PAHIRA,
demography 169-182; melody 131

PANDARAM,
Hill Pandaram worldview 114, 115
PANGGI,
77; cosmogonic myth 64, 82
PARJA,
melody 131
PURUM (Chote),
demography 169-182

SANTAL,
20, 27, 28, 30, 37, 43, 50, 115, 117, 119, 221; industrialization 240, 241, 242, 243; music 21, 131-148; polytechnic behaviour 20, 193-214; value-pattern 183-192

SENTINELESE,
19, 100, 102, 179; population 178
SHERDUKPEN,
cosmogonic myth 54, 69, 72, 83
SINGPHO,
cosmogonic myth 64, 68, 69, 70, 71, 72, 83

TAGIN,
cosmogonic myth 71

VARLI,
mural painting 8

WANCHO,
77; cosmogonic myth 67, 68, 69, 71

YAO,
of Nyasaland 53